914.203
Col

84271

Cole.
Persons & periods.

Date Due

PERSONS AND PERIODS

PERSONS & PERIODS

Studies

by

G. D. H. COLE

Essay Index Reprint Series

BOOKS FOR LIBRARIES PRESS, INC.
FREEPORT, NEW YORK

First published 1938
Reprinted 1967

84271

LIBRARY OF CONGRESS CATALOG CARD NUMBER:

67-26726

PRINTED IN THE UNITED STATES OF AMERICA

CONTENTS

PREFACE

FOR permission to make use of certain of these studies my particular thanks are due to the Oxford University Press, Messrs. J. M. Dent & Sons, Mr. Peter Davies, and Messrs. Cassell. A note showing what has been previously published, and where, will be found at the end of the volume.

G. D. H. C.

OXFORD, *December* 1937

Daniel Defoe
(*1660–1731*)

DANIEL DEFOE was known best during his
own life as ' the Author of *The True-born Englishman* ' or ' the Author of the *Review* '. Posterity
knows him best as ' the Author of *Robinson Crusoe* '.
Among his contemporaries he had the distinction of
being the most abused of all writers. Pope reviled him
in *The Dunciad*, pretending to believe that he had lost
his ears as well as stood in the pillory : Swift again and
again referred to him contemptuously as an illiterate
scribbler : Whig and Tory, Jacobite and Hanoverian,
alike slung mud at him. He was accused of dishonesty
in his business relations, of being a secret spy in Government pay, ready at all times to turn his coat in order to
keep his place, of writing only for pay and caring not at
all what he wrote. Even in his own day no one could say
with certainty how much that was attributed to him was
really his ; and on this issue the critics are still dis-
puting, and will dispute as long as he is remembered
at all. He was twice imprisoned, and twice pilloried :
he became a bankrupt, and was haunted by creditors
most of his life. He made several fortunes and lost
them ; and, amid many mysteries that still attend his
career, the last year of his life remains the greatest
mystery of all. For Defoe died in hiding ; but no endeavour of his biographers has availed to discover what
or who pursued him. It may even be that he was flying
only from his own too lively imagination.

Defoe was in his day a merchant, and he never
ceased for long to meddle with commercial concerns,
over and above his writing, which was for him very
much a matter of business. But he was above all else

a writer with an itch to write. He could not possibly have stopped writing, even if nobody would have paid him a penny for what he wrote. He was more than thirty when the first work we know to be his appeared in print, and he seems to have published little for six or seven years after that. But then the spate began ; and when Defoe had once set up as an author it was quite impossible for him ever to stop. He began with political pamphlets, some in prose and some in verse that is near doggerel at its worst but has pungency and rises at its best into effective satire. He was in his forty-fourth year before he had written anything more extensive than an enlarged pamphlet. Then, in 1704, he made his bow as a journalist, with the famous *Review* which, published usually two or three times a week, he conducted practically single-handed for more than nine years. All this time he went on writing pamphlets and verses, in addition to his journalism ; but when he was fifty-five he had published, apart from two collected volumes of his shorter writings, only two books of any account—*The Consolidator*, a satirical account of a journey to the moon which in some ways foreshadows *Gulliver*, and his elaborate *History of the Union of Great Britain*, dealing with the Union of the English and Scottish Parliaments, with which he had been throughout the negotiations very closely concerned. Even then, four years were still to pass before the opening of his great period of writing. *Robinson Crusoe*, the first of his novels, appeared in 1719, when he was nearly fifty-nine ; and within the next six years he produced in swift succession *Memoirs of a Cavalier, Captain Singleton, Moll Flanders, A Journal of the Plague Year, Colonel Jacque, Roxana*, and *A New Voyage Round the World*, to say nothing of his *Tour through the Whole Island of Great Britain*, and the first volume of his *Complete English Tradesman*, or of a host of minor writings of any and every sort. Moreover, through these crowded years he was still the assiduous journalist. He conducted a daily newspaper, wrote

2

regularly for more than one weekly, and had a finger in many other journalistic pies. His last years are hardly less crowded with writing : up to the moment of the illness which preceded his mysterious flight he went on scribbling hard. It is even difficult to believe that he did not die with a pen in his hand.

An author who wrote so much had no leisure to polish what he wrote. But Defoe would not have bettered his writing by being at greater pains. He wrote as the words came ; without elegance, but with directness, force and simplicity. His best effects depend upon these qualities : he has a supreme naturalness, an ordinariness of phrasing that makes his fancy seem truth, and gets right home to his readers. With this he has an ordinary mind, so that, whatever extraordinary things his characters may do or suffer, they are all ordinary people, acting or reacting in ways that anyone can immediately understand. This is as true of Roxana, or of Moll Flanders, in their most disreputable adventures, as it is of Crusoe on his island, or of any of those real people whose lives Defoe translated into stories to amuse or instruct his public. There is no difference between Defoe the reporter and Defoe the novelist. His real and his fictitious characters are just the same. *The Apparition of Mrs. Veal* passed for a masterly flight of his imagination till, quite recently, some industrious delver found out that it was all true.

Defoe's contemporaries called him an illiterate scribbler because the wits of the age—Swift and Pope, Addison and Prior—loved polish, and Defoe had none. The polite world of his day despised him, and resented his circulation among the vulgar. Their contempt riled Defoe, who liked to think himself a man of culture, and was proud of being a wit and scholar who knew how to be a ' complete English tradesman ' as well. He hated ' fops ' and aristocrats who looked down their noses at honest commercial gentlemen, and deemed the latter of the more use to the country because they lived not at its expense but to its gain as well as their own. But he wanted his claims to intellectual equality to be admitted. There were only two charges, among the many flung at him, that he really resented. One was that he was a mere hireling, writing only for bread. The other was that he was illiterate ; and I think the second rankled the more.

Defoe wrote many people's lives, real or imaginary, but never his own, save to the extent to which *Robinson Crusoe* is to be regarded as an allegory of his own experience. But he wrote much about himself, not only in his *Appeal to Honour and Justice*, in which he defended himself against his critics, but also in his journalism, which he was constantly seasoning with personal allusion and anecdote. A good part of an autobiography could be pieced together out of his own words ; but it would not tell the whole story. For one vital part of the story could not be fully told at the time, though even then much of it was half known. Defoe was for many years, first probably under William III and certainly later under Anne and George I, a political agent in the Government's pay ; and estimates of him as a man, and of his honesty as a writer, turn largely on what is made of this aspect of his crowded career. Let me say at once one thing about what I make of it. After a fairly extensive study of his writings, I feel confident that he never wrote a word against his convictions, though he often edited for the press other men's writings with which he did not agree, and often kept out of his own writings things that he would have said if he had felt free to speak his whole mind. Few professional journalists, I think, can claim more than that.

But before we come to Defoe the journalist, something must be said of his earlier career. Daniel Foe—the ' De ' is of his own adding—was born in 1660, the son of a London butcher who was an active Dissenter. He was meant for the ministry, and educated at a Dissenting Academy in Newington, where he returned later to live in a substantial house of his own building. But he felt

4

himself unsuited for the ministry, though he remained a staunch Dissenter all his life ; and instead he was apprenticed to a merchant who dealt in hosiery and wine, exporting the one and importing the other. His time out, he set up for himself as a hose-factor in 1685, became a City liveryman in 1688, and failed in business in 1692, partly by his own fault, but also partly because of losses due to the war. In 1694 he received a small Government post as accountant to the Commissioners of the Glass Duty, and kept it till the duty was abolished in 1699. Meanwhile, he had become secretary and manager to a company which set up a brick and pantile factory at Tilbury—a new branch of the manufacture designed to rival the Dutch. This lasted till 1703, when his imprisonment ruined his business—or so he explained his severance from it. Thereafter, although he engaged from time to time in commercial speculations, especially in his latter years, his business career was over. He lived mainly by writing, and by serving the Government as a secret agent.

Defoe had achieved fame as an author two years before he published the pamphlet which brought him into conflict with the law. Until 1701 he was merely one of a host of pamphleteers on the Whig side, devoted to the ' glorious Revolution ' of 1688 and the cause of Protestantism, though he had already written one book which posterity ranks among the best of his secondary works. His *Essay on Projects*, published in 1698, foreshadows much of his later economic and social writing. It has often been praised for its anticipations of reforms which were long in coming, for its enlightened outlook on women's education, and for its plain common sense amid the darkness and confusion of the times. But it was not much noticed by his contemporaries. Nor did his vigorous controversial pamphlets against the practice of Occasional Conformity do more than embroil him with his own friends, the Dissenters ; for even those who were not prepared, in Defoe's own phrase, ' to play bo-peep with God Almighty' resented his action in writing openly against those who did, on the ground that what he said might strengthen the hands of the ' High-flyers ' (the High-Church Tories) in procuring more drastic penal laws against Dissent. Defoe found fame, not by solemn argument, but by satire, through *The True-born Englishman*, which is undoubtedly by far the best of his verse.

The True-born Englishman was a political squib, in defence of ' Dutch William ' and his foreign favourites at Court. John Tutchin, in *The Foreigners*, and many others had sought to rouse their countrymen against the King's foreign friends. Defoe retorted with an effective exposure of the Englishman's own mongrel antecedents :

> A true-born Englishman's a contradiction,
> In speech an irony, in fact a fiction.

and

> The silent nations undistinguished fall,
> And Englishman's the common name of all.
> Fate jumbled them together, God knows how ;
> Whate'er they were, they're true-born English now.

At this, and much more like it, the true-born Englishman knew how to laugh. And the satire brought Defoe King William's favour, so that, till his death the following year, the poet had clearly some degree of the King's confidence, and was his adviser in more than one commercial and political scheme. Perhaps, indeed, the connection had begun earlier, while Defoe still held his minor official post. Whether or no, there is no reason to doubt his repeated assertions that he was on terms of trust and service with William III during the last years of his reign. But the King's death ended that, and ended too the immunity from prosecution which printers and authors had for the most part enjoyed under his rule.

It will be remembered that, when Royal Anne became our Queen, the Vicar of Bray hastened to turn Tory. The press was kept busy with ' High-flying ' pamphlets; and the Dissenters felt themselves in imminent danger of a renewal of severely repressive measures. Dr. Sacheverell preached his 'Oxford' sermon against them; and Bills for suppressing Dissenting conventicles and academies and for the rigid exclusion of Dissenters from all forms of public office were everywhere under discussion. Into the very midst of the prevailing excitement the 'Author of *The True-born Englishman*' flung forth his pamphlet, *The Shortest Way with the Dissenters*.

The Shortest Way was anonymous—on the face of it, the work of the highest-flyer of all the Church of England covey. It advocated, in so many words, not repressing the Dissenters, but exterminating them—stamping them out till no such thing as a Dissenter should be left in the land. Defoe's aim was, by invoking the help of irony, to laugh the persecutors out of court. He carried their doctrine to a ridiculous extreme; but, instead of raising a laugh, as he had done with *The True-born Englishman*, he had the misfortune this time to be taken seriously. Tory High-flyers lauded his work from the pulpit—and then discovered that *The Shortest Way* was a hoax.

The true-born Englishman has a sense of humour; but it does not embrace irony. In England a man is ironical at his peril. What Butler met with when he published *The Fair Haven*, Defoe had to encounter over *The Shortest Way*. For there are few things so infuriating as to be the victim of a joke one has not seen. Nearly everybody was rabid against Defoe; for his Dissenting friends could appreciate his irony as little as his Tory enemies. The Tories, however, had more immediate power to hurt him. He was prosecuted for a seditious libel, shut up in Newgate, and in due course sentenced to be fined and imprisoned, and to stand in the pillory, where it was hoped all parties would unite to pelt him with stones and rotten eggs.

But the ironist was not left wholly without friends.

John Tutchin, known as *Observator* from his news-paper, and a fellow-pamphleteer, did see the joke, and organised a Whig mob to protect him from the missiles of the Tories—his Dissenting critics, as sober citizens, not being addicted to the throwing of rotten eggs. Moreover, Defoe entered into the spirit of the occasion with his *Hymn to the Pillory*, written from Newgate and hawked as a broadside among the crowd that came to watch his exposure. His humiliation was turned into a popular triumph—for the moment. Nevertheless, haled back to prison with a prospect of prolonged confinement before him, ruined in business and still pursued by his creditors of ten years before, out of credit with the Dissenters and hated inveterately by the Tories, Defoe was in no position to glory overmuch in turning the tables on his adversaries. By his own testimony he was in despair ; and out of his despair came the negotiations which procured him, within a few months, the Queen's pardon for his ' offence ' and a new rôle as the con-fidential agent of Harley and, through Harley, of the Government itself.

Defoe's relations with Harley, which long remained obscure, have been partly cleared up by the publication of his correspondence found by the Historical Manu-scripts Commission among the Portland Papers. Defoe was enlisted in Harley's service, with Lord Godolphin's approval and the Queen's, to report on the state of opinion in the country, to build up a body of local correspondents who would inform him of currents of feeling in each area, and to influence opinion as well as to sound and record it. But he was not asked—that is plain from the correspondence—nor did he undertake to do anything against his own convictions. For a long time past Defoe, despite his capacity for embroiling himself, had been essentially a ' moderate ', deprecating violent quarrels between parties and seeking a tolerant pacification that would secure the Protestant succession on a foundation of ' live, and let live '. This suited

Harley, who was himself a friend to the Dissenters, and Godolphin, who saw in political assuagement the best hope of retaining power for himself and Marlborough and the Whig-cum-Protestant interest. Defoe's post with the Government was as honourable as any part in the secret service can be. Indeed, his record over the next few years fully vindicates his honesty—for he freely criticised the Government in print on many matters, even while he was drawing its pay. He attacked its measures against the Dissenters, which Harley no doubt disliked as much as he. But he also freely criticised the terms of the Treaty of Utrecht, and ventured on other occasions to dissent publicly from the policy of his official paymaster.

What Defoe wanted from the Government was a regular office, such as he had enjoyed previously under William III. But, though the hope of this was again and again held out to him, he had to make the best of irregular subventions through Harley, either from that astute politician's own pocket, or, more probably, from the secret service funds. Before long he went touring England on his mission of sounding and influencing opinion, especially among the provincial Dissenters, whom he sought to turn to moderate support of the Government for fear its fall might let in something worse. Already he was taking an interest in the affairs of Scotland, where the question of Union with England was being hotly discussed. In 1706 Harley sent him to Scotland as a secret agent, to mingle with the Scots without revealing his mission, to register and to mould opinion, and to lend a hand, out of his commercial knowledge, in drafting the economic terms of the Act of Union.

There can be no doubt that Defoe, posing usually as a merchant on the look-out for commercial openings, did his work in Scotland well. During the next few years, first as Harley's agent and later as Godolphin's after Harley's fall from office, he was in Scotland most

9   B

of the time ; and he did many things there besides his
official work on behalf of the Government. All this
while, despite the extreme badness of communication by
road—of which we hear a great deal in his letters—he
managed regularly to bring out his *Review* in London.
He had established it in 1704, at the same time as he
entered into the Government's service ; and it was
doubtless run with the aid of Government money, for
Defoe is emphatic that it never paid its way. Part of the
time he published it also in a special Scottish edition ;
and after he had dropped this he conducted for a time a
Scottish newspaper of his own—the *Edinburgh Courant*.
Beyond all this, he found time to pour out from the
press a stream of pamphlets, to write *The Consolidator*
and his elaborate *History of the Union*, and to make
numerous journeys about the country and keep in touch
with a host of correspondents upon political affairs. Of
course he must have had ' ghosts ' to help him do all
this—at the least a faithful ' man Friday ' to take charge
of his affairs in London when he was away. But whatever
hands helped him with his journalism, there is no reason
for supposing that any hand but his wrote the numerous
books and pamphlets that went out from him during
these years, or that he failed to keep full control over
any of his numerous affairs. He was assuredly sincere in
his protest that he had never accepted dictation from any
source about what he should write, or shown Harley
any of his writings with a view to censorship before they
were put into print.

Nevertheless, being a secret agent is an equivocal
business, especially when the agency is only half a secret.
Defoe's close relations with Harley were, almost from
the beginning, pretty widely known, though their exact
nature was not ; and accordingly the worst construction
was put upon them by Harley's political opponents—
Whigs and High-flyers alike. Nor was Defoe himself
immune from the effects of his employment. He developed a habit of mystification beyond the need ; and

this never left him afterwards. Indeed, it grew upon him in later life, till, in the words of his son-in-law, Henry Baker, he had become a man who loved ' to hide himself in mists ', and was quite incapable of giving a plain relation of his own affairs. This foible had, however, its literary compensations ; for without it he would hardly have written with so astonishing a semblance of reality the histories of Moll Flanders, or Roxana, or Robinson Crusoe himself.

As long as Harley or Godolphin remained in office, Defoe's position was assured ; for he was far too valuable an agent for them to lose, whatever liberties he might venture to take. His taste for irony did, indeed, threaten to get him again into serious trouble in 1713, when, despite his connection with the Government, he had a second short spell in gaol. This was over his ' Hanover ' pamphlets, of which the first, *Reasons against the Succession of the House of Hanover*, was seriously mistaken for a Jacobite tract, though it was in fact an ironical exposition of the absurdity of the Jacobite case, and it is very difficult to understand how anybody ever managed to mistake its real meaning. On this occasion Harley, suspect himself of coquetting with the Pretender, nevertheless speedily got his indiscreet employee the Queen's pardon, and his jest was forgiven, even if it was not appreciated. But in the next year Harley fell from office; and the accession of the Whigs and George I landed him in the Tower, under a charge of treason. Defoe was let alone; but his irony, and his association with Harley, had offended the Whigs : his protector and his employment were gone.

The *Review* had ended before that, in 1713, killed by the newspaper stamp tax imposed in the previous year ; and though for a time *Mercator* took its place, Defoe was only a regular contributor, and not the responsible proprietor of the new venture. *Mercator*, in which he strongly pressed the case for freer trade, ended in 1714, and left him without a regular journal, though he con-

ducted for a time Hurt's *Flying Post*. To top his misfortunes, he fell seriously ill, in the midst of writing his
Appeal to Honour and Justice, in which he set out to
defend his political conduct and incidentally provided
his biographers with a great deal of material to record
and to quarrel over concerning his career. At one point,
his life was despaired of ; but he got better, and began
to look about him for a new way of earning his living,
on the assumption that his career as a Government agent
was over and done with.

In all probability it is to this break in Defoe's career
that we owe *Robinson Crusoe* and the rest of his romances.
True, he began his new career as a writer apart from
politics not with a story, but with a highly moral and
instructive manual of conduct, after the pattern of many
Puritan manuals of the previous century. It is difficult
now, despite enlivening passages here and there, to recapture the quality that made Defoe's *Family Instructor*,
for a century and more, close neighbour to the family
Bible in the parlours of the devout. It is as dead as
mutton now, save as an historical document. But that it
was very much alive until well on in the nineteenth
century is proved by its many editions and by its ubiquity
in the second-hand bookshops even to-day.

The Family Instructor was probably written while
Defoe was sick, and minded to be a saint. Many will
reckon his next action as a sign of renewed health. In
1715 he became involved in another prosecution, for
criminal libel against the Earl of Anglesey, a prominent
leader of the ' Hanoverian Tories ', and an active mover
in the proceedings against Harley. Defoe was released
on bail : sure that he would be convicted, he first ab-
sconded, and then threw himself upon the Government's mercy, offering his services to it as a loyal
Hanoverian, who had nevertheless friends in the opposite
camp, and was well equipped for keeping the Government informed about what was toward. The sequel was
the acceptance of his offer, and his re-enlistment, far

more secretly than under Harley, in the public service. In 1716 we find him re-established as a journalist, writing regularly for a newspaper, *Mercurius Politicus*, over which he had, however, no absolute or exclusive control, and, presumably, drawing again a salary of some sort from the secret service funds.

It would not be fair to pass to this new phase of Defoe's career without recording that, both before and after his new appointment, he exerted himself energetically on behalf of his former patron. In *The Secret History of the White Staff* and in other pamphlets he did his best to defend Harley against the charge of treason, and to put his conduct in a favourable light. That Harley seems not to have appreciated his help does not alter the fact of Defoe's loyalty, when loyalty could not possibly pay.

The nature of the services expected from Defoe by the Government was not made fully plain until 1718, when he entered into a formal arrangement. As a secret agent, he was to connect himself with the Jacobite press, to write and edit for it, with the purpose of keeping its expressions of opinion within moderate limits. Apart from his connection with the openly moderate *Mercurius Politicus*, Defoe began to write for, and soon to edit, *Mist's Weekly Journal*, the leading Jacobite organ, and to contribute to other Tory and Jacobite papers, seeking to suppress contributions that were plainly seditious, to modify offensive expressions against the Government and the dynasty, and to guide the Jacobites towards reconciliation with the new order—always without betraying his purpose, or openly changing the character of the papers for which he wrote. From time to time, despite his endeavours, seditious articles would slip in ; for Mist did not give his editor absolute control. But on these occasions Defoe was able more than once to save Mist from the consequences of prosecution, to exact guarantees of moderation, and to persuade the Government to let the case drop—still without betraying his position as a

Government agent. The affair ended, as such things will, in a quarrel, when Mist discovered what Defoe had been about. But their connection lasted in all for seven years ; and when it was over Defoe was able to go on playing the same rôle for two years more as editor of *Applebee's Weekly Journal*, another Tory organ of a complexion somewhat less pronouncedly Jacobite. Indeed, for four years, from 1720 to 1724, Defoe wrote for both *Mist's* and *Applebee's*, and at the same time conducted a succession of journals of his own. In 1718 he founded the *Whitehall Evening Post*, which he sold in 1720 ; but meanwhile he had founded, in 1719, the *Daily Post*, over which he kept his control till 1725. Then, in 1726, something happened—we do not know precisely what—to sever Defoe's connection with popular journalism for good and all. Possibly it was a full exposure of his relations with the Government : more probably a cessation of the Government payments that made such journalism worth his while. He seems to have come back to journalism, as contributor to and perhaps as editor of the Whig *Political State of Great Britain*, on Abel Boyer's death in 1729. But, apart from that doubtful exception and a few occasional articles, he wrote no more for the papers after 1726.

This record of Defoe's activities as journalist and secret agent has taken me on far beyond his ' arrival ' as a great teller of stories. From 1715 to 1718 he had been writing pamphlets with almost incredible activity—the list of works that are probably his runs to thirty-three in 1715, fourteen in 1716, twenty-six in 1717 and thirteen in 1718. But then, in 1719, appeared the two narrative volumes of *Robinson Crusoe* ; and he was instantly established as pre-eminent in a new field. The publishing ' pirates ', from whom he had suffered before—over *The True-born Englishman*, for example—instantly attested his popularity with a flood of unauthorised and abridged editions. *Robinson Crusoe* became immediately a popular classic ; and so it has remained ever since.

Having found the new vein, Defoe, despite all his journalistic preoccupations, was prompt to develop it. In addition to the *Serious Reflections of Robinson Crusoe*, which only quarriers in Defoe's biography can bear to read, 1720 gave the world *Captain Singleton*, with its romance of piracy and its delightful Quaker (Defoe had known William Penn well, and had several times assumed the character of a Quaker in his political writings), *Duncan Campbell*, forecasting his later preoccupation with magic and the supernatural, and, most important, *Memoirs of a Cavalier*. In 1721, apart from journalism, he was almost silent; but in 1722 came *Moll Flanders*, *Colonel Jacque*, and *A Journal of the Plague Year*. His publications in 1723 do not count; but then, in 1724, came *Roxana*, and the first volume of his *Tour*, and in 1725 the second volume of the *Tour*, *A New Voyage Round the World*, and the first volume of *The Complete English Tradesman*. 1726 completes the *Tour*, and adds *The Political History of the Devil* and *A System of Magic*. 1727 brings the rest of *The Complete English Tradesman*, *A General History of Discoveries in the Useful Arts*, and *The History and Reality of Apparitions*. 1728 adds *Augusta Triumphans* and *A Plan of the English Commerce*, and also *Captain Carleton*, if that be Defoe's, as I incline to think it is. Then at last the flood turns to a trickle, and there is nothing more of note till *The Compleat English Gentleman*, which was stopped in the press in 1730, and left unfinished at the author's death in 1731.

Apart from *The True-born Englishman*, and perhaps *The Shortest Way with the Dissenters*, most people nowadays know nothing of Defoe's that was written before *Robinson Crusoe*. His works, for most readers, mean *Robinson Crusoe* and the stories and narratives which followed it during the next few years. Defoe's great literary following and reputation rest on these products of his latter years. Nor is the verdict unjust, from the purely literary standpoint. Defoe was a great political journalist and a great occasional pamphleteer.

15

But it is of the nature of most political journalism and of most pamphleteering not long to outlive the occasion. Literary journalism can, witness *The Spectator* ; and so can journalism in which politics is mingled inextricably with more durable and personal impressions—witness *Rural Rides*. But most of Addison, or of Swift, and most of Cobbett, is dead to the reader of to-day; and so is most of Defoe's journalism, even at its best. Arguments die : only personality, and the human story, go on living for ever.

Defoe, then, lives by his stories—by *Robinson Crusoe* most of all, and thereafter by *Roxana*, by *Moll Flanders*, by *Memoirs of a Cavalier*, and *by the Journal of the Plague Year*. *Robinson Crusoe* comes first ; but what next ? Opinions differ. To-day, the *Cavalier* and the *Plague Year* are for highbrows only, or at the most do not go beyond the middle-brows. *Moll Flanders* and *Roxana*, however—especially *Moll Flanders*—have also a second public. You can find them, in a dress that shamefully suggests obscenity, cheek by jowl with *Aristotle's Works* and other salacious morsels, in shops where ' high-class rubber goods ' rub cheeks with vigour-restorers to re-inforce the energies of ' weak men '. Inevitably, this second blossoming invites a doubt. Was Daniel Defoe, Dissenter and pious author of *The Family Instructor* and other elevating works of piety, also a conscious purveyor of pornographic delights ? Did he moralise only with his tongue in his cheek, and write his *Lives* of Jack Sheppard, Jonathan Wild, Captain Avery, and other notorious malefactors, his fictions about *Moll Flanders* and *The Lady Roxana*, and the moral reflections of *Robinson Crusoe*, only to conceal his own immorality and screen his prurience behind a show of moralising ?

The answer, I am sure, is that he did not. *The Family Instructor* is writ serious ; and when *Robinson Crusoe* moralises, the reader is meant to take his pious reflections to heart. The repentance of Moll Flanders and of Roxana is meant in all seriousness : there is no consciousness of hypocrisy in the author's mind. Other times, other manners; and what attracts by its exceptional frankness now was then only a serious representation of what was written in levity by a host of other writers. Defoe is no more 'frank' than Congreve, or Wycherley, or Aphra Behn ; but he meant to point the moral, where they were content merely to adorn the tale. He was, no doubt, fully conscious that it is more interesting to read about vice than about virtue, and quite ready to play on his readers' desire for sensation and the amorous *macabre*. But there was no insincerity about his giving his stories of crime and passion and mere mercenary pandering to lust a moral twist. The underworld, which he had met with in Newgate and in the Mint as prisoner, as fugitive from his creditors, and then as journalist, interested him and stirred his fancy. He knew it, and how to write about it ; but he regarded it in all sincerity as evil, and meant to make it so appear. If *Moll Flanders* has become a *conte sale* to many of its modern readers, that is not Defoe's fault. He was as outspoken, and as reticent, as his contemporaries : his work outlives theirs in popular appeal, because of its abounding realism. His readers of to-day may skip his moralisings ; but he meant them to be read and taken to heart.

It is true that Defoe had an illegitimate child, *plus* seven legitimate. Wordsworth had one too. It is true that you can read *Moll Flanders* as a ' filthy book ', and enjoy it so, if your taste runs that way. It is true that for many years Defoe played an equivocal part, acting the Government spy upon the Jacobites, and concealing his receipt of public money under the cloak of the honest journalist, deeply maligned by his inveterate enemies. It is true that a sensitive character could never have sustained such a part. But Defoe was not sensitive. He was coarse-grained—even, if you will, a little vulgar. He did enjoy, as well as reprehend, Moll Flanders ; and, I am not ashamed to say, so do I. He did do things which, to-day, no decent man could do, and continue to deem himself honest. But it is ridiculous to judge men out of the standards of their time. After all, Defoe was no more a hired scribbler than Swift; and he stuck at least as close in his writings to what he really felt and believed.

This is not an exculpation, but plain justice. For Defoe has been dubbed ' rogue ', both in his own day and subsequently, far oftener than he deserves. He was, I feel sure, far less a rogue than St. John, or Harley, or Marlborough, or even Swift. As for his public life, it was of the times, dusty ; but not dustier than the rest. At any rate, he stuck to two principles through all his troubles and—whoever paid him for what he wrote—to toleration and, what goes with it, the desire to appease violent political or religious passions. He was a Dissenter without hostility to the Church ; for he regarded the Church's security as an essential shield against Papists and Jacobites. He was a Whig, who was ready to steer a middle course with the moderate Tories—or a Tory, ready to join hands with the moderate Whigs. But he was a moderator and a conciliator only on the basis of pre-serving certain fundamentals in which he believed. As a young man, he joined Monmouth's rebellion, and was lucky enough to escape Jeffreys's vengeance. He joined the Prince of Orange in 1688. All his moderation was based on preserving the Revolution settlement intact. On that point he never compromised. If Harley had dealings with the Pretender, Defoe had not.

Yet, about all this, who really cares ? What matters is that Defoe wrote *Robinson Crusoe* and, much less, that he wrote *Moll Flanders* and the *Journal of the Plague Year*. Having largely created English journalism, he went on to create the English novel. For, in truth, there were no novels before Defoe's—no naturalism in story-telling, no attempts to create in fiction the sense of reality in the reader's mind. Defoe achieved at one blow this realism—so thoroughly that even to-day no one can quite tell what in his books is based on real happenings

18

and what is sheer invention. That does not matter : nor does it matter whether this achievement was the outcome of supreme literary art, or craftsmanship, or of the lack of it—as Boswell's faults made his *Life of Johnson* the best biography ever written. The accomplishment is Defoe's, whatever lies behind it ; and the inheritance is ours. We can afford to be grateful for it, highbrows and lowbrows together ; for Defoe appeals to both.

Defoe's England

DEFOE'S *Tour through the Whole Island of Great Britain* is one of those books which many quote, but few read. Almost every social or economic history of the eighteenth century makes some reference to it ; and there are half a dozen passages from it that everybody knows. But to the best of my belief, apart from short extracts and two popular re-prints of special sections, there had been no re-issue of the book since 1779 until I reprinted it in 1927. It is not included in any of the collected editions of Defoe's writings, and even the quotations from it are mostly mere copyings and recopyings of a very few familiar passages.

At first sight, this is surprising ; for the book was very popular in the eighteenth century, and it is to-day both readable and of great value to the student of eighteenth-century England. No one is likely to accuse Defoe of a passion for accuracy, or of hesitation in allowing his lively invention to supply the gaps in his knowledge. But, with all his capacity for romancing, he was a highly competent observer, with a very keen eye for significant facts, and a point of view which makes his observations exceptionally valuable and interesting to the modern reader. For he was essentially a man of the transition from the old to the new order, and the things he looked for on his journeys were by no means those which appealed to the ordinary tourist of his day or of our own. For ' antiquities ' he had something of scorn ; he liked towns which excelled not in the ' tumbledown picturesque ', but in good, clean, well-built modern houses ; he liked a countryside full of corn and cattle, rather than of views and romantic wildness ; and, above

20

all, his interest was always in the present rather than the past. Not that he was unable to appreciate a fine old building, or a 'view' which conformed to his sense of beauty. But these were not the things he was in search of, and he gave them but a passing mention. What really interested him was the state of the country in a social and economic sense. Wherever he went, his first concern was to find out all he could about the social habits of the people, the products, the industry, and the trade and commerce of the various parts of the country, and to form some estimate of their contributions to the wealth and well-being of Great Britain as a whole.

For some readers, this preoccupation with the affairs of trade and commerce will doubtless detract from the interest of Defoe's *Tour*. Indeed, the eighteenth century itself seems to have thought that he had overdone the commercialism of his observations. The later editions, revised by other hands than Defoe's, steadily whittled down the economic and commercial information, and replaced it with more accounts of 'gentlemen's seats', more touches of the picturesque, more glimpses of antiquity such as Defoe had deliberately left out of his book.

In fact, the *Tour* was not a guide-book; but the eighteenth century chose to treat it as one. In the successive editions through which it passed, the revisers so maimed and refashioned it that by the ninth and final edition, the original spirit and plan were quite lost in the mass of excisions and accretions. There was little of Defoe left in it, by the time Samuel Richardson and other editors, of a temper very different from the original author's, had done their worst.

Moreover, the *Tour*, treated merely as a guide-book, grew, despite the frequent botchings, more and more out of date. It was first revised and 'brought up to date' in 1738, more than a decade after its original appearance. The process of amendment was repeated in 1742, 1748, 1753, 1764, 1769, and, finally, 1778 and 1779. But a description of British conditions as they were in 1724–6 was obviously quite inadequate as a basis for a description of Britain in 1779 or at any later time. The changes were far too numerous and too fundamental to be incorporated in any mere revision of Defoe's text. The *Tour* had, for a guide-book, an extraordinarily long life : as a guide-book, it waned and perished ; for the Britain of the rising Industrial Revolution needed, and found, fresh interpreters of its own. But, in its original conception, it was not a guide-book in any ordinary sense ; and that is why it is alive and important to-day.

This record of the *Tour's* adventures explains why it dropped out of print ; but it does not explain its long neglect in our own day. It was not worth while to tinker again with the already mangled edition of 1779 ; but it has long been well worth while to reprint the original edition of 1724–6. For, if we have no use for Defoe revised as a variant on Murray or Baedeker, we can make great use of Defoe unrevised to tell us what England was really like in the early eighteenth century.

On such a quest, we could hardly fall into better hands. For Defoe had both an extraordinarily wide knowledge of the country, and an intimate and first-hand acquaintance with its economic and commercial organisation. He does not, indeed, pretend to have made at any time precisely the ' circuits ' or journeys which he describes in his book ; and there is no doubt that he borrowed freely from guide-books and works of reference in supplementing what he knew by direct observation. He certainly had as little scruple in writing about places to which he had never been as in composing the *Memoirs of a Cavalier*, or the *Journal of the Plague Year*, or in issuing, despite his confinement in Newgate at the time, his narrative of the *Great Storm*. What he says can never be taken, on points of detail, as necessarily first-hand and unimpeachable evidence, unless we have reason to be quite sure that he had actually visited the scenes which he describes. And, with Defoe, it is extraordinarily difficult to be quite sure. That is half the secret of his skill.

This, however, matters very little. For what we want from Defoe is not an accumulation of accurate details, but a general and correct impression. This he was undoubtedly in a very good position to supply. We know that, during his years of secret employment in the Government service, he travelled a great deal over most parts of the country. In all probability, there were few places of importance which he did not at some time visit. And his general accuracy is confirmed by the very small number of definite and ascertainable mistakes into which we know him to have fallen.

Fully as important as Defoe's wide knowledge of the country is his no less wide familiarity with trade and commercial affairs. In the course of his career, he was himself both a trader and merchant and an industrial employer on a considerable scale. It has often been brought up against him that he failed in business, both as a hose-factor in London and as a brick and tile manufacturer at Tilbury. But this is hardly fair, not merely because he never, after he had once tasted authorship, gave undivided attention to business, but because at least one of his failures was at any rate in part due to his imprisonment for writing the *Shortest Way with the Dissenters*, and may well have been independent of any business cause. Indeed, if we can believe his word, he had repaid to his creditors, out of the profits of his tile business, the entire £17,000 which had been owing after his first failure, before his imprisonment brought his second venture down. There is no reason to believe that Defoe was an incompetent business man, though he certainly loved a speculative flutter, and probably fell into the vice of ' over-trading ' on an inadequate capital when he was engaged as a hose-factor in London. His warnings against this error in the *Complete English Tradesman* have, at any rate, a distinctly personal ring. The main trouble was, not that Defoe did not understand business, but that his first and most real interests were in other parts of his work.

Apart from his direct experience as merchant and employer, Defoe had an exceedingly wide knowledge of commercial conditions. The *Plan of the English Commerce* and the *Complete English Tradesman* are both really vigorous and intimate pieces of economic writing; *Mercator* and that astonishingly good periodical, the *Review*, of which he wrote every word himself, are abundant store-houses of economic information and pointed comment. It is not necessary to contend that Defoe was a great original economic thinker, or above the current commercial prejudices of his time. He was not. But he was an exceedingly good observer, a most acute critic, and a man of astonishingly wide economic and commercial knowledge, of which the Government, under both William III and Anne, often availed itself to excellent advantage.

It is, then, primarily as a guide to social and economic conditions that Defoe's *Tour* is important. It is an invaluable picture of the state of Great Britain about midway between the ' Glorious Revolution ' of 1688 and the period of the great inventions which we are used to call the ' Industrial Revolution '. For such a picture Defoe had just the right upbringing, interests, and experience. He was a Dissenter and a tradesman, brought up in that middle walk of life of which he so often and so loudly sung the praise. He was acutely ' middle-class conscious ', to use a modern term. The prosperity of Britain, he believed, was bound up indissolubly with that of the trading and trafficking classes to which he belonged. His scorn of ' poor, decayed borough towns ', which returned members to Parliament and served to keep the trading interest subordinate in the nation's counsels, was worthy of a Manchester cotton spinner a hundred years later. He was indeed prepared to give due respect to the ' nobility and gentry ', but only on condition that they should requite him by behaving themselves as true gentlemen, and giving due respect to his own class. His praises were all for the solid virtues of the rising *bourgeoisie* : he looked askance at the loose diversions of the rich, and wrote a whole book, the *Compleat English Gentleman*, at least half in order to prove that the respectable merchant or tradesman was the best gentleman after all.

Yet Defoe was certainly no mere Puritan in the ordinary sense. He wrote, indeed, such books as the *Family Instructor*, full of sage moral precepts for the use of his own class. But he is as the poles apart from, say, John Bunyan's *Life and Death of Mr. Badman*, to which some of his writings bear a superficial resemblance. For Defoe is very much a man of the world, and his point of view is that of the newer moderate and tolerant Dissent which was gaining ground with the rapid advance of the trading class in wealth, power, and social prestige. He represents, with singular accuracy, the mental outlook of the middle classes in the early eighteenth century, the direct precursors of the men who made, and were made by, the Industrial Revolution a generation or two later on.

The picture which such a man presents of the Britain of his time is naturally coloured by his outlook and interests, and cannot be accepted without qualification as complete. But it is probably less one-sided than any other picture made at the time would be likely to be. If it exaggerates, at certain points, the growth and importance of trade and commerce, the effect is at most only to anticipate a little, and not to distort ; for the forces which Defoe describes were rising rapidly at the time when he wrote, and represented essentially the coming power in the national society. Behind and underlying the world of Pope and Addison was a new world of *bourgeois* habits and culture, which, still insignificant politically even after 1688, was swiftly building itself up into the most creative influence in the nation. Fine Society had already recognised and largely assimilated

C

Sir Josiah Child and the magnates of city commerce and finance. But behind these giants was the rising host of ' complete tradesmen ' who, too numerous to be assimilated, were destined in time to assimilate society itself to their own habits and ideals.

The *Tour*, then, shows us Britain through a tradesman's eyes. But that tradesman is not merely an exceptionally keen observer, but also, for all the haste of his writing, one of the first masters of modern English prose. For a plain tale there is no one like Defoe. His is not a literary English, but a plain, half-colloquial, way of speech, which suits well the purpose of his *Tour*. His writing is always simple and to the point. True, he digresses often and at length, as the fancy takes him. But he always comes back, and, in a few vivid sentences, tells us of every place just what we need to know in order to get a clear vision of its commercial quality and standing.

What is the impression conveyed by this spirited picture of the condition of Great Britain two centuries ago ? It is, at first sight, somewhat startling, especially for those who have learnt from the text-books to date the beginning of England's industrial-greatness from the mechanical changes of the later eighteenth century, and to regard the England of the days before the Industrial Revolution as a placid agricultural country in which the wool industry alone possessed substantial economic importance. Defoe, indeed, is no agriculturist, and has little to tell us of the methods of tillage and relatively little of the march of agricultural improvement. He has a keen eye for good corn-lands, fat flocks and herds, flourishing orchards and hop-gardens, and all the manifestations of rural wealth. But he is not an expert, and there is nothing in his work that enables us to compare his observations with those of Arthur Young half a century later. In agriculture, as in industry, it is mainly the commercial side of things that attracts his observation. He never misses a corn-market or a fair, or omits to tell us how and where the food products of the various districts find their markets. But there his interest usually stops short ; and almost his only comments on agricultural methods, as distinct from results, are his account of the conversion of down-land to arable by the folding of sheep on the hill-sides between Winchester and Salisbury, and his reference to the use of turnips in fattening the Suffolk cattle for the London market. Usually, he contents himself with telling his readers that the husbandry is good or bad, without entering into the how it is done.

Industrially, too, it is the sale and marketing of the product rather than its manufacture that commonly attracts his attention. He does indeed describe the lead-mining of Derbyshire ; but he only records the com-mercial importance, without giving any description of the working, of the iron-works of Sussex, the tin and copper mines of Cornwall and Cumberland, the coal mines of South Wales and the North-Eastern Counties. He is not an industrialist, but a tradesman, and always his test of economic growth and prosperity is the number and wealth of the merchants rather than the size or ex-tent of the industrial undertakings. He is, however, always concerned to record the employments of the common people ; and in this especially his work is valu-able as presenting by far the clearest picture of the dis-tribution of industries and occupations two hundred years ago.

In his account of the Sussex iron industry, indeed, Defoe makes one notable false prophecy. After speaking of the ' prodigious expense of wood ' for the furnaces, he alludes to the current fears of the impending ex-haustion of the supply. ' I must own, however,' he adds, ' that I found that complaint perfectly groundless, the three counties of Kent, Sussex, and Hampshire . . . being one inexhaustible store-house of timber never to be destroyed, but by a general conflagration, and able at this time to supply timber to re-build all the Royal

Navies of Europe.' Rebuilding the Royal Navies would have been a light task in comparison with keeping the Sussex iron furnaces supplied ; and within a short time the iron industry was migrating rapidly from Sussex in search of fresh woodlands. Only the introduction of coal as a fuel for use in all processes of the iron trades saved the woods of England from complete destruction through the development of the metal industries. We may, however, forgive Defoe this mistake in a matter on which he had no pretension to be more than a casual observer. His conclusion was natural enough, though it was entirely wrong.

Next to corn, sheep and cattle, the wool industry in its various branches naturally bulks largest in his account. For the manufacture of woollen goods was beyond dispute the pre-eminent industry of eighteenth-century England. Defoe's description of the cloth trade of the West Riding has been, perhaps, more often quoted than any other piece of writing about economic conditions. His accounts of the cloth trade in other areas are less well known, but quite as important.

If the wool and worsted trades occupied a pre-eminent position, they were by no means alone in having reached a considerably advanced stage of economic development. Already, most of the coalfields with which we are familiar to-day were at least beginning to be worked. Northumberland and Durham, which chiefly supplied the London market, were much the furthest advanced ; but in Yorkshire, Lancashire, Cumberland, and the Midland Counties, as well as in Wales and Scotland, the coal industry had already assumed a considerable magnitude, and coal was of account for industrial as well as for domestic use. The iron trade was growing in importance, not only in the old Sussex iron district, but in Yorkshire, Derbyshire, and other Northern and Midland Counties. The lead mines were being developed, not only in Derbyshire, but in Wales, Yorkshire, and Scotland, in addition to the old workings in the Mendips and in Cornwall. The

Cornish tin and copper mines, and the copper mines of Wales and Lancashire, were increasing their output to keep pace with the growth of ' battery ' works and other metal-working establishments. The salt-mining industry was prospering as the trade in fish developed. The free-stone quarries of Portland and Purbeck had greatly expanded with the growth of fine building. This extract-ive group of industries came next in importance to the wool and worsted trades, and absorbed a large and growing mass of wage-labour. Manufactures of metal goods were already settled round Sheffield, for the tool and cutlery trades, and round Birmingham, especially for the lighter wares. Newcastle was also developing as a centre for the making of heavier metal goods. Shipbuild-ing was a flourishing industry, especially in the southern parts, which were still well supplied with building timber from the forests of Kent, Sussex, and the neigh-bouring counties. The glass and bottle trades flourished in London, Bristol, Stourbridge, Newcastle, and other centres.

Most of these trades, and many others which Defoe notices in the course of his survey, were of course still carried on mainly on a quite small scale. But there were some very considerable establishments ; and from their very nature most of these industries were organised definitely on capitalistic lines. The miner or iron-worker, the shipwright or battery worker, the bottle-maker or paper-mill operative, was definitely a wage-labourer, working under capitalist discipline in an establishment belonging to an employer. The ' domestic system ', of which we have heard so much as the precursor of the modern factory system, was not only never universal, but applied only in part even to the textile industries to which it was for the most part confined. For a large section of the industrial workers, though the factory unit was smaller, the discipline was already not vastly different from that whose coming we are apt to associate with the Industrial Revolution.

Indeed, it is even easy to misinterpret Defoe's famous account of the organisation of the woollen industry in the West Riding of Yorkshire. Commentators have often written as if Defoe had described the country round Halifax as a paradise of prosperous artificers, each earning a good competence by the sale of his own products in the market at Leeds or Halifax, owning no master and treating no man as servant.

In fact, Defoe's own picture is widely different from this. ' At every considerable house,' we are indeed told, ' was a manufactory or work-house', with its little stream of water to supply its needs ; but we are also told that ' among the manufacturers' houses are scattered an infinite number of cottages or small dwellings, in which dwell the workmen who are employed '. In these cottages the women and children were busy combing, spinning, and carrying out other simple preparatory processes ; but the men were employed, and at any rate some of the weaving, as well as the dyeing, bleaching, and finishing processes, were executed, not in the workman's *cottage*, but in the workshop attached to the *house* of the manufacturer. In fact, Defoe's West Riding manufacturer was not an independent craftsman so much as a small employer of labour, the scale of whose productive operations was still limited by the absence of power-driven machinery.

The difference between the cloth trade of the West Riding and of the South-Western Counties was not that, in Yorkshire, capitalism and wage-employment did not exist, but that there the small employers enjoyed a high degree of independence and a direct access to markets for the sale of their goods, whereas, in the West Country, though more weavers and other craftsmen worked in or about their own homes, most of them were virtually in the employment of larger capitalist clothiers, who owned the materials and saw to the marketing of the products. The latter system was in a sense the more capitalistic ; but the former lent itself more readily to transformation under the influence of machinery into capitalism of the modern type. Under both, the mass of the operatives were practically wage-workers.

A careful reading of Defoe's *Tour* is, by itself, enough to show that much that has been written about the ' domestic system ' is based on a misunderstanding of the facts. Everywhere, save in the West Riding, weaving was largely an urban occupation, and the work which chiefly occupied the villagers was the simpler labour of preparing the yarn for the weaver. This simpler labour was, indeed, everywhere carried on in the workers' homes, and formed a most important auxiliary source of income, throughout the woollen districts, for the families of the agricultural labourers as well as of the craftsmen. The making of stockings, before the great development of the new frames, of gloves and of bone-lace, and the straw-plaiting of Bedfordshire, are other examples of ' domestic ' industry properly so called. But weaving and other skilled processes were already partly carried on in work-shops, and in the strict sense many of the dyeing and finishing processes were never really ' domestic ' at all. The workshop, if not the fully developed factory, had a very important place in the economy of England before the Industrial Revolution. And, of course, not only mining and quarrying, but also most branches of metal work, never admitted of any ' domestic system ' at all.

The famous figures of Gregory King, estimating the population and the occupations of the people at the end of the seventeenth century, have often been quoted in order to show the overwhelming preponderance of agriculture over industry at that time. In fact they show nothing of the sort. Gregory King does, indeed, estimate the number of artisans and handicraftsmen, with their families, at only 240,000, whereas he gives the number of labourers with their families as 1,275,000, and that of cottagers and paupers as 1,300,000. But a large mass of industrial employment is really included under the last heading; for by artisans King means skilled workers following a definite trade. Not merely the spinner and the lace-maker, but also the miner and the quarry-worker, are presumably counted as 'labourers' or 'cottagers' rather than as ' artisans '.

There is accordingly nothing inconsistent between Gregory King's enumeration and the considerable industrial development which, only thirty years later, Defoe's descriptions seem to imply. To ask what was the distribution of the people between industry and agriculture before the Industrial Revolution is to pose an unanswerable question. There was no clear division between the agricultural and the industrial population. Agriculture was doubtless still by far the greatest of all employments. The woollen industry followed next ; and then there was a very big gap. But the total employment in the rising industries of mining and metal-work must have been already very considerable.

If Defoe presents a picture of substantial industrial production and activity, that only confronts us with another problem. How was this rapidly growing mass of commodities transported ? To this point he returns again and again, especially when he is discussing his favourite theme of the vast importance of the London market in the economy of the entire nation. Here, once more, our text-books are apt to offer us a misleading account of the actual situation. One would often suppose, from what they say, that it was nearly impossible to move any large quantity of heavy goods for any considerable distance until the canals and the turnpike roads had temporarily solved the problem under pressure of the urgent needs created by the Industrial Revolution. That, in the latter part of the eighteenth century, the growth of industry was sorely hampered by defective transport is a fact well known and beyond dispute. But earlier generations were by no means so helpless or so apathetic in dealing with their problems of transport as either the diatribes against bad roads, or the praises of new turnpikes and canals, sung by their descendants would lead us to suppose.

Defoe's narrative is, indeed, one in which the difficulties of transport are by no means left out of the account. He comments strongly on the bad state of the roads in the Midlands and in the South-Eastern Counties. He dwells, again and again, on the difficulties and the expense of long-distance land carriage. He tells us of rivers silted up, and of ports gone to ruin from that cause. The provisioning of the London market presents itself to him as, above all, a problem of the organisation of transport, and he explains the growth or decay of towns largely in terms of their good fortune in the matter of facilities for the carriage of their goods. His accounts of the Suffolk turkeys walking to the London market, and of the loss of weight by fat cattle performing the same operation, are well known, and have often been quoted.

But, while transport was a terribly difficult problem for the men of Defoe's day, it was by no means, in his view, either insoluble or unregarded. His account of the river navigation of England, and especially of the Eastern and Midland Counties, is impressive, and gives large credit to the successful attempts at improvement by the deepening of river-beds, the preservation of channels, and even the making of new cuts—the forerunners of the canals. The barge traffic by river was, of course, at the best extraordinarily slow and circuitous. But there is no doubt of its vital importance, or of the substantial achievements of river improvement in coping with the difficult problem of transporting heavy goods. The volume of commodities needing transport was steadily and rapidly increasing throughout the eighteenth century. The inland parts of England, especially in the Midlands, were being steadily and rapidly developed. And, until the coming of steam power presented a problem of heavy transport of coal and iron which imperatively demanded new means, the improvement of the navigable rivers at least did a great deal towards keeping pace with the growing need.

On the subject of roads, too, Defoe is illuminating. That the turnpikes began away back in the seventeenth century we are all aware ; but Defoe's estimate of the great improvements which they had already brought about by his time contradicts the popular view that nothing much was done to improve the roads until the Industrial Revolution was in full swing. Standards, of course, changed ; and what seemed to Defoe a vast improvement appeared to his successors a generation or two later almost less than nothing. The problem which the men of the Industrial Revolution had to face was vastly greater ; and the huge growth of traffic in their day made what had been done seem very insignificant beside what needed doing. But something had been done in Defoe's day ; and in relation to the problems of his time it was not insignificant, but full of promise.

A glance at any old ' Road Book ' of the early eighteenth century will show, indeed, how great the problem was even then. I have two before me as I write —John Senex's improved *Ogilby* of 1719, and John Owen's of 1736. In both, what stands out is the extent, even on important lines of communication, of unenclosed roads—in other words, of mere open tracks leading across the countryside. Almost every considerable route included, even in 1736, long stretches of unenclosed track. The turnpikes still covered only a tiny mileage ; and, in the winter at least, heavy road transport was impossible over long distances, and in any case so expensive as to give water-carriage, wherever it could be made available, an incontestable advantage. Nevertheless, something was being done, even in Defoe's day ; and the state of the roads was improving and not, as later grumblers were disposed to allege, already getting worse. The position was bad enough ; but the growing need for improvement was already evoking a response.

34

Of the progress of shipping itself Defoe has little to say. At every port he gleans what information he can about the ships belonging to the local merchants, the countries to which they trade, and the nature of their outward cargoes and ' returns '. But of the ships themselves he tells us little, though he takes careful note of the main shipbuilding centres, such as Yarmouth and Ipswich on the East Coast, famed for strong building, Shoreham, which builds ' neat ' ships, the other South Coast centres, and the Tyne, famous for its colliers.

But, if he tells us little of the ships, he says much of the ports and their commerce. He writes fully of the decline of Southampton, whose trade, like that of many other ports, has been eaten up by London ; the decay of the Ipswich coal trade ; the great commercial import-ance of Bristol, especially in the West Indian trade ; the extraordinarily rapid rise of Liverpool, and its flourishing commerce with the North American planta-tions ; and the growing enterprise of the Glasgow mer-chants, who have developed a system of land transport to the Firth of Forth, and opened a depot at Alloa, in order to get easier access for their imports from America to the London and continental markets. We see, side by side with the growth of the great new commercial ports, the continued importance of those smaller ports which serve the adjacent manufacturing areas ; and we realise how, before the coming of good internal trans-port, a large number of widely diffused small ports was essential in order to carry off the produce and manu-factures of the country to the main centres of popula-tion both at home and abroad.

And so we are led to London, by far the greatest port and the greatest market of all. Defoe is always in-sisting how every part of the country makes its vital contribution to the provisioning of the Metropolis. He never forgets to note what goods are carried from each port or fair to the London market, or to celebrate the importance of London as the pivot on which the whole

35

productive system of the country turns. Foreign commerce, indeed, is important, especially in relation to the woollen manufacture. But for all the trade in foodstuffs London is pre-eminent as the great market which it takes a whole country to supply with the means of life.

When he describes London itself, he is astonished at its bigness, and its continual increase. He takes his readers a journey round this—by eighteenth-century standards—vast urban agglomeration, extending from Deptford to Vauxhall south of the Thames, and from Westminster to Limehouse on the north—a total circuit, he proudly exclaims, of more than thirty-five miles. And even so he has left out Chelsea and Knightsbridge on the west, and Poplar, Blackwall, and Greenwich on the east, though they are practically continuous with London proper—to say nothing of all the growing suburbs north and south of the city.

Again and again, Defoe dwells on the astonishing growth of London. It has, he believes, fully a million and a half of inhabitants within the limits he has assigned to it, and many more if the surburban districts are included. And, every year, this huge population is rapidly increasing. Defoe, no doubt, greatly exaggerated the populousness of the London of his day; but he was right in his broad conclusions about it, even though his figures were a long way wide of the mark.[1]

Nor is he less eloquent on the subject of its growing wealth. Wherever he goes around London, he finds substantial houses of the citizens springing up in great numbers, from the magnificent mansions of ennobled financiers like Josiah Child's son, who became Lord Castlemain, to the pretty villas of merchants and tradesmen of the lesser sort, who have either retired from the City or maintain a summer residence in the country as well as a house in town. Croydon and Carshalton and many other places on the south, Stratford, Leyton, Walthamstow, Woodford, and many more on the north,

[1] See page 75.

are full of good new houses, handsome and large, all the habitations of wealthy citizens of London. In 1724, the year in which the first volume of the *Tour* appeared, we know that Defoe built himself a substantial new house at Stoke Newington.

In these, as in all the triumphs of trade and commerce, Defoe feels a real satisfaction. He pauses, indeed, to lament the late ' Bubble ', which brought many worthy citizens of wealth to ruin, though he himself is said to have done well out of it by skilful speculation. But, on the whole, he has reason to be well pleased with what he finds—ample evidence of rising wealth, prosperity, and standards of comfort and social consideration, among the class to which he himself belongs.

So much for what I may call the ' economics ' of Defoe's Grand *Tour*. A few words, finally, about its relation to the rest of his work. The book belongs, with the other writings most closely allied to it, to the last period of his life. Nearly all his most enduring work was written when he was round about sixty years of age. Before writing the *Tour*, he had, in the five years between 1719 and 1724, produced in quick succession *Robinson Crusoe, Duncan Campbell, Memoirs of a Cavalier, Captain Singleton, Moll Flanders, Journal of the Plague Year, Colonel Jacque*, and *Roxana*, to say nothing of a host of minor writings. Then came the first volume of the *Tour*, followed by the two parts of the *Complete English Tradesman* in 1725 and 1727, and by the *Plan of English Commerce* in 1728. This was really his last important work ; and he died in 1731 at the age of about seventy.

These last three books therefore represent the gleanings of a busy life, in the course of which Defoe had repeatedly travelled up and down the country, and come into contact with all sorts and conditions of men. They bring together the results of many years' observations, and of ceaseless journalistic writing about the affairs of trade and commerce. They are unlike anything else in the language in the diversified and authentic picture of social and economic conditions which they offer to the reader.

The difference appears plainly if the *Tour* is contrasted with other writings of a similar kind. And there is one comparison in particular which it irresistibly provokes. In 1714 there appeared the first volume of *A Journey through England, in Familiar Letters from A Gentleman Here to His Friend Abroad*. A second volume followed in 1822, and *A Journey through Scotland* in 1823. These books, which almost certainly suggested to Defoe the plan of his own *Tour*, were written by John Macky—like Defoe an agent employed in the secret service of the Government, and on his own behalf an enterprising projector of commercial schemes. Defoe unblushingly borrowed a good many particulars from Macky's book ; but far more significant than their resemblances are their points of difference. Macky's style is not unlike Defoe's, without its peculiar pungency ; his *Journey* is readable, and by no means devoid of social and economic information ; yet, in its general effect, it is as far apart from Defoe's work as chalk from cheese. In his journey through Yorkshire, Macky makes no reference at all to the cloth trade ; he dismisses Lancashire, except Liverpool, as not worth seeing ; and even in his account of the south-western counties the wool manufacture is only casually mentioned. Instead, there is more description of gentlemen's seats, of scenery, and of places of public resort. In short, Macky's volumes are a guide-book, whereas Defoe's present a social picture.

In another way, Defoe's book provokes comparison with the later *Tours* of Arthur Young, and with Cobbett's *Rural Rides*. But both these are concerned more with the country than with the town, and Cobbett's especially is far more a political commentary than a bare description. Doubtless Defoe, like Young and Cobbett, had an axe of his own to grind. His object was to sing the praises of British commercial prosperity, and to glorify the trader and merchant for their successful services to themselves and to the public. But this was only secondary. Defoe's primary purpose was to make a book that would sell, and direct propaganda formed no part of his plan. When he knew, he just described; when he did not know, he copied or invented a plausible account; and usually he knew enough to make his inventions approximate to the truth. He might not have hesitated to distort the facts if distortion had suited his purpose and he had seen his way to make it sound like truth. But he had no reason to distort the facts, and generally it is fairly safe to believe what he says, with only a reasonable scepticism upon points of detail.

It is no part of my aim in this essay to discuss the still unsolved enigma of Defoe's personality. Was he a rogue, or an honest man? When did he mean what he said, and when was he writing merely for his public, or with his tongue in his cheek? It is a fascinating problem : but it does not arise in connection with this particular book. For, here at least, there was no call for irony; and writing for the public happened to be consistent with writing the truth.

Here then I leave the *Tour*, making for it no extravagant claim as a work of exceptional genius, but rather suggesting that its very plainness and the prosaic purpose it was designed to serve give it a special value as a work of historical record. It is well written, in clear quickly-moving sentences that make it easy and pleasant reading. That is all Defoe tried to make it ; but, as long as men are interested in the past, that should be enough to give it an appeal.

BIBLIOGRAPHICAL NOTE

Daniel Defoe's *Tour through the Whole Island of Great Britain* was first published in three volumes, which were issued by G. Strahan of Cornhill, in association with a number of other booksellers. The first volume appeared in 1724 and the second in 1725 ; the third is mentioned as ' published this day ' in the advertisement columns of *Mist's Weekly Journal* on August 13, 1726. This seems to fix the date, which is given as 1726 in both Lee's and Dottin's bibliographies. But in every copy purporting to be a first edition that I have seen (including, besides my own and the copy from which the present reprint is made, those in the British Museum, the Bodleian, the Goldsmiths' and the London Library), while the first and second volumes are dated 1724 and 1725, the third is dated 1727. Unless a copy dated 1726 can be proved to be somewhere extant, I can only assume that the first edition of the third volume, though published in 1726, bore the date ' 1727 ' on the title-page.

Lee, in his bibliography, mentions a second edition of the complete work as appearing in 1727. This, if it exists, I have never seen ; and I doubt if it ever existed, save perhaps as a binding up of the original volumes. At all events, a Second Edition, so described on the title-page, was issued in 1738, by J. Osborn, S. Birt, D. Browne, A. Millar, F. Cogan, J. Whisten, and J. Robinson. It is described as embodying ' very great Additions, Improvements, and Corrections, which bring it down to the beginning of the year 1738 '. ' A Gentleman ' is still given as the author ; but the Preface makes it plain that all the changes are the work of a different hand. This Second Edition is also in three volumes.

A Third Edition, this time in four volumes, appeared in 1742, printed for J. Osborn, S. Birt, D. Browne, J. Hodges, A. Millar, J. Whisten, and J. Robinson. This edition was again substantially revised, and the sections dealing with the Northern Counties and Scotland considerably expanded. The editor is believed to have been Samuel Richardson, the novelist.

A Fourth Edition appeared in 1748, a Fifth in 1753, a Sixth in 1746, a Seventh in 1769, an Eighth in 1778, and a Ninth, the latest I can trace, in Dublin in 1779. Further revisions were made with each reissue, except the last ; but the general form of the work remained unchanged. All editions after the Second were in four volumes. Defoe's name, as that of the original author, first appeared on the title-page of the Seventh Edition, which also states that the work was at one time revised by Samuel Richardson.

Of all these issues, the first alone is Defoe's. The later editors not only added, but also excised a great deal that he had written ; and the effect of the changes was not merely to bring the book up to date (which was very imperfectly done) but to alter its character.

Town Life in the Eighteenth Century

Here sit poor I, with nothing but my own solitary individuality ; doing little, and suffering no more than I have
often suffered ; hearing nothing that I can repeat ; seeing
nothing that I can relate ; talking, when I do talk, to those
whom you cannot regard, and at this moment hearing the
curfew which you cannot hear.—*Johnson to Mrs. Thrale
from Lichfield* (July 26, 1775).

A small country town is not the place in which one would
choose to quarrel with a wife ; every human being in such
places is a spy.—*Johnson to Dr. Taylor* (Sept. 3, 1763).

WHY do men live in towns ? One reason is
'Because they like it' ; and there are towns
which appear to exist only for this reason. But
the great majority of men cannot simply follow their
inclinations in deciding where to dwell. They have to
earn their livings, and to take up their habitation where
their business lies. Most towns, in modern times at any
rate, exist because they serve an economic end ; and
accordingly their character reflects the forms and needs
of the dominant economic system.

In eighteenth-century England there were pleasure-
towns, such as Tunbridge Wells and Cheltenham and,
above all, Bath. There were seaside holiday resorts, such
as Scarborough, and later in the century Margate,
Brighthelmstone, and Weymouth ; for this was the age
in which the fashionable world discovered sea-bathing in
addition to popularising the inland spas. There were
cities and towns, such as Exeter and King's Lynn and
Stamford, that, apart from their trade, were noted for
the number of gentlemen who had good houses in and
around them. There were decayed boroughs, such as
Winchelsea and Great Bedwin, that seemed to have no
reason for existing at all. There were, finally, cathedral

towns, such as Wells and Johnson's Lichfield, that owed most of their importance to the church, and clustered, almost in medieval fashion, about the Close ; and there were, hardly less ecclesiastical in tone, the ancient university towns of Oxford and Cambridge.

But most English towns in the age of Dr. Johnson owed the greatest part of their wealth and activity to some form of trade. There were, first of all, market towns, any number of them, scattered over the entire face of the country, and serving the surrounding villages as centres of exchange. Thither the rural producer brought many of his wares to sell, either directly to the consumer, or to a middleman who would carry them away to some greater market. And thither the country dweller, too, came to buy, either from stalls or booths in the market-place, or from regular shops. For in eighteenth-century England every town, even the smallest, already had some shops ; and their number and importance increased steadily and rapidly as the century advanced. Markets and fairs were indeed far more important then than now ; and most towns had a regular market once or twice a week. The poorer people dealt not at the shops, but in the market ; but in or near most market towns there were enough of the richer sort to keep at least some shops alive.

The shops flourished especially in those market towns which served a countryside well filled with seats and villas of the gentry. Stamford, for example, where Robert Owen served his apprenticeship as a linen-draper, was a famous shopping-centre throughout the century. Guildford, where the old clothing trade had almost completely disappeared, was another ; and, indeed, towns of this sort, which lived largely by supplying the gentry, were scattered thick and fast over most of southern England. No one who glances through one of the old *Road Books* of Cary or Paterson will take long to discover that ' gentlemen's seats ' were regarded as the most important feature of the eighteenth-century landscape, or that every road in the south was studded with them. The number of

these country houses increased very greatly as the
century advanced ; for it was a great time for building.
But they were plentiful throughout Dr. Johnson's age ;
and the latter half of the century was especially fertile
not only in mansions for noblemen and successful
merchants, but also in eligible villa residences for the
lesser gentry.

Many market towns in the south were places of little
trade apart from this lucrative business of supplying the
gentlefolk with provisions and draperies, and catering
for their more occasional needs of travel and amusement. If the town stood on a main road, it would have
at least one tolerable inn, over and above the alehouses
and lesser ' publics ' which drove a thriving trade on
market days. At this inn there would probably be a
local Assembly Room, which could be used for balls,
dinners, and other entertainments, and would sometimes house a troop of players—for there were regular
theatres only in the larger towns. If the place was a
borough or the county town, and accustomed to con-
tested elections, it would almost certainly have two
rival inns, used as headquarters by the contending parties.
But some boroughs, where the representation was
virtually owned by a single landlord, or put up to the
highest bidder by a close corporation, were not used to
election contests, and recked little of political affairs.
One inn, in addition to the many public houses, might
serve their needs.

Other market towns in the south were much more
than mere shopping centres for the surrounding gentry,
and for the country folk on market days. For they were
also the focus of a vigorous industrial life. The west of
England, especially, was full of little towns which lived
chiefly by their activities in the woollen trade. These
were industrial towns long before the coming of the
Industrial Revolution, which indeed to a great extent
stole their industry away. The growing competition of
the Yorkshire manufacturers, who were undercutting

44

its old-established products by new methods of production and with cheaper and less durable goods, though much complained of, had not yet prevented the growth of the industry in east or west ; for the total demand was expanding rapidly with the increase of foreign markets. The western counties lived by sheep and by the woollen manufacture ; and on this trade and industry the life of their towns was chiefly based.

These west-country towns were not merely centres for buying and selling, but active hives of manufacturing industry. The rich merchant clothiers, whose chief business was trade, were mainly concentrated in the larger towns, such as Exeter and Taunton. But in each smaller town—Bradford-on-Avon, Devizes, Witney, Malmesbury, Honiton, Axminster, and a host of others —there were gathered the actual producers of woollen stuffs. For whereas spinning of wool was at this time carried on by unskilled labour, chiefly that of women and children, scattered among innumerable villages all over the country as well as in the towns, weaving was for the most part a skilled urban occupation. The weavers had little or no connection with the land, though they might help at harvest time ; and they were mainly gathered together in towns and large villages that were far more urban than rural. Wool-combing, too, was a highly skilled and highly paid urban occupation, even more concentrated in the larger centres than weaving. Wool-combers, and to some extent workers in the finishing trades, might labour under the roof of a substantial employer ; but the vast majority of the weavers were home-workers, plying their craft in their own cottages or in work-rooms attached thereto. The west-country weaving town was a place not of factories but of substantial cottages each containing a loom, or perhaps two or three.

Very similar conditions existed in the eastern counties, save that there Norwich was the metropolis of the woollen trade to a far greater extent than any single town

45

or city in the west. Indeed, anyone who wishes to recapture the spirit of the old English woollen industry will find in Sudbury, Lavenham, Long Melford, Stoke-by-Neyland, and other old clothing towns and villages of the eastern counties, an outward shape less changed by time than anywhere in the west.

The western counties and East Anglia, with Yorkshire, of which more anon, were the greatest centres of the woollen manufacture. But many other counties had their clothing towns and villages not greatly unlike those of Suffolk or Devonshire. Kendal, Rochdale, Burnley, Bacup, Knutsford, Darlington, Godalming, Leominster —the list could be almost indefinitely prolonged, even without going to Scotland or Wales for additional examples. The woollen manufacture was in the eighteenth century England's most widely diffused, as well as her greatest, industry ; and it stamped its peculiar imprint on half the towns in the country. Moreover, the less important, but still considerable, manufactures of linen and silk, the knitting trade in the east Midlands, and cotton itself before the introduction of the new machines, created towns and villages of very similar appearance and social structure.

In Yorkshire, however, the woollen manufacture was carried on under somewhat different conditions, and with different effects on the structure of town life. For the representative figure of the Yorkshire woollen trade in the eighteenth century was neither the rich merchant clothier nor the urban home-worker, but rather the small master-craftsman working with his own hands and employing one or two journeymen under his own roof. There were, of course, rich merchants in Leeds and Halifax and Bradford ; but they were not for the most part nearly so rich or so gentlemanly as the merchant clothiers of Exeter or Taunton. There were home-workers too ; and spinning was, until about the end of the century, an unskilled occupation carried on by women and children in town and country alike. But weaving, the main skilled occupation, was a good deal less urbanised than in the south ; and Defoe's famous description of the country round Halifax continued to hold good in the latter part of the century. The Yorkshire manufactures grew up scattered, wherever a river or streamlet afforded a supply of good water for washing and bleaching and, later, for the application of water-power. Its typical unit was a substantial workshop attached to a farm-house ; and the typical employer remained at least one part a farmer till quite late in the century.

In these circumstances, there grew up in Yorkshire no such plenty of small clothing towns and large villages as in the west. The Yorkshire clothing towns—Leeds, Halifax, Bradford, and the rest—were centres rather of trade than of actual production. Their chief importance lay in their famous cloth markets, to which the small masters from all the country round brought in their wares. Only with the introduction of steam-power and the factory system did Leeds and Halifax and Bradford become primarily manufacturing, rather than trading, towns.

This, of course, does not mean that no manufacturing was carried on within their limits. Wool-combing and carding, and the pressing and finishing of the woven stuffs, were urban occupations in the north as well as in the south ; and there were weavers and spinners in Leeds and Halifax as well as in the surrounding country. But the towns themselves got their social atmosphere and their importance from trade rather than manufacture ; and their leading citizens were merchants rather than employers.

Our journey to the north has carried us from the small market towns with which we began to larger urban centres ; for Leeds, Huddersfield, and Halifax were all considerable places in the eighteenth century. Richard Price gives the population of Leeds as 17,000 in 1775, and Halifax, with its surrounding countryside, had long been noted as the ' most populous parish in England '. But, even so, Leeds was only a third as populous as Norwich, and about half the size of Birmingham or Liverpool. Chester was nearly as big as Leeds as late as 1750.

Of course it is necessary to speak with great caution of town populations in the eighteenth century, when there was no such thing as an official census, and different authorities often gave wildly different estimates. Sometimes these differences arise because the varying estimates are not for the same areas, some being confined to the borough limits and some including the surrounding suburbs. For example, very different figures are given for Manchester, according as the quotation is for the town itself, or for the wider parish, or for the whole area of the Manor of Manchester.

It is, however, possible, from the estimates quoted by Arthur Young, Macpherson, and other economic writers and travellers, and by Richard Price in his famous *Essay on the Population of England*, and sometimes from local censuses of varying accuracy, to get some idea of the size of the principal towns in the third quarter of the eighteenth century. London was, of course, immensely the largest—nearly as big in relation to the total population of eighteenth-century England as modern London is in relation to the England of to-day. For London was the great centre of trade as well as of fashion, arts, and government ; and, at any rate in the south, the London market dominated the trade of the smaller towns to a very great extent. In the south, London's only serious rival was Bristol, which alone drove a thriving independent import and export trade, and provided an alternative point of focus for the industries of South Wales and the western counties, including the Severn country and even, to a great extent, Birmingham and the west Midlands with their rapidly growing manufactures of iron and brass.

Bristol was, indeed, easily the second town in England,

with a population approaching 100,000, and a flourishing glass and china manufacture in addition to the trade of its port. Manchester, growing at a very rapid rate, had only 30,000 inhabitants in 1769, according to Arthur Young, and even with Salford and the suburbs no more than 50,000. Young put the population of Liverpool at 40,000 in 1769 ; but Price made it only 34,500 in 1773, and the latter estimate is probably nearer the truth unless the surrounding villages are included with it. Birmingham in 1770 had about 30,000 people according to several authorities, Hull from 20,000 (Young) to 24,000 (Macpherson), and Sheffield from 20,000 (Macpherson) to 30,000 (Young). These, with Norwich, variously estimated at from 40,000 (Young) to 60,000 (Macpherson), were the largest towns, followed by Nottingham and Leeds, each with about 17,000. Chester had about 15,000, Shrewsbury about 13,000, and Worcester from 11,000 to 12,000, according to varying estimates by Price and Young, while Bolton had only 5,000, and Northampton no more. Newbury, in Berkshire, with 4000 people, was as big as Bradford ; and the great majority even of the more flourishing lesser towns had only from two to four thousand inhabitants. Chippenham, for example, had 2400 (Price), and High Wycombe 2500 (also Price).[1]

Ordinary market towns and even flourishing industrial centres were, then, even in the latter part of the eighteenth century, no larger than populous villages of to-day ; and even the great trading centres, except Bristol, were no larger than very minor modern provincial towns. We must bear this smallness of the typical eighteenth-century town constantly in mind if we mean to get a true picture of its character and way of life. For a town even of forty or fifty thousand people cannot be far removed from the country ; and a town of five thousand will, unless it be quite excep-

[1] In 1781 Lichfield had less than 4000 inhabitants (Harwood) and in 1789 Oxford rather more than 8000 (Parker).

tional in its way of life, still retain many of the characteristics of a village.

It is necessary to keep this consideration in mind above all in passing judgment on the sanitation and methods of government of the towns of the eighteenth century. For it is very easy to condemn them, on both grounds, by the application of wholly inappropriate standards. We read of the lack of a proper water-supply, of paved streets, of an adequate police force, and of one after another of the essentials of modern town life, in, say, Leeds or Birmingham ; and we are apt to think what these great cities would be like now if they had to do without these vital services. But, in fact, neither Leeds nor Birmingham in the eighteenth century was in the least like the Leeds or the Birmingham of to-day ; and we cannot afford to be so proud of the water-supply or the urban amenities of many of our large modern villages as to cast stones very readily at the great majority of eighteenth-century towns for doing without them. Doubtless, the towns of the eighteenth century would have been healthier, and perhaps happier, if they had been better ' policed ', in the eighteenth-century sense of that term. But they were by no means so ill off for want of this as the modern reader is apt to imagine, or as the scandalised Utilitarians who drew up the *Report on Municipal Corporations* in 1835 were disposed to suggest. The sanitary problem became desperately urgent only when the trading and hand-working towns of the eighteenth century turned into industrial towns under the factory system and steam-power, and found their populations vastly increased in a few years by the concentration of workers which the factory system involved.

It is, however, true enough that urban government throughout the eighteenth century was in a bad way. Many of the newer towns, like Manchester and Birmingham, were not incorporated, and had no fully developed municipal institutions of their own. But this did not always mean that they were any worse off than a borough in possession of a fully fledged Municipal Corporation, with a charter from the Crown, and valued privileges which rendered it immune from the jurisdiction of the county. For the typical Municipal Corporation of the eighteenth century hardly regarded itself as a local government authority in the modern sense, or accepted any responsibility for the adequate development of sanitary services and amenities on behalf of the whole body of inhabitants. There was an immense variety of municipal constitutions; and the municipal corporations ranged from bodies regularly elected, at least in theory, by nearly all the householders to narrow oligarchies of the wealthier tradesmen and merchants, with perhaps a few independent ' gentlemen ', renewing themselves by co-option without any shadow of a representative method of choice. These self-elected oligarchies were indeed the predominant type; and bodies elected by the householders were relatively few. But there is positively, through all the century, no sign of serious objection on a national scale to the principle of self-election, or of a sense that things ought to be otherwise arranged, though it is significant that the more progressive towns, when they needed new services, seldom thought of entrusting them to the existing Municipal Corporations. There were plenty of movements in the latter part of the century, like that of the Yorkshire freeholders and the agitations led by Cartwright and Horne Tooke, for a reform of parliamentary representation. But neither the earlier reformers nor the democrats at the end of the century had ever turned their attention seriously towards municipal reform.

The eighteenth-century Municipal Corporation was indeed, and considered itself as being, far less an organ of local government in the modern sense than an institution for the management of a corporate property. Membership of this privileged body had come to be regarded

51

almost as a property right, and the property of the Corporation almost as belonging to its members as individuals rather than to the town. Civic feasts, such as we associate with the London Livery Companies of to-day, seemed a more appropriate use for the civic funds than the provision of an adequate water-supply or the paving or lighting of the streets ; and the right to send Members to Parliament came to be regarded rather as a property right of the members of the Corporation than as a right of representation in the counsels of the country. The right of electing Members to serve in Parliament was often vested in the Corporation, and seats were often put up for sale, without shame or sense of shame, to the highest bidder. Indeed, the buying of seats was often justified as a desirable means of securing the return to Parliament of men of property who lacked territorial influence ; and often the best and most independent Members sat for the rottenest boroughs. Sometimes, of course, when a large part of the borough was owned by a single great landowner, the Corporation simply carried out his will in the election of Members to Parliament ; but, where property was more widely distributed and the Corporation free to act as it chose, it was usually far less inclined to aim at getting its own point of view represented in the House of Commons than to return some man of wealth who was prepared to pay for the privilege. The truth is that most of the eighteenth-century boroughs had no particular desire to be represented in Parliament. They wanted, not to be better governed, but to be left alone.

Nor did things usually work out any better when the parliamentary franchise was vested, not in the Corporation, but in a wider body of freemen, or in all the householders paying scot and lot. For this, as a rule, only diffused corruption over a wider field, causing a plentiful outpouring, at election time, of free dinners, free beer, and very often free money as well. These wider bodies of electors were no more disposed than the oligarchical

Corporations to take their privilege of representation seriously. Even such famous open constituencies as Westminster, Preston, and Coventry, where real elections were fought in the early nineteenth century on real issues of political principle—though not without a good deal of corruption even then—only gained their reputation after the revolutions in America and France had sent men back to political first principles, and effectively roused the democratic spirit from its long sleep. Whatever virtues the eighteenth century had, it was assuredly not democratic. It did not want to be democratic ; and accordingly, even when democratic instruments were placed in its hands, it did not commonly care or trouble to use them.

Parliament, however, was far away ; and it may seem surprising that the provincial notables, even if they could not be bothered with governing the country, did not make more effort to provide for the good government of their own towns. But, in fact, in many of the older towns the members of the Municipal Corporation were hardly conscious that a problem of local administration existed at all. As Mr. and Mrs. Webb have pointed out in their monumental study of English Local Government, the very phrase ' Local Government ' was not coined until after the middle of the nineteenth century. This, of course, is not to say that the notion had not existed for many centuries. But it had been associated, in the minds of the Municipal Corporations of Tudor and Stuart times, primarily with the regulation of local trades and industries, that is, with forms of administration which changing economic conditions had rendered obsolete. What remained of the old functions was judicial rather than administrative ; and the Borough Justices, inferior in social status to the country gentlemen who manned the county bench, were in most towns a good deal more active in local affairs than the Municipal Corporations. Here and there, as at Liverpool, an energetic and on the whole enlightened Corporation was to be found. But

53

Liverpool was exceptional; for its rapidly growing prosperity depended obviously on the efficiency of its docks and its trading organisation, and the merchants who controlled its administration had a strong interest in the proper conduct of municipal affairs. Manchester might have been just as efficient if it had possessed the appropriate local institutions. But Manchester was not a Corporation at all; it was still under the old manorial jurisdiction.

Most of the English towns in the mid-eighteenth century were still unconscious of problems calling for strong municipal government. Such a matter as the cleaning of the streets was still imposed as an obligation on each individual householder, whose duty it was to keep the space in front of his own dwelling clear, as far as the middle of the road. Street cleaning was thus a citizen's obligation, to be enforced by the justices, rather than a public obligation. The supply of water was indeed coming in the early part of the century to be felt as a pressing need in some of the larger towns; and this service was sometimes taken in hand by the Corporation. But eighteenth-century travellers always commented with surprised fervour when they found a town, such as Exeter, publicly supplied with water in leaden pipes; wells and pumps still supplied the needs of townsmen in most places, as they do to this day the needs of the majority of villages.

What is remarkable is that when, as the century advanced, increasing population and improving sanitary knowledge began to force the problems of municipal organisation into public notice, the commonest way of getting new services developed was not by means of the Municipal Corporations, but by the establishment, side by side with them, of new and independent authorities. Under various names, one town after another set up in the course of the eighteenth century bodies of Improvement Commissioners, created by a special Act of Parliament, and given power to lay a limited rate upon the whole of the householders. These bodies of Commissioners were doing, in the latter part of the century, far more to introduce new municipal services than all the Municipal Corporations taken together. They chiefly set about lighting, cleaning, and paving the streets, providing a rudimentary police force of night-watchmen, regulating traffic, and in many ways both removing nuisances and improving local amenities. This is not surprising in towns such as Manchester, which lacked corporate rights and organisation : what is at first sight astonishing is that bodies of this sort were set up almost as much in towns which already had Municipal Corporations, and that in most cases the entrusting of the new duties to the existing authorities seems not to have been even considered. There could be no clearer sign of the extent to which incorporation had come to be regarded as conferring not duties but privileges on the members of the corporate body. This attitude fitted in well enough with the common opinion of eighteenth-century England about the scope of government and the rights of property. *Laissez-faire*, save in matters of foreign trade, was not a nineteenth-century invention, or a product of the machine age. It flourished even more, inside the country, after the ' Glorious Revolution ' of 1689 had established the country gentleman's right to be let alone by Parliament, and the spread of the ' domestic system ' through the market towns and country districts had destroyed the old regulative functions of Gilds and Municipal Corporations.

Another important reason for the lethargy of the Municipal Corporations was the prevalence of religious Dissent among the merchants and tradesmen of the developing towns. For though the Test and Corporation Acts were not enforced, and Acts of Indemnity were regularly passed on behalf of those Dissenters of an accommodating spirit who took office in spite of them, the Municipal Corporations retained throughout the century a strong flavour of religious orthodoxy, enough to exclude the more vigorous and conscientious members of the dissenting connexions. It was partly under the influence of the latter, and in order to secure their collaboration, that the new purely secular and undenominational bodies of Improvement Commissioners were brought into being ; and it was through these new bodies that the Dissenters came to be a power in the municipal world.

Apart from such clearly public functions as the lighting, paving, cleaning and watching of the streets, there were plenty of other municipal duties awaiting the energies of the local reformers as the century advanced. Outside London, the movement to establish hospitals for the use of the poor seems to have begun with the opening of a public hospital at Winchester in 1736. This was intended to serve the needs of the entire county ; and the funds for it were raised by public subscription among the wealthier inhabitants—a method followed for most subsequent institutions of a similar kind. Bristol, York, and Exeter all established hospitals within the next few years. Liverpool's Infirmary was founded in 1749 and Manchester's in 1752. Manchester added a Lunatic Asylum in 1765, and Public Baths in 1751. Newcastle-on-Tyne began a Lying-in Charity in 1765, and Norwich a hospital in 1771. Finally, in 1784, came Dr. Thomas Percival's famous Report on the Health of Manchester to the County Justices, followed by the setting-up of the Manchester Board of Health.

Thus, even before the middle of the century, attention was already turning towards medical and sanitary reform, and thereafter this movement rapidly gained force in several of the larger towns. In this field of action, Manchester, under the vigorous leadership of Dr. Percival, was well to the front ; and indirectly John Howard's national crusade for prison reform, which began in 1773, exerted a powerful influence on the movement. Howard's *State of the Prisons* appeared in 1777 ; and he included hospitals and similar institutions within the scope of his enlightening surveys. But reform was slow. William Tuke's Retreat at York—the first humane Lunatic Asylum—was not founded until 1791 ; and the creation of separate fever hospitals was only beginning at the end of the century. The Manchester Fever Hospital, created under Percival's influence, dates only from 1796.

The spirit of philanthropy was not confined to hospital subscriptions. The latter half of the century was also marked by the growth of other charitable bodies, from Friendly Societies, under the patronage of the rich, to such institutions as the Norwich Society of Universal Good Will, first founded as the Scots Society in 1776, for the relief of poor strangers in the town. The movement to set up Charity Schools connected with the Church of England had by 1750 exhausted its impetus and ceased to expand ; but sporadic Sunday Schools, such as Hannah Ball's at High Wycombe (1768), were founded even before Robert Raikes began work at Bristol in 1780. Hannah More was at that time still pursuing her literary career in London, on intimate terms with Dr. Johnson and his circle. Her philanthropic ventures at Cowslip Green, near Bristol, began only after 1785.

This growth of philanthropic activities is closely bound up with the rise of Wesleyanism and the Evangelical movement. Of these, Wesleyanism counted for much the more in the provincial towns. Wesley's famous *Journal* is full of accounts of his visits and preachings not only in Bath and Bristol, but also in the growing towns of the north, in all of which from the middle of the century he began to have a considerable following. Wesleyanism was, indeed, concerned with men's souls far more than with their bodies ; and Wesley himself, as well as his leading followers, abhorred all forms of Radicalism. This came to matter greatly at a later stage, when the age of political excitements had set in with the Revolutions in America and France. But in the middle part of the century there was little political unrest to impel the religious reformers to turn their backs on the demand for social reform ; and in the provincial towns the Wesleyan revival was undoubtedly a factor making for the development of the social conscience.

The lead, however, was taken at this stage not by the Wesleyans, but by older types of Dissenters, and especially by Unitarians and Independents, and in some places, such as York, by the Quakers. The Unitarians, headed by Richard Price and Joseph Priestley, were made up of far more intellectual elements than any other group of Dissenters; and their Academies, such as the New College at Warrington, where Priestley taught, followed by Dalton the chemist after its removal to Manchester, were notable centres of social as well as religious enlightenment. Certain of the most successful merchants of Liverpool and other fast-growing centres of industry and commerce got their education at the Dissenting Academies, which spread a knowledge of popular science as well as of religious and political speculation.

Closely connected with the growth of education and enlightenment among the younger generation of merchants is the creation of Literary and Philosophical Societies in the leading mercantile towns. Robert Owen has left, in his *Autobiography*, a graphic record of the impression made on him in his youth by the discussions at the Manchester Society, which was led by Dr. Percival and Dr. Barnes, and included Dalton, as well as Owen, among its members. Coleridge came to address it while Owen was there ; and in other towns besides Manchester societies of this type became centres of reforming zeal as well as of literary and philosophical illumination. They gathered together valuable libraries for their members' use ; and their debates and discussions were taken very seriously indeed.

In some cases the formation of a subscription library came first. Liverpool, well to the front as usual, began one in 1757, and added a weekly ' Academy ' in 1774, the year in which the Chamber of Commerce was founded. Manchester, on the other hand, began with informal weekly discussions in an hotel ; and out of them the ' Lit. and Phil.' developed in 1781. No lasting subscription library came into existence till 1792, though there had been earlier attempts. Leeds, under Priestley's influence, formed a Subscription Library in 1768 ; and a Debating Society followed in 1793, but died out in a few years. The Leeds Philosophical and Literary Society dates only from 1818.[1]

By these and other means, standards of taste and knowledge rose very rapidly in the larger manufacturing towns during the latter half of the eighteenth century. A further contribution to the development of more polished manners and a less rude way of living, and perhaps, though not so certainly, to higher cultural standards as well, came from the growing number of boys from the families of the squirearchy who were being apprenticed to trade, especially in the merchant houses of Liverpool. There were many tales narrated about the discontent of these new recruits at the rough ways of speech and living current even among the richer members of the merchant class, at the very early and long hours of work, and at the Puritan ideas so widely spread in the industrial districts. The gentry who took to trade brought with them some shadow of the habits and customs of the fashionable world—a cultivation of dancing, concerts and assemblies, and a taste for music and the fine arts. The Liverpool Musical Society grew out of the great Musical Festival held there in 1784 ; and exhibitions of pictures began about the same time to be shown in some of the leading provincial towns.

The theatre and the newspaper also spread through the leading provincial centres in the course of the eighteenth century, and especially after 1750. In the

[1] The circulating libraries established by booksellers in the larger provincial towns also helped to spread knowledge and to encourage the liking for books.

earlier part of the century, strolling players used mainly tents or booths, and the superior travelling companies and the ' stock ' or repertory companies which existed already here and there used any available hall, and did not provide regular daily performances. But in the latter part of the century there was a rapid building of provincial theatres, such as the Nottingham Theatre of 1760 and the Manchester Theatre Royal of 1775. Often the theatres in several towns were under the same management ; and companies changed places one with another. Bath, indeed, had its first theatre as early as 1705, with a stock company, and the plays selected by the leaders of fashion who were there to take the waters. But the venture came to an end about 1738, and for a time plays were given at an inn or in a cellar under the Rooms. Not until 1750 did the elder John Palmer, of whom more anon, open his theatre in Orchard Street (now the Masonic Rooms). His son, who succeeded to the control, developed a group of theatres in Bristol and other neighbouring towns, with circulating companies in which many of the leading actors and actresses of the day made their names. Mrs. Siddons, who had begun her career at Birmingham, was a member of the Bath company from 1788 to 1792, when she went to Drury Lane. Elliston, Macready, and Kean, as well as Henderson, the leading Bath star, also first made their reputations at the Bath theatres under Palmer's management.

Booksellers' shops and printing houses, often associated with a local newspaper, already existed by the middle of the century in most provincial towns of any size. Dr. Johnson's father was a bookseller in Lichfield ; for his parchment-making, at which he lost money, was only an auxiliary venture. New and second-hand bookselling were not then divided ; and the trade was a much less stable one than it is to-day. It was also more laborious ; for the provincial bookseller used often to go from town to town, opening a stall on market days, in addition to his permanent shop in some one centre. Johnson's father, for example, went regularly to Birmingham with his wares on market days ; and William Hutton, the historian of Birmingham, travelled a regular round of towns for some time, carrying his books long distances upon his back. We also find him walking in 1749 from Nottingham to London and back, in order to buy better tools for his trade as a bookbinder. There is no eighteenth-century autobiography so rich as Hutton's in materials for the study of the provincial life of tradesman and artisan in the Midland counties.

Apart from theatres and concert-rooms and the assembly rooms of the fashionable resorts and the county towns, the centre of the recreative life of the provinces was very often the racecourse. At Manchester, regular race-meetings at Kersal Moor began about 1729, and gave rise to a great deal of controversy. A pamphlet, attributed to John Byrom, was written denouncing them ; and in 1745 they were suppressed for a time. But they were renewed in 1760, and a grand stand built by subscription in 1777, followed by a ladies' stand, equipped for refreshments, in 1780. Nottingham racecourse, which belonged to the Corporation, was leased to the noblemen and gentlemen of the county in 1777, under a trust deed, and did not revert to the Corporation until 1845. Doncaster, already celebrated for its races, was also a famous hunting centre ; and Defoe tells how, about 1725, it was full of great inns, and the Mayor, who kept one of them, had a pack of hounds, and was deemed fit company for the gentry. Another sport was also gaining in popularity. In 1771 Nottingham and Sheffield met in their first cricket match. Less innocuous was the prevalence of cock-fighting and bull-baiting as sports of rich and poor alike.

This consideration of amusements and recreations leads us naturally back to the world of fashion ; for in the eighteenth century almost all sports and recreative arts depended on the noblemen and gentlemen for their patronage. And, in the world of fashion, all roads seem to lead to Bath, which began its career of triumph right at the beginning of the century and kept its ascendancy undimmed to the very end.

Bath, the city of Beau Nash, of John Wood, John Palmer, and Ralph Allen, of Dr. Oliver and Sally Lunn, and, incongruously, of Lady Huntingdon as well, had its first Pump Room in 1704—three years before its first theatre, and its first Assembly Room (Harrison's) in 1708. Nash, Allen, Oliver, the elder Wood, and the elder Palmer were all dead and gone before Dr. Johnson visited Bath with the Thrales in 1776 ; but the younger Wood with his new buildings and the younger and more celebrated Palmer with his mail-coaches, were in the height of their glory. Most of Bath's notable buildings had already been erected, and the new Assembly Rooms, built by the younger Wood, had recently been opened (1771). Henderson was already playing Shakespeare at the theatre, and Thomas Sheridan and Linley were there, teaching elocution and music. Ralph Allen's house at Prior Park was no longer a great resort of literary folk as in Pope's day, and Bath society was broken up far more into sets and coteries than earlier in the century. But, save in one important respect, Bath was still much as Nash had striven to make it in the early years, a place of resort for the upper and middle classes alike, where the observed routine of bathing and drinking the waters was in fact subordinated to the hardly less regular discipline of social events. The company still gathered largely for breakfast in the Assembly Rooms, with a dip in the Baths still earlier for those who fancied it. After breakfast they resorted to the Pump Room to drink the waters, and then, if so disposed, to morning service in the Abbey. Walking, riding, or driving filled in the time until dinner, varied by a visit to the booksellers to read the papers ; and after dinner there were more parades in the Pump Room or the

Orange Groves, followed by five o'clock tea, often taken at the Rooms, and a ball or a visit to the theatre in the evening.

By the time Dr. Johnson paid his visit, Bath was in the third and most enduring phase of its popularity. It began its career, like Harrogate and other places of resort to the waters, as a centre of attraction for invalids. It passed, under Nash's influence, rapidly into a haunt of fashion ; but in this second phase one of its chief attractions was the opportunity which it afforded for open and organised gambling. Till 1745 Nash made most of his money out of the commission of 2½ per cent which he received from the bank on its takings at each EO table—for EO was the favourite form of gambling. But in 1745 public gambling was suppressed by law, to Nash's heavy loss ; and thereafter, while it went on to some extent in taverns and private houses, it ceased to count as an important attraction of Bath life. Gamblers resorted abroad, or to the new racecourses ; and Bath society was none the less fashionable or enticing to the mind of the public for its disappearance. Thereafter Bath, haunt of wickedness as it appeared to John Wesley and the circle of Lady Huntingdon—who lived there none the less—followed in the main a very innocuous round of pleasures. Its favourite plays were classical tragedies, by Otway or the Elizabethans, and its favourite dance was the stately minuet. It was, indeed, the great match-making centre of England, and a great place for innocent flirtations. But as a den of vice, save the minor vices of idleness and frivolity, it left much to the Wesleyan imagination.

Bath's appeal was in no wise weakened by the rapid growth of other centres of fashionable resort, such as Cheltenham and Tunbridge Wells and Harrogate, or by the growing popularity of seaside watering-places as the century advanced. Of other inland spas, Knaresborough, near the Harrogate waters, was the oldest, and Harrogate grew up as a separate place of resort by the middle of the century. Tunbridge Wells also developed about the same time as a new town grouped round the waters ; and Cheltenham was just becoming popular when Richard Pococke visited it in 1750. But its lodgings were then, in his view, no more than tolerable. Cheltenham and Tunbridge Wells modelled themselves on Bath, and reproduced faithfully its routines and observances, whereas Harrogate, frequented chiefly by Northerners, was a good deal less ceremonious.

But the chief resort in the north, and the pioneer of all seaside watering-places, was Scarborough, already famous for its waters in the seventeenth century. From Dr. Wittie's encomium on the virtues of. Scarborough Spa in 1667 to Dr. Peter Shaw's *Inquiry into the Contents, Virtues and Uses of Scarborough Spaw Water* in 1734 much was written about the special health-giving properties of the place ; and Sir John Floyer's *History of Cold Bathing* (1734) and Shaw's *Inquiry* gave it a new accession of popularity. Sea-bathing was by this time coming much into fashion as a cure ; and, in imitation of the inland spas, drinking the sea-water was also widely recommended. These new fashions led to a great growth of watering-places in the south. Brighton, or Brighthelmstone, was only a poor fishing village in Defoe's day ; but by 1750 Pococke records it as ' greatly improved of late by the concourse of people who come to it to bathe and drink the sea-water ', and as possessing a good coffee-house, a large room for company, and carriages for the convenience of bathing. Pococke has much the same to say of Margate, where he notices especially ' the conveniency of covered carriages, at the end of which there is a covering that lets down with hoops, so that people can go down a ladder into the water and not be seen, and those who please may jump in and swim '. Deal and Eastbourne and Portsmouth were among other resorts that became popular in the first half of the eighteenth century, followed a little later by Weymouth and many other places. Much of the fashionable world went

64

on to a seaside resort after passing the earlier part of the summer at Bath or some other inland spa.

But no more space can be devoted to the haunts and habits of the noblemen and gentlemen, or of those prosperous merchants and tradesmen who came more and more either to imitate their manners, or to work out a round of pleasure for themselves as standards of living advanced and the earlier forms of Puritanism relaxed their hold. For in the eighteenth century, as at other times, towns were mainly workaday places, and the great majority of their inhabitants belonged to the working classes. It is time, then, to glance at the position of the urban workers, their wages and conditions of work, and the environment in which they spent their leisure.

It must be observed in the first place that it is of even less use to generalise about working-class conditions before the Industrial Revolution than in the nineteenth century or to-day. For prior to the coming of the factory system the distinction between the working classes and the social groups nearest to them was even less clear-cut than it is in the modern world. A prosperous skilled artisan earning a weekly wage might be quite as well off, and as respectable in his social status, as a small master or shopkeeper ; and in the days of the ' domestic system ', the lines between small masters, sub-contractors, and working journeymen were not at all easy to draw. In the building trades especially, the same man often worked sometimes as a small contractor and sometimes as a journeyman drawing a wage ; while the ' domestic ' worker might be either an independent producer working with his own tools and upon his own materials or a dependent using tools and materials which were the property of someone who was virtually his employer, and paying rent for the use of the instruments of production—' loom-rent ' for example. There was, in addition, a far wider gulf between skilled artisans and mere labourers than there is to-day, both in wages and in degree of education and social standing. The cultural gulf between labourer and artisan was usually much wider than the gulf between artisan and small employer or tradesman.

For information about wages outside London, the most valuable sources are Arthur Young's *Tours* ; for he recorded, wherever he could, the prevailing wages for urban as well as rural workers. His figures have, however, to be taken as very rough estimates, mostly derived from employers' information ; and statements about the earnings of piece-workers under the domestic system are especially liable to error. It is, nevertheless, possible to obtain from his writings, with such confirmation as can be secured from other sources, a fairly clear picture of prevailing wage-standards in many of the principal towns.

Thus, in Manchester it appears that, about 1770, the wages of highly skilled male workers in the textile trades did not often rise above 7s. 6d. a week, though a few exceptionally skilled hands might sometimes get up to 12s. A large number of skilled men got no more than 5s. or 6s. and some as little as 4s. a week. Skilled women workers appear to have made less, but not a great deal less, than the majority of men ; and in a number of cases Young records that they were paid at the same rates. Children earned from 1s. 6d. a week upwards, according to age and trade. Eden, writing almost thirty years later, in the midst of the great rise in prices during the French War, put the wages of skilled men as high as 18s. a week, and women's from 6s. to 12s., with unskilled labour at 2s. or 2s. 6d. a day.

This sharp advance in men's wages was due in part to the rise in prices, but also to the rapid growth of the cotton trade. Lancashire was a low-wage area until the Industrial Revolution. The old-established woollen industry in Yorkshire paid the male workers rather better. Thus, in Leeds, Arthur Young gave the earnings of men weavers as from 5s. to 12s. a week, with an average of 7s., and of broadcloth weavers at 10s. 6d., and

66

wool-combers 6s. to 12s. But, while highly skilled women weavers made in some cases as much as men, their average earnings were only from 3s. 6d. to 4s., and at spinning—an unskilled occupation—women got only from 2s. 6d. to 3s. Moreover, all these rates were for full-time work ; and Young comments that they were often seriously reduced by intermittent employment.

Earnings tended to be lower in the north of England than in the south, at least for the most highly skilled grades of workers. Thus, dyers in Norwich are said to have earned 15s. a week, and cloth pressers 13s., while wool-combers in the Western Counties averaged 13s. Weavers in Witney got from 10s. to 12s. a week all the year round—an exceptionally prosperous group ; for weavers even in London earned on the average no more than from 12s. to 15s. a week. Young gives the average earnings of men employed in industry in the western counties as 11s. a week, in the eastern counties as 6s. 6d., and in the south as 9s. 4d.

There were, thus, wide differences in wages both from trade to trade and from place to place. Artisans in the older crafts in the larger towns—shoemakers, tailors, cabinet-makers, and so on—and the minority of highly specialised craftsmen, such as wool-combers and dyers, in the larger industries did best, while the condition of the main body of wage-earners varied very greatly from one town to another. But it has to be remembered that costs of living were a good deal lower in the north and east than in the south, and in the market towns than in the larger cities.

It is exceedingly difficult to say how far the industrial workers in the eighteenth century were organised in Trade Unions for collective bargaining about wages and conditions of labour. No modern Trade Union dates from this period ; and those which did exist have left no records of their own behind them. But there is plenty of evidence of the widespread existence of certain forms of combination. The journeymen in the larger towns

certainly had their regular Trade Clubs, which were often
Friendly Societies as well as Trade Unions, and negotiat-
ated freely with the small masters, usually without any
interference from the law. There was, indeed, on the
Statute Book a general embargo on working-class combinations enacted under Edward VI ; and many specific
statutes were passed in the eighteenth century prohibit-
ing combinations in particular trades. But the small
Trade Clubs of the urban artisans were seldom molested,
the severities of the law being directed rather against the
larger Unions which arose from time to time among the
weavers of a whole county, or some similar widespread
group. The wool-combers seem to have maintained a
nation-wide organisation without being suppressed ; and
persecution of Trade Unionism was intermittent and
casual until the fears of Jacobinism came to render all
working-class bodies suspect of treasonable designs.

These eighteenth-century combinations often sought
to influence wage-rates not so much by collective bargaining as by appeals to the law. Again and again the
weavers and other groups are found petitioning Parliament or the Justices for the fixing of a legal rate of wages.
This method was hardly used by the smaller urban
groups ; but they were fully prepared to invoke the law
when a master endeavoured to employ unapprenticed
labour, and so to break down the monopoly of the trained
craftsmen. These appeals to the law took place under the
Elizabethan Statute of Artificers, which was still in force,
though the justices had long ceased to fix regular rates of
wages for the various urban trades, and even the fixing
of agricultural rates had largely lapsed or become formal
and meaningless. The restrictions on apprenticeship continued to be enforced to a substantial extent in the older
crafts and towns ; but over the greater part of the textile
trades these too had lapsed. They were never enforced
in the case of the new Lancashire cotton industry, or in
the woollen industry except in Norwich and a very few
other places.

The real strength of working-class bargaining power in the eighteenth century lay among the minority of highly skilled craftsmen in the small-scale industries of the towns ; for the expansion of wealth gave these skilled groups a valuable monopoly of labour, and the small scale on which their trades were carried on put them nearly on a bargaining equality with their employers. Their small Trade Clubs were powerful monopolies, within their narrow range. But they showed little disposition either to combine on a national scale, or to establish federal relations between club and club, even in the same town. The urban artisans formed less a class than a number of groups of persons lifted well above the common run of labour in both status and earning power, and divided by no more than a narrow line from the typical urban employer. The employer, indeed, was much further removed from the merchant than from his own journeymen until the new class of factory employers began to develop with the advent of power-driven machinery.

It follows from what has been said that it is impossible to generalise about the habits and social conditions of the eighteenth-century workers, any more than about their wages and industrial status. The colliers of the midland and northern counties, the metal-workers of the Black Country, the iron-workers and certain other groups not primarily urban, were doubtless rough and uncivilised enough. But most of the urban workers who responded to the preaching of Wesley and his followers, or were soon to be roused by the appeal of Radical doctrines, had at least some education and some pretension to a civilised way of living.

It has to be remembered that, in many of the urban crafts, apprenticeship was still fully in force, and the apprentice still often went to dwell in his master's house, under conditions which made his master responsible for his training in manners as well as at his trade. William Hutton learnt his trade in his uncle's house at Nottingham, and Robert Owen was apprenticed first to a draper at Stamford. Such men, whatever their origin, usually emerged from their period of servitude with manners like their masters' ; and while these might be rough and brutal enough at times, there were many Dissenting or Wesleyan households in which high moral standards were enforced, while in places like Liverpool and Bristol and Norwich the main body of the skilled craftsmen had a long tradition of self-respect and importance in the town's affairs. The common labourers were much below the artisans in these respects ; but even for them Wesley and Whitefield did much as the century advanced. Nor must we regard deliberate efforts at working-class education as beginning with Robert Raikes or the Sunday School movement. They were in fact going on all the time, in chapels, Trade Clubs, and other societies, as well as in the course of apprenticeship and in the daily contacts of ordinary life.

There was, however, a town mob in most of the larger cities, and it made its presence felt long before the Gordon Riots in London or the burning of Joseph Priestley's house and laboratory in Birmingham at the time of the French Revolution. Arkwright had his first factory burnt down ; and there were frame-breaking troubles in Nottingham and other east Midland towns half a century before the Luddites. But the commonest cause of mob action in the middle of the eighteenth century was the high price of provisions ; and again and again, in town after town, we hear of more or less serious bread-riots in times of scarcity and unemployment. These movements had, however, little or no political complexion. What Radicalism there was existed among the most highly skilled of the artisans and among the tradesmen who formed the backbone of the Revolution Societies for celebrating the triumphs of 1688, and not among the mob. For some time after the French Revolution, the mobs were loyalist, and not Jacobin, and far more liable to demonstrate against Popery or Jacobinism than against an iniquitous Government.

But that there existed the material for intense mass excitement the preaching of Wesley and Whitefield and their followers abundantly demonstrated. There are many passages, even in Wesley's *Journal*, which cannot but fill the modern reader with sheer astonishment. We read of sinners who, listening to Wesley's preaching, were overcome with terrible physical pains, and rolled in torment on the ground, while the enthusiasts of the new gospel knelt round and prayed for their spiritual deliverance. We read of vast masses moved out of themselves by the call to repentance far beyond anything that has marked the revivalism of more recent times, though not perhaps beyond the achievements of latter-day American evangelists. We get an impression throughout Wesley's *Journal* that he is appealing to persons incapable of an intellectual response, whose souls must be saved by other and more ferocious means, and we are confirmed in this impression by the attitude of many of Wesley's own contemporaries towards his preaching. It was not only among the votaries of the Established Church that the Wesleyan enthusiasts were derided as throw-backs to an earlier and less civilised age, but almost equally among the more intellectual members of the earlier Dissenting congregations. It is customary nowadays to regard Wesleyanism as a great humanising and civilising influence ; and so in many ways it was. But it has its other aspect as well ; for, setting out to catch men's souls by all means, it used methods of approach which played upon the fears of the uneducated and the illiterate without qualm or remorse. And it was able to do this with the less compunction because from the outset it would have no truck with political democracy in any form.

But Wesleyanism after the days of the early preachings was speedily toned down as the Methodists gathered regular bodies of adherents in the various towns and built themselves chapels. They developed into orderly

Dissenting congregations which had much in common with the Nonconformist groups already in existence. Throughout the middle of the eighteenth century the Methodists were busy creating for themselves regular places of worship in one after another of the towns where Wesley had gathered his first disciples by preaching in the streets or on the open moor. The Methodists did not cease to remind their hearers of hell fire even in these changed surroundings ; but when once they had settled down they began to educate men for this world as well as to save their souls, and perhaps the most important part of the education which they provided was the training in self-government which arose out of the working and organisation of the local chapel and its contact with the wider Wesleyan connexion.

Go to-day to some small town—Sudbury, in Suffolk, Chipping Norton, in Oxfordshire, or even Appleby in Westmorland—which has preserved much of its outer appearance as it was in the eighteenth century, and you have the means, with a little imagination, of visualising the outer appearance of the typical town, or even city, of two hundred years ago. But in order to make the picture correct, you have to people these towns very differently, and to think of many of them far more as independent manufacturing centres than as markets and shopping-places. Some, indeed, such as Stamford, owed their importance to their use as markets and meeting-places for the surrounding countryside ; but, taking the country as a whole, many more had some special manufacture of their own—some branch of one of the textile trades, or pin-making as at Gloucester, or pottery as at Burslem, or tanning (not yet brewing) at Burton-on-Trent. Industry was much more scattered then than now ; but, contrary to a common opinion, it was even then mainly urban, if market towns as well as boroughs are included in the conception of a town. Urban areas were very numerous, and for the most part very small ; and they were also, as we have seen, exceedingly diverse in their character and ways of life. And above them all stood London, the only town worthy to be thought of as a considerable town at all by our modern standards. But London deserves—and gets—in this volume an essay to itself.

London—One-Fifth of England

MORE than two hundred years have gone by since Daniel Defoe, in his *Tour Through the Whole Island of Great Britain*, expressed his amazement and admiration at the prodigious growth of building in the neighbourhood of London, and at the extraordinary increase of houses and people within London itself. In Defoe's eyes these things were very good. His heart rejoiced when he saw the houses of prosperous merchants perching themselves in every vantage-point of high land around the metropolis ; and as he journeyed about England and Scotland on his equivocal missions for Robert Harley, reporting on the state of opinion in the country and organising everywhere a service of correspondents who would keep him, and through him the Government, regularly informed of what people were thinking, he never wearied of recording how much London's greatness contributed to the prosperity of the whole country. In eighteenth-century England all roads, by land or by water, seemed to lead to London ; and nearly all trade appeared to be an exchange between London and the provinces, to the advantage of both.

London was, in Defoe's day, the only town in England that could be reckoned large by modern standards. Bristol and Norwich, which came next to it in population, had in the 1720's probably no more than about 30,000 inhabitants ; and most other important towns were no bigger than many villages are to-day. No wonder London seemed to Defoe and his contemporaries a prodigious place, overshadowing the whole country with the multitude and wealth of its consuming public.

And yet, by the standards of our time, how small a place Defoe's London was ! Half a century before, at

the time of the Great Plague, Greater London probably
had about half a million inhabitants. After the Plague
and the Fire, the number fell perhaps by a fifth. Then it
increased again very fast. Defoe, in 1724, asserted that
London and its environs had a population of a million
and a half. This, however, like most of Defoe's estimates,
was obviously wild exaggeration ; for when the first
Census was officially taken in 1801, Greater London—
reckoning it as including the area which is now administered by the London County Council—had still
less than a million people. For this same area, which was
in 1801 fully adequate to include all veritable Londoners,
Defoe's figure was not reached until about 1826 ; and
a population of two millions was not achieved until the
early 'forties. The three-million mark was passed in the
middle 'sixties, and the four-million mark in the middle
'eighties, but the four and a half millions enumerated
in the Census of 1901 proved to be the summit of growth
within the area of the London County Council. Since
then London's population, within this area, has been
actually declining.

At the time of the Plague and the Fire roughly one
citizen out of every eleven in England and Wales could
be called a Londoner. In Defoe's day the proportion was
perhaps one in ten. At the date of the first Census it was
one in nine. London had been gaining in relative population, but not very rapidly. But in the nineteenth
century the relative rate of increase became much
greater. By 1880 Greater London could claim one
citizen out of every six in England and Wales. To-day
it can claim one out of every five.

These proportions are not, of course, for the same
areas at different dates. They represent the population
of a Greater London which has been continuously
spreading out over a larger space. The area which was
assigned to the Metropolitan Board of Works on its
establishment in 1855 seemed generously adequate to
include all London, though the powers assigned to the

75

new body were confined to the single function of co-ordinating the system of main drainage. Thirty-three years later, when inner London at length acquired, in the London County Council, a unifying authority with reasonably sufficient powers, the boundaries of 1855 were left unchanged ; and perhaps they still seemed barely adequate to include all London. These boundaries remain the same to-day, for London in an administrative sense ; but they are now quite ludicrously too narrow. Fully half the people of London live nowadays outside the area administered by the London County Council ; and it is a safe conjecture that before long the number of outer inhabitants will be greatly in excess of the number of Londoners in the administrative area—that is, of course, unless London's frontiers are enlarged. In terms of extent of territory, the disparity is naturally even greater than in the number of inhabitants ; for the outlying suburbs are much less densely populated than the districts within the inner ring. In these days a growing population requires much more room to house than even a generation ago. Dwellings are built less thick on the ground ; and more land is given to gardens and open spaces, public or private—though still, especially in the poorer areas, not nearly enough. Moreover, in these days, families are smaller, so that for a given population houses need to be more numerous as well as further apart.

Thus it has come about that the area assigned to the London County Council forms nowadays only a small part of Greater London. Still more startling is the contrast if we compare even the L.C.C. area with that of the Greater London which Defoe thought so vast and marvellous. London County includes, in addition to the City, the twenty-eight Metropolitan Boroughs created by Parliament in 1899 out of the previous confusion of parishes and district boards which had sent their representatives to the Metropolitan Board of Works. Of these boroughs, only two—Holborn and Southwark

76

—fall wholly within the area which Defoe marked out as constituting the Greater London of his day. Five other boroughs—Westminster, Finsbury, Shoreditch, Stepney, and Bermondsey—fall to a substantial extent within Defoe's area ; and three more—Lambeth, Deptford, and Battersea—include small districts which Defoe regarded as lying within the boundaries of Greater London. But no less than eighteen of the present boroughs of inner London—quite apart from the numerous boroughs and urban districts of the outer ring—fall entirely outside the frontiers of the great metropolis as Defoe described it in his *Tour*. Yet Defoe, with his abounding enthusiasm for London's greatness, was certainly much more likely to exaggerate than to minimise its extent.

It is interesting to compare the frontiers of Defoe's London rather more in detail with those of London to-day. What Defoe regarded as Greater London began, in the west, at a point not far distant from Westminster Abbey, say somewhere on the river about midway between the Abbey and the present Vauxhall Bridge. From this point the boundary ran north, stretching over towards Vauxhall Bridge Road and then along it to Buckingham House—now Buckingham Palace—and thence to Hyde Park Corner. There it turned east, taking in Piccadilly, and spread again to the north in the neighbourhood of Bond Street, reaching what is now Oxford Street, and throwing out one or two small projections to the north of Oxford Street. At Tottenham Court the buildings spread a little way up Tottenham Court Road, but then the boundary ran due East just to the north of the British Museum—then Montague House—taking in a fraction of what is now Bloomsbury. Thence the limit of building went roughly by Guilford Street across Gray's Inn Road, where there was another outlying spur towards St. Pancras. East of Gray's Inn Road the frontier becomes harder to define ; for the houses were already reaching out to join up with

Islington past Mount Pleasant, and there was a good deal of recent building in the neighbourhood of Sadler's Wells. To the east of the northern projection towards Islington, the frontier went a little to the north of Old Street; but on the south side of Old Street there were large open spaces, occupied by the Artillery Ground and Moorfields, and these open spaces stretched down almost into the heart of the City. To the east of this expanse the northern boundary continued the Old Street line, taking in Shoreditch. Then it began to slope south, round the edges of the New Town of Mile End. Bethnal Green and the Old Town of Mile End were still well outside the area of continuous building, which ended at this point approximately where the Whitechapel Road turns into the Mile End Road to-day. To the south of this developing area the boundary receded sharply westwards, leaving a large open space, then partly occupied by rope-walks—broadly where the Commercial Road district is now. But further south, beyond this unbuilt area, the houses had pushed out a long way to the east along the north bank of the river through Wapping and Shadwell as far as Limehouse. Limehouse in its turn was already almost joined in the far east to Poplar and Blackwall beyond it.

On the south side of the river, continuous building began in the east at Deptford and extended as far as Lambeth in the west, about opposite the point at which London's frontier north of the river then lay. On the Surrey side, however, there was, for most of this distance, only a thin strip of built-up land along the river-bank, with only one considerable stretch of building away to the south, in the growing town of Southwark beyond London Bridge. London Bridge still remained the only dry crossing of the river until Westminster Bridge was opened in 1750. Apart from the considerable town of Southwark, the buildings lay much thicker to the east than to the west of London Bridge. Redriff, or Rotherhithe, and Bermondsey were already substantial places, whereas to the west of the Borough the districts of Newington and Lambeth were still very thinly peopled. In Southwark itself the built-up area was being extended southwards in a sort of ribbon development along the Kent and Croydon roads past St. George's.

Such was Defoe's London, of which he reckoned the complete circuit, leaving out Poplar and Blackwall, at between seventeen and eighteen miles. This he regarded as an altogether unexampled immensity of continuous building, though, as we have seen, it covers but a tiny fraction of the area now administered by the London County Council, and a still tinier fraction of the Greater London of to-day.

Not till the nineteenth century did the area covered by continuous building spread out far beyond the limits of Defoe's Greater London. Study any London map of the early nineteenth century—say Cary's of 1822—practically a century after Defoe's survey. The changes in the built-up area are very much smaller than the figures of the increase in population would suggest. Indeed, the really continuous spread of London was still relatively small. Independent towns and villages such as Islington, Hackney, and Stoke Newington to the north, and Peckham, Battersea, and Clapham to the south, had come into much closer contact with London, without being actually engulfed. So had Woolwich in the east, and Kensington and Hammersmith in the west. The Greater London of 1855 was already being foreshadowed ; but it was not yet in being. The railway age, which was soon to suburbanise a host of towns and villages beyond the built-up area, had not yet begun. London's first steam railway was not opened until 1833. The network of suburban lines was mostly built in the 1850's.

Indeed, at many points the solid growth of the London area was rendered possible only by the draining of the marsh lands, especially to the east, where even to-day low-lying districts along the courses of the

Thames and the Lea still account for considerable open spaces within the circuit of the built-up area. The story of London's expansion until well on into the nineteenth century is bound up with the drainage of low-lying lands. As rivers were canalised, or even put into pipes and lost to sight, as marshes were drained and filled up with all manner of rubbish, Londoners populated spaces where building had been quite out of the question at an earlier date. East London, as we know it, has been erected largely on the low lands along the valleys of the Thames and the Lea.

To the north and to the south Nature offered fewer obstacles to expansion than to the east ; but in these regions also contours have been important. In both these directions the higher lands were usually filled up first, as residential suburbs for the well-to-do. The lower lands were for the most part developed later for cheaper houses and for poorer folk. Westwards, population was able to pour out more evenly than in other directions, along the relatively flat clay land of Middlesex. But even in this region, expansion usually came earliest on such rising ground as there was. In Greater London, except in the central districts, it is broadly true that the rich, or the well-to-do, live on higher ground than the poor.

There is of course no difficulty in finding reasons for London's continuous tendency to expand. London is the capital city of one of the richest countries in the world ; and this country is itself the centre of the world's most populous empire. London has been for generations the world's financial capital, with a vastly greater accumulation of experience than any other city in the handling of large and delicate financial transactions. London is the only great capital city in Europe which is also a first-class port ; so that foreign commerce, as well as government and high finance, finds in it a natural home. It is well placed for contact with the continent of Europe, so that it became at an early date the clearing-house for tourists as well as for commercial traffic. Many causes have conspired together to make London great ; and the greater it becomes, the more compelling grows its attractive power. Great populations mean great markets for the wares of culture and commerce alike. The more people come to live in London, and the more industries settle there, the stronger grow the reasons why even more should follow. Nor are there, now that the marshes in the vicinity have mostly been drained, any serious natural obstacles to further expansion. Physically, there is no reason why London should not be stretched out continuously to Brighton, or to Oxford, or to Colchester, without encountering any worse hindrances than have been overcome in the course of its growth up to the present day.

Is this proliferation of the metropolis good or bad—first from the standpoint of the Londoners themselves, and secondly from that of the country as a whole ? From certain points of view it is obviously bad. For one thing —much in men's thoughts in these unhappy days—it increases the vulnerability of London to attack from the air ; for a stampede of any considerable section of London's vast population into the surrounding country would obviously dislocate the entire system of food-supply and public administration. Again, London's development aggravates the problem of the depressed areas ; for London offers a peculiar attraction to the lighter finishing trades, which grow most rapidly in these days with the expansion and diversification of the consuming market. But it is just these finishing trades that are needed in the depressed areas to make up for the decline of the older basic industries.

Moreover, the bigger London grows, the more evident become the disadvantages of its growing without any sort of comprehensive plan. It is costing millions to establish some sort of green belt of open land around Greater London ; and even so, in face of the chaotic development of the past, this belt is bound to be broken by many stretches of built-up land. This might have

81

been avoided if, at an earlier stage, London had possessed any sort of unified governing authority with power to plan its development on rational lines. But no such Greater London authority has ever existed ; and unhappily none exists to-day, or seems likely to exist in the near future.

The disputation about the advantages and disadvantages of London's vastness is almost as old as the recorded history of the place. For centuries before William Cobbett railed at London as ' The Wen ', one generation of Englishmen after another had been marvelling at its prodigious size. Foreigners, too, and half-foreigners from North Britain, have often recorded their wonder at London's greatness—from William Dunbar's ' London, thou art of townes *A per se* ', to the most eloquent star in Baedeker. Indeed, foreigners have been much more inclined to approve of London's vastness than Londoners themselves. For there have been many voices uplifted on the other side. Queen Elizabeth issued a number of proclamations designed to check the growth of building in London ; Shelley capped Dunbar by proclaiming ' Hell is a city much like London ' ; and Cobbett regarded the growth of ' The Great Wen ' as the main cause of the decay which he saw in the countryside of England. No one who lives in or near London, whether he likes it or not, can help observing with wonder the apparently limitless capacity of the Great City for taking all things unto itself—a capacity which has appeared in our own time to be unaffected, if not positively stimulated, by economic depression elsewhere.

It is, indeed, easy to see why London has been growing so fast in recent years. Just now the face of England is changing, economically, almost as rapidly as it changed in the days of the Industrial Revolution, when cotton factories and coal mines and iron works were piling up populations in the new industrial areas of the north. Nowadays the current is setting the other way. Finished commodities are made with a smaller expenditure of

82

raw material; and the semi-manufactures used in the making of them take much less fuel to produce. Labour is being shifted out of the extractive and primary producing industries into the lighter finishing trades, which, unrestricted to any particular locality by physical causes, are for the most part free to settle where they please. At the same time, as productivity increases and standards of living rise, fewer workers come to be employed in making things, and more in carrying them about, handling them in warehouses and shops, or making book entries about them in ledgers. More people find employment in rendering direct services to the consumers whose incomes allow them a surplus over the bare needs of living. There is rapid growth, for example, of the entertainment and catering industries; and more labour is needed to man the public utility services, from gas, water, and electricity to roadmaking and the erection of public buildings, and all the host of subordinate occupations dependent on these services. Maintenance work in garages, in house-repairs, and in a host of minor services, grows apace. The public departments, national and local, assume new functions, and therewith take on a larger number of employees. Finally, the professions wax in numbers; and more and more hitherto unorganised and unrecognised callings acquire a defined professional status.

All these changes in the character of employment serve to foster the growth of London. Both the official Census and the recent *New Survey of London Life and Labour* reveal very plainly the special characteristics of London's economic life. In the area covered by the *New Survey*, the figures showing the numbers engaged in different occupations are very significant. Domestic service heads the list, with 418,000 employees. Next comes transport, with 316,000, followed by the food and catering trades with 272,000, the dress trades with 264,000, and commercial occupations with 227,000.

So far the list of occupations of the people of London

does not include a single major 'industry' in the ordinary sense of the term. Next, however, comes building (165,000); and then follow in order professional occupations (153,000), metal and machinery trades (150,000), printing and paper trades (102,000), Government services (86,000), wood and furniture trades (83,000), and textile trades (72,000).

Thus, among productive industries in the narrower sense, excluding the food and dress trades, which are largely concerned with 'making-up', building comes easily first, followed by the metal and engineering group and by the printing and paper trades. Domestic service, the food and catering trades, and the clothing trades occupy a far larger proportion of the working population than in any other region, and the same is true of transport and of commerce, including distribution. London's professional population is also quite abnormally high. If the persons engaged in domestic service are added to the 'non-manual' group, the numbers of the combined population of 'non-manual workers' rise to nearly half the whole number of the people.

These figures bear out the impression that London is predominantly a commercial and residential rather than an industrial centre. Yet the total amount of manufacture is very considerable. Even if the food and dress trades, as well as building, are left out, manufactures employ at least one-fifth of the total occupied population inside the survey area. A division of the total occupied population within this area into eight broad groups, *plus* one miscellaneous group of unclassified workers, yields the following results : manufacturing, 446,000 ; domestic, 418,000 ; commerce and professions, 381,000 ; dress and textiles, 336,000 ; transport 316,000 ; food and catering, 272,000 ; building, 165,000 ; Government and defence, 104,000 ; miscellaneous, 227,000.

Interpreting these figures, we can reach the broad conclusion that even in London manual workers predominate over 'black-coats' if domestic servants are

excluded from both groups. An analysis of the unemployment insurance figures yields the very rough
conclusion that London's ' black-coats ' number about
40 per cent of the total of insured workers. These figures
of course leave out the more highly paid salary earners :
so that, in effect, only about one-half of London's working population is engaged in industry and transport,
while of the other half about one in three is in
domestic service, and the other two in commerce,
finance, and the professions or public services.

It is not easy to make any comparison between these
proportions and the distribution of London's occupied
population at earlier periods. The Census returns give
occupational figures from 1851, but not on a comparable
basis ; for the earlier Censuses classified workers largely
according to the materials on which they worked, and
not according to the industry or the precise occupation in
which they were engaged. In these circumstances only
the broadest comparison is possible. It is roughly true
that since 1851 the numbers employed in transport,
commerce, the professions, the public services, and other
non-industrial occupations show not very different rates
of increase, whereas the population engaged in manufactures has grown much more slowly, and domestic
service more slowly still. The great increase in non-
manual as against manual occupations has thus been
offset to a substantial extent by a relative decline in
domestic service. In 1851 manufactures and the domestic
services (including the dress trades) each accounted for
nearly 40 per cent of the total of occupied persons :
to-day manufactures account for about 44 per cent and
domestic service and the dress trades together for only
about 25 per cent. Meanwhile transport has risen from
8 to 12 per cent, and commerce from 5 to 9 per cent.
Government service has increased from 2 per cent to
about 3½ per cent, and professional work from about
4 to about 6 per cent. These proportions are of course
only approximate, and not for fully comparable areas ;

but they serve to give a broad indication of the main changes that have been taking place.

As a manufacturing centre, London is concerned mainly with the trades making finished consumers' goods. In this there is nothing new. Although the predominant trades have changed, it was as much the case in the eighteenth century as it is to-day. In 1750, or thereabouts, London's principal occupations included watch-making, silk-weaving, and boot-making—all consumers' industries which have now for the most part disappeared. Shipbuilding, which was in the eighteenth century the principal London industry not catering directly for the consumer, has also deserted the Thames, the last London shipyard having been shut down within living memory. Silk-throwing disappeared to provincial factories in the course of the eighteenth century, and silk-weaving died away fast after the removal of the prohibition upon imported silk goods in 1826. Watch-making and boot-making, for which London had once a great reputation, migrated from the metropolis much more slowly, the former to Birmingham and Switzerland, and the latter to the developing factory areas in East Anglia and the Midlands and around Bristol. Coach-making, which was among the most important of all London's industries in the eighteenth and early nineteenth centuries, died away gradually with the advent of the railway age.

These London industries of the eighteenth century were for the most part conducted on a small scale, in workshops rather than factories, or even in the workers' homes. But eighteenth-century London had other industries which were organised in a much more capitalistic fashion. Shipbuilding, of course, belongs to this group, apart from boat-building, and to it must be assigned brewing and distilling, sugar-refining, and soap-boiling—London trades which were carried on in the eighteenth century for a more than local market, and exported a substantial proportion of their products.

The treating of produce imported from the Far East and from the Colonies was also of importance among the London trades of the eighteenth century ; for the *entrepôt* business played a large part in British commercial activity in the age before the Industrial Revolution.

Broadly, the workers in these trades of eighteenth-century London were distinguished by contemporaries into two classes—the skilled artisans and the ' mob ' of unskilled labour, with the poorly paid Spitalfields silk-weavers ranking somewhere between the two groups. The London artisans had in those days a very high reputation for skill ; and the wages of skilled men tended to be relatively higher in London as compared with the provinces than they are to-day. On the other hand, by the unanimous verdict of contemporaries, the London ' mob ' stood unsurpassed in drunkenness, ill-manners, and boisterous depravity. The writings of foreign visitors to England are filled with adverse comment on the perpetual disorder of the London streets and the perpetual rudeness of the people. These criticisms should doubtless be discounted to some extent—for the eighteenth-century traveller usually belonged to the higher social classes and was very ready to mistake independence for insubordination—but they cannot be altogether disregarded in face of the evidence of such Londoners as the Fieldings, or of the actual circumstances which accompanied the recurrent outbreaks of mob violence, such as the Gordon Riots.

As the nineteenth century advanced London's old staple trades, except those which were directly connected with commerce and transport, began to melt away, and the relative importance of manufactures in London's total economy for a time declined. But the expansion of the dress trades largely filled up the gap left by the decline of silk-weaving ; and especially in the latter part of the century there was a very rapid growth of new consumers' trades in the east end, in the neighbourhood of the Docks. Furniture-making, match-making, jam-making, and many other food trades settled in London to an increasing extent ; printing expanded with the growth of newspapers and commercial advertising, and the lighter metal trades became rapidly more important with the advent of telephones, gramophones, and, in our own day, electrical apparatus and wireless sets. Assembling works, especially for motor-cars, grew numerous in the twentieth century, and many manufacturing industries established big depots as well as offices in the metropolitan area. London's manufacturing activity again increased. It has been growing faster than ever during the past few years—though not so fast as the catering and amusement services.

Thus London's attractive power, as the focus of a great local market, as the capital of a world-wide empire and as the principal money-centre of the world, has given it to an increasing extent the capacity to adapt itself to all manner of economic activities which are not tied to a particular region by inescapable physical limitations. This power was great enough to prevent London from falling in relative population even during the period when industry, based on coal and iron, was making its most rapid advances in the North of England and in the industrial areas of the Clyde and South Wales. And to-day this power is increasing, because the attracting influence of coal and iron has been very greatly reduced.

It would seem obvious that so great and rapidly developing a centre of economic and social life as London needs to be planned and governed as a whole. Yet never has London, since it overflowed the narrow boundaries of the medieval city, possessed a common government. In 1855, the year in which the Metropolis Management Act set up the Metropolitan Board of Works, a writer in *The Times* could even maintain that London did not really exist :

We may really say that there is no such place as London at all, the huge city passing under this title being rent into an infinity

of divisions, districts and areas. . . . Within the metropolitan limits
the local administration is carried on by no less than three
hundred different bodies deriving powers from about two hundred and fifty different local Acts, independent of General Acts.
The number of Commissioners employed, though not precisely
ascertainable, Sir Benjamin Hall estimated by his own computa-
tion at about fifteen thousand.

In the sense given to the phrase by *The Times* in
1855, London still does not exist. The number of separate administrative bodies responsible for the government of the inner metropolitan area has indeed been
reduced, and there has been a considerable co-ordination
of certain essential services. But even inner London is
still administered by a host of separate bodies with no
complete system of unifying control ; and the development of Greater London has brought into being a host
of new administrative authorities fully as confusing and
formidable in obstruction as those of the years before
1855.

When the Metropolitan Board of Works was set up,
for the purpose of equipping London with a main
drainage ' grid '—for that is what we should call it
nowadays—the area allotted to it could reasonably be
regarded as at any rate roughly coterminous with
Greater London. But the Board of Works was never an
effective central authority. It had no power to supersede
the chaos of local bodies whose activities it was merely
given the task of co-ordinating within one particular
field ; and, as it was indirectly elected on a federal basis
by these very authorities, it was incapable of transcending the parochial spirit. It is true that a number of Acts
of Parliament passed between 1855 and 1888 added
considerably to the powers and functions of the Metropolitan Board of Works ; but to the end it remained
purely a federal sanitary authority, without any power
to assume wider functions or to envisage the problem
of London government as a whole.

Thirty-three years after the establishment of the

Board of Works, when Parliament at last decided to set up the London County Council on a basis of direct election by the whole body of London ratepayers, the Metropolis had already sprawled much further afield ; but the boundaries laid down in 1855 were retained without alteration. They remain exactly the same to-day ; for every year since 1888 has made extension more difficult. For most administrative purposes, London to-day is still the London of 1855. Yet in that year Greater London had only about two and a half million inhabitants, whereas it has to-day between eight and nine millions, living in what is essentially a continuous urban area.

Even in 1888 London was already spreading fast beyond the frontiers of 1855, so that the new London County Council set to work under a tremendous handicap. The districts in which the most rapid development was taking place were already beyond its grasp, and it had to watch the metropolitan population spreading fast over suburban areas wholly beyond its co-ordinating control. Moreover, even after 1888 it took Parliament another eleven years to straighten out the tangle of local administrations within the restricted area assigned to the London County Council. The twenty-eight Metropolitan Boroughs, with their separate Councils and their responsibility for local duties which it had not been regarded as necessary to centralise in the hands of the L.C.C., were not established until 1899, though they were largely based upon the twenty-seven London Parliamentary Boroughs which had been set up purely as electoral districts under the Redistribution Act of 1885.

This is London's tragedy—never to have had a government, and to seem to-day further off than ever from acquiring one. For it grows harder every year to rectify the old mistakes. Only a few years ago a Royal Commission on London Government practically abandoned its task in despair. Much more now than in 1888 will any attempt to include the sprawling suburbs within London's government be fought by bitter and determined opponents. The County Boroughs, and many of the Municipal Boroughs, of Greater London will fight hard to preserve their independence—in many cases less from civic pride than because they have lower rates than they could hope for if they were within the L.C.C. area, so that to some extent their citizens can enjoy London's common services without paying for them. Still more energetically will the County Councils of Middlesex, Surrey, Essex, Kent, and Hertfordshire resist any attempt to transfer to the London County Council, or to any unifying authority for Greater London, a substantial part of their present populations and a still larger proportion of their rateable values. To-day the London County Council, when it sets to work to clear slums or to re-house the overcrowded inhabitants of the poorer districts in the inner ring, is compelled largely to build its new houses outside its administrative area, so that they constitute an addition to the rateable value of the neighbouring districts. This may be a powerful logical argument for including these districts in the area of London government; but politically it makes their inclusion all the harder.

London, then, has grown up without a plan, for it has been without any authority capable of making a plan. Since Wren and Evelyn drew up their comprehensive schemes for the rebuilding of London on the morrow of the Great Fire of 1666, no one, I think, has been venturesome enough to make, even on paper, a comprehensive plan for the redevelopment of the metropolis as a whole. After the Great Fire Wren's and Evelyn's plans were promptly jettisoned in face of the objections of London property-owners to being told what they were to do with their land. Vested interests were strong enough even then to veto planning on any adequate scale.

Since then a great many projectors have dreamed of planning London in one or another of its parts; but few of them have been given the opportunity, even on a small scale, of taking the task in hand. One of the few really considerable pieces of planning that have been carried through—the laying-out afresh of the area round Regent's Park, and the driving of a new line of communication thence to Charing Cross, with Nash's Regent Street as its principal architectural accomplishment—was made possible only because it could for the most part be developed upon Crown Lands, for which the existing leases had fortunately expired at the same time. There have been, of course, many other pieces of planning here and there on a smaller scale. The construction of Kingsway is a notable example. But in the main London has been left to grow without any sort of planning beyond the private plans drawn up by the proprietors of particular estates. There has been no one, and despite the strengthening of town-planning authority, there still is no one, with sufficient authority to plan for the development of London as a whole, even in areas which are not yet fully built up—much less for the re-development of districts in which every inch of land is already exploited to the full, in a purely commercial sense. And, if no one has been able to plan London architecturally, or in relation to its problems of traffic and communication, much less has its economic growth ever been subjected to any sort of co-ordinating review, or to any sytematic attempt at balanced expansion of its various industries and services.

But, it may be asked, will London continue to grow ? We are told, in these days, that before long the population of England and Wales will begin falling fast, and that within a generation or so the decline is destined to become catastrophic. About these matters I do not profess to know ; for in the long run, at any rate, population has a way of playing the game of ' Cheat the Prophet '. But in the fairly near future some fall of population in Great Britain is certain. How will this affect London's continuing growth ?

A good deal less, I think, than might be imagined at first sight. For there is still abundant room for the improvement of our housing standards, even if the population gets smaller. We shall continue, I hope, to empty the overcrowded areas in the centre of London, and to spread the people out more thinly in better and pleasanter surroundings. We shall continue to do this, even if standards of flat-building improve, so that a larger population can be decently re-housed in inner London itself. Moreover, unless war comes to devastate the city, London is likely, under modern economic conditions, to retain its attractive power, and, in default of a major change in the course of economic development, to go on gathering people unto itself. It will not be surprising if before long one Englishman in every four, instead of one in every five, comes to be a Londoner.

Therefore, the need for planning exists now more than ever, and planning needs to be economic and not simply social. We ought to be planning not only the buildings and open spaces of London, but the industries as well ; and accordingly we require, now more than ever before, a common government for London as a whole—not to supersede lesser authorities, but to complement and co-ordinate their work. But are we likely to get such an authority for Greater London—a regional, as distinct from a merely local, governing body ? Not, I fear, until the notion of London as a city has sunk much deeper into the minds of most of its citizens than it has to-day ; and not, I fear, until we set to work seriously to plan, not merely London, but the ordered development of Great Britain as a whole.

Roads, Rivers, and Canals

AS recently as the middle of the eighteenth century, most travellers still went on horseback or on foot, and most goods were transported either by water, coastwise or on the river navigations, or, if they went by road, on pack-horses rather than in wheeled vehicles. Stage coaches had indeed begun to ply regularly on a few routes in the seventeenth century; and by 1750 there had been a considerable increase in the number and regularity of the routes in the South of England. Moreover, the service of horses for travelling by post-chaise had been improved; and this method was used increasingly during the summer. There were also great lumbering stage-waggons, used mainly for transporting goods, but carrying poorer passengers who could not afford more expensive conveyances. There were ' railways ' or trackways, especially in some of the mining areas; but these were for horse-drawn vehicles, and were used only for conveying heavy goods to the nearest available river navigation, or to the sea.

Roads and waterways were thus the two means of communication which dominated the economic life of the eighteenth century, as they had dominated that of centuries before. But before the advent of the railways as a completely new and revolutionary force, a profound transformation was brought about in both these earlier channels of intercourse and exchange of goods. The roads of Great Britain were largely revolutionised by the turnpike system; and the waterways acquired a new economic significance with the construction of canals. Over the same period, the potentialities of sea-borne commerce were immensely enlarged, before the coming of steamships, by the improvement of the art of ship-designing, and by the building of docks and harbours of greater capacity and convenience.

Yet travellers who moved about England in the eighteenth century—and still more those whose affairs took them into Scotland—seldom omitted to grumble about the roads. Many of these grumbles have been cited over and over again by later writers—above all those of Arthur Young. But there were voices raised on the other side. Defoe, in the 1720's, and a writer in the *Gentleman's Magazine* of 1754, both dwelt with admiration on the immense improvements that had recently been made in the facilities of travel; and a French traveller, De Saussure, writing in the time of George II, actually described the roads, especially in the neighbourhood of London, as ' magnificent ' by comparison with the roads of France.

There is, in effect, no doubt, despite the prevalent censures, that throughout the eighteenth century the English roads were being rapidly improved. The trouble was, not that the roads were getting worse, but that they were being called upon to carry a quite unprecedentedly heavy volume of traffic. Passenger travel was increasing fast, and the number and weight of passenger vehicles on the roads were growing every year at a pace comparable in proportion with that of the recent growth of motor traffic. At the same time the expansion of industry, and the rapidly developing trade of the provinces with London and with overseas markets, were causing a big increase in the quantity of goods which had to be carried by road, at least to the sea or to the nearest available waterway. The development of towns was swelling the development of traffic proceeding from the surrounding country towards the market centres; and over the greater part of the country the pack-horse was steadily being replaced by the cart or waggon.

Under these conditions, the entire road surface of England needed to be re-made, in order to endure a quite different type of traffic from that for which it had been meant. Up to the eighteenth century, most roads were soft roads, intended principally for horses or at the most for light vehicles not carrying heavy loads. Sometimes there was a stone causeway, broad enough to take a horseman or a pack-horse, but not designed for wheeled vehicles, which had to use the soft road. In summer, when most of the travelling was done, such roads often served well enough until they were called upon to bear the impact of heavy coaches and waggons carrying big loads of merchandise. When vehicles of these types did begin to ply upon them, they collapsed. The heavy vehicles wore deep ruts, which made the roads difficult for lighter vehicles or for travellers on horseback ; and when goods came to be moved, and people to travel, extensively in winter as well as in summer, the roads became mere strips of slush between the fields on either side.

The difficulty was seriously aggravated by the de-velopment of agricultural enclosure. In many parts of the country until well on in the eighteenth century the road was, over long stretches, not so much a made road as a right of way across open stretches of common land. When the existing track became impassable, the traveller merely took another beside it across the fields ; and this his right of passage gave him a full legal right to do. In certain counties, where the land had already been enclosed, these conditions did not exist ; and in these areas, notably in parts of Kent and Sussex, the roads were notoriously bad. In the course of the eight-eenth century the enclosure movement spread rapidly over most of the country, except in the far north. Hedges and fences were put up on each side of the road ; and it became impossible for horses and vehicles to take a new track, however rutted or bogged with mud the defined road might have become. This largely accounts for the perpetual complaints of actual road deteriora-tion, especially in the case of cross-country journeys ; for, as we shall see, the road improvements of the eighteenth century affected mainly the major roads, and it was not till well on in the nineteenth century that the problem of the by-roads was taken seriously in hand.

Let us try to illustrate the effect of the enclosure by an example. Let us follow an imaginary traveller in the middle of the eighteenth century on a journey from Berwick-on-Tweed as far as the crossing of the Thames at Tilbury, supposing his mission to require that he should turn aside to visit a number of important places by the way. Let us, in effect, imagine a traveller bound a generation later on the same sort of mission as Defoe undertook again and again for Harley at the beginning of the century. Let us see, as far as we can, what manner of roads he would have found.

From Berwick-on-Tweed to Newcastle-on-Tyne he would have followed an ' open '—that is, unenclosed— road all the way, except for short stretches in the neighbourhood of the towns of Alnwick and Morpeth. South of Newcastle, on leaving Gateshead, he would have found more open road till he came to the ' streetway '—so named in the old guides—leading to Chester-le-Street. Thence to Durham he would have followed mostly a made road ; and from Durham to Darlington he would have found only about a quarter of the distance unenclosed.

From Darlington southwards he would have been on an enclosed road as far as Topcliff—not a great distance ; but thence to York, via Boroughbridge, was still mainly open road. From York we may suppose him turning away towards the West Riding towns, along enclosed roads except over the long open stretch of Bramham Moor to Leeds. From Leeds to Halifax was partly made road, but with a number of open stretches.

But now comes a difficulty. Suppose our traveller had wished to return from Halifax across Yorkshire by Sheffield and Doncaster to Hull. In 1750 he would have found such a journey very difficult even on horseback, except in the summer months ; for it would have meant riding along endless lanes and across stretches of open country with practically no roads at all. Let us assume, then, that our traveller was making his journey in the summer ; for assuredly no sane man would in 1746 have set out on such a pilgrimage in winter-time.

From Hull our traveller could have ferried over to Barton in Lincolnshire. Right across this county, through Lincoln to Sleaford, the roads were still unenclosed. From Sleaford let us suppose that he turned aside to Boston, then an important commercial town. This would have meant a journey with enclosed roads at either end, but all the middle part over open land. From Boston to King's Lynn he would have ridden among muddy lanes—a very trying journey—and from Lynn to Thetford across open country, and then from Thetford to Norwich he would have found a made road. From Norwich to Yarmouth and thence to Ipswich was again made road ; but from Ipswich to Bury St. Edmunds involved either a cross-country journey mainly by narrow lanes and some open country, or else a long detour half-way back to Norwich. From Bury St. Edmunds to Sudbury meant again a winding course through narrow lanes, and from Sudbury to Colchester the conditions were much the same.

Thereafter from Colchester to Chelmsford our traveller could have followed the relatively well-made London road ; but from Chelmsford to Tilbury would have been again a cross-country journey by lanes and by-ways, largely through sodden and marshy land.

A similar traveller in 1820 would have found the journey a very different matter. Right from Berwick-on-Tweed as far as Tadcaster south of York he would have been following the road of the Royal Mail, made and adapted for heavy vehicled traffic in winter and summer alike. From Tadcaster to Leeds and Halifax and back through Wakefield to Doncaster he would have found the roads less good, but still quite tolerable in all weathers ; and he would have been able to use a regular, though not a mail, road from Doncaster to Hull. From Barton-on-Humber right across Lincolnshire he would have been back on a great mail road, turning off at Sleaford by a quite tolerable direct road to Boston, where he would again have picked up the mail road. He could then either have turned along a by-road direct to King's Lynn, ferrying across a narrow channel of the Wash at the mouth of the Welland ; or he could have gone round by a better road through Wisbech. From Lynn to Norwich direct was still poor road ; but there was a good road to Thetford, and a mail road thence to Norwich, whence there was a fair road to Yarmouth, and a mail road again from Yarmouth to Ipswich.

From Ipswich to Bury St. Edmunds there was a good road as far as Stowmarket, and thence only a fair one. From Bury to Sudbury was a good made road, from Sudbury a fair road to Neyland, and then a good one to Colchester. From Colchester to Chelmsford was excellent mail road, and a few miles beyond Chelmsford a fair direct road turned off to Tilbury.

Even in 1820 our second traveller could still have found a good deal of unenclosed road in the northern part of the country, and elsewhere across heaths and commons, as he might even to-day. But in 1820 he would have been journeying over most of the distance along hard roads, adapted to heavy traffic and to use in all weathers. Only cross-country connecting roads, and occasional notorious stretches of main road, were still in a deplorable condition.

This great change had been proceeding continuously for more than a century. The stage coach, which gave the same impetus to road improvement as the motor-car is giving to-day, had been introduced during the first half of the seventeenth century, and had begun to ply over long distances before 1660. The first ' flying ' coach, between Oxford and London, began running in 1669. The big rumbling stage waggon, carrying impecunious passengers as well as goods, had begun even earlier, in the reign of Elizabeth. But until about 1750 stage coaches were not very numerous; and there was about the same time a rapid increase in the number of stage waggons and other heavy vehicles on the roads. This caused an immense spate of road legislation in Parliament: apart from public Acts dealing with roads and highways, there were over 1600 private Turnpike Acts between 1751 and 1790, and 2450 more between 1790 and 1830, as against about 400 in the first half of the eighteenth century.

This brings us to the question of the methods by which the roads were maintained and improved. In the middle ages road maintenance had been extensively undertaken by the monasteries; and their dissolution compelled the State to make alternative provision. This was done under the Highways Acts of 1555, 1562, and 1586, which established temporarily, then renewed, and then made permanent the system of ' statute labour ' for the upkeep of the roads.

Under this system, which was still in force in the eighteenth century, each parish was made responsible for the roads in its own area, and was compelled to appoint an unpaid Surveyor of Highways, whose task it was to keep the roads repaired with the aid of the compulsory labour of the parishioners, and of carts and road materials compulsorily supplied by them. For certain days in each year everyone in the parish was compelled to labour on the highways, or to send a substitute; and carts and materials had to be supplied free of charge by landlords and farmers. The Surveyors, amateurs at the task, and with no funds to requisition skilled assistance, had to do the best they could with this ' statute labour '; but in fact they often did much less than their best—for the office of Surveyor was compulsory, and no one nominated by the parish could refuse to serve. The parishioners, more-over, were usually reluctant to supply labour, or carts and horses, or materials; and commonly the work of repair was at best perfunctorily done. The worst holes were mended by throwing earth and stone into them; and sometimes wattles were used to make a foundation of sorts. But improvement, as distinct from mere casual mending, was seldom attempted by the parishes. The County Justices from time to time made some attempt to improve the roads by ordering parishes which were 'presented' before them to mend their habits; but these efforts were sporadic and for the most part ineffective. The parish system, with its use of unskilled and reluctant labour, was inevitably ineffective.

Under the Commonwealth an attempt was made to get rid of this unsatisfactory system, and to replace it by the levying of local rates for highway repair, assessed on local property-owners, and also by spreading the burden more evenly between neighbouring parishes. But in 1662 the Parliament of Charles II undid the Commonwealth's work, and put back the system of statute labour, with only the difference that optional power was now given to the Surveyors to levy rates in order to supplement the statute work. This power, though it was more than once reaffirmed by Parliament before 1700, was in fact little used; for rates were unpopular both among the dominant landlord class and among the farmers, who particularly resented being made to maintain roads designed for through traffic.

In 1663 came the first experimental use of a new method which was to be responsible for the main road improvements of the eighteenth century. The first Turnpikes were set up, under an Act empowering the Justices of Hertfordshire, Cambridgeshire, and Huntingdonshire to levy tolls and apply the proceeds to repairing and improving the roads. This was done because the bad condition of the roads in these counties was interfering seriously with communications with East Anglia, the Midlands, and the North. But this Act was not permanent; and after something had been done under it to set the roads in order, it was allowed to expire. The tolls were taken off, and the turnpikes removed.

But the new device, of making road-users themselves pay for the upkeep of the roads, was too good to be abandoned. It was much preferred to statute labour by many landowners and farmers. There were several more Turnpike Acts between 1663 and 1706, when the new system entered on a fresh phase. Hitherto, the power to levy tolls and erect turnpikes had been given to the County Justices; but in 1706 Parliament created the first Turnpike Trust.

A Turnpike Trust was an institution for maintaining the roads, administered by a body of Commissioners, at first usually local gentry, nominated under a private Act of Parliament. The Trust was empowered to erect toll-gates, and to levy tolls on vehicles using the road, according to prescribed scales. The Trusts were not profit-making bodies—or were not supposed to be—though they had power to borrow capital at interest in anticipation of revenue. They took over from the parishes the maintenance of the stretches of road for which they were set up; but at first the establishment of a Turnpike Trust did not exempt the parishioners from statute labour. In 1716, however, power was given to the parishes to pay a sum of money, raised by a rate, in lieu of statute labour to the Turnpike Trust, and this practice gradually became fairly general.

Most of the Trusts were set up for quite short stretches of road, on the initiative of local landowners or business people. The system spread gradually; but there was little turnpiking except on main roads—for elsewhere the tolls would not have met the cost—nor were the main roads nearly all turnpiked. A traveller even along a main road in the late eighteenth century would have found stretches of turnpike, especially near towns or between neighbouring towns, alternating with long tracts of road still under statute labour. Consequently, there were immense variations in the condition of the same road at different points. Some turnpikes, especially where the tolls had failed to come up to expectations, were very ill maintained ; and many were badly, and some fraudulently, managed. But in general the turnpiked stretches of road were very much superior to those which were left under the older system.

The turnpikes were, however, for a long time exceedingly unpopular. The ' Turnpike Riots ', most extensive between 1735 and 1750, were among the most widespread and turbulent manifestations of popular discontent in the eighteenth century. The turnpike gates were again and again broken down, and even the tollhouses burnt, by angry crowds resentful at being made to pay for the right of passage. Nor were the riots without warrant. The House of Commons Committee of Enquiry in 1752 found many abuses and extortions in the conduct of the Trusts ; and something was done to put them right. Thereafter there was less rioting, as people got used to the system ; but right up to 1830 popular feeling continued to flare up from time to time, and then gates would be broken down, and there would be trials for rioting, and the outcry against the Trusts would be taken up in the more Radical newspapers.

The early Turnpike Commissioners were for the most part country gentlemen. But, as the system developed, this social exclusiveness tended to disappear. Tradesmen, and especially innkeepers, often managed to get chosen as Commissioners, though Parliament legislated from time to time in order to keep them out. Innkeepers were objected to most of all, on the grounds that they tried to turn their office into a source of profit. But where gentlemen were responsible for the Trusts they could not be expected to do the work of management themselves. It was the regular practice to farm out the tolls to contractors who offered a fixed payment to the trustees, and then depended for their profit on collecting from the road-users more than they had undertaken to pay. These contractors in turn commonly entered into special bargains with regular users of the road—stage coach or waggon proprietors—who compounded for a fixed annual payment in return for a free passage for their vehicles.

This system opened the way to the regular evasion of the limits upon the loads to be carried ; and the actual gate-keepers could often be bribed by road-users into connivance in breaches of the law about loads and breadth of wheels. The consequence was that turnpike charges fell very unevenly upon different vehicles, and that occasional travellers were in most cases charged more than regular users of the road.

Moreover, Parliament persistently kept up the fiction that the turnpikes were meant to be temporary. Powers were usually given to the Trusts for a period of twenty-one years ; and their renewal involved the promotion of a new private Bill in Parliament. This was an expensive business ; and an appreciable part of the receipts from the tolls had to be spent in legal and parliamentary expenses. There was also a temptation, whenever renewal was uncertain, for the Trusts to let the roads deteriorate as much as possible towards the end of their terms, in order both to secure a larger profit and to strengthen the case for a further grant of powers on a promise to put them in better condition.

Meanwhile, Parliament had also been trying to remedy the condition of the highways by other means. In the early seventeenth century there had been an attempt, by a Royal Proclamation of 1621, to restrict the size and weight of vehicles using the roads ; but there was so much opposition that the order had to be withdrawn. In 1718 Parliament tried to secure the same object by restricting the number of horses that were to be allowed to draw a vehicle on the public roads ; and in 1741 ' weighing engines ' were authorised on the turnpikes, with discriminative tolls against heavy vehicles. These ' engines ' were made compulsory in 1751 ; and in 1753 Parliament passed the ' Broad Wheels Act ', laying down nine inches as the minimum breadth for the wheels of vehicles, except light carts and traps, using the roads. The idea of this was that the broad wheels, instead of wearing ruts, would roll out the roads, and so keep them fit for traffic. There was much more legislation about the weight of vehicles, the breadth of wheels and their distance apart, and similar matters in the following decades, especially in the Turnpike and Highways Acts of 1767 and 1773.

These two Acts embody the principal attempt made during the eighteenth century to render more efficient the system of statute labour on the general highways, as distinct from the turnpike roads. They readjusted the burden of providing labour, cartage, and materials, so as to make it bear less heavily on the poorer inhabitants ; and they also legalised the compounding system, which had already been applied extensively without legal sanction, and gave definite power to the parish authorities to levy rates if statute labour proved to be inadequate. But at the same time they conferred on Justices of the Peace powers to divert highways, or to stop them up altogether, on grounds of redundancy. This power was often abused, both where an influential Justice objected to a highway crossing his own land and where it was used in order to reduce expenditure by closing roads which were really needed. The idea behind the Acts was that the parishes, if they were given fewer roads to maintain, would be able to keep them in better order. But this was by no means always what actually happened.

At the same time Parliament attempted to establish some supervision over the Turnpike Trusts, by making them amenable to control by the County Justices, of whom they had previously been independent because they derived their powers directly from Parliament. A property qualification for Trustees was also introduced ; but neither change produced much effect. Nor did subsequent attempts, in 1778 and 1790, to restrict the number of passengers allowed to be carried on stage coaches meet with a better fate ; for the provisions

H

remained for the most part a dead letter in face of the compounding system used by the coach proprietors.

Meanwhile the attempt to enforce broad wheels was still continued even in the Turnpike Act of 1822, and was only abandoned in the General Highways Act of 1835, which abolished all regulations of wheels and weights, and also did away at a blow with the entire system of statute labour, and substituted local rates for highway purposes. Thus statute labour on the roads disappeared under the Reformed Parliament at the same time as the old Poor Law, under which extensive use had been made of pauper labour for highway maintenance.

The reform of the Poor Law had, in fact, made a new system indispensable. After the introduction of the Speenhamland system of poor relief in the 1790's, the labour of paupers—agricultural labourers displaced by enclosure or domestic workers ruined by the migration of domestic industries to the factory districts —was more and more substituted for the older system of compulsory ' statute labour '. The parishes, with a mass of unwanted paupers on their hands all over the South and West of England, naturally found employment for them on the roads, and thus released the rest of the inhabitants from an irksome and unpopular obligation. But, when statute labour had once been allowed to fall largely into disuse, it was impossible to reimpose it with success. The road engineers, by this time able to speak with some authority, were emphatic in asserting the inefficiency of both pauper and statute labour, and the superior economy of employing regular workers and paying them out of public rates—where the roads were not turnpiked, so as to provide a revenue from the tolls. Accordingly, the year after the enactment of the new Poor Law of 1834, Parliament swept the old system of statute labour finally away ; and thereafter road maintenance became, on the highways as well as the turnpikes, a contractor's job, to be paid for on an ordinary commercial basis.

This, however, was only after a century of vain endeavour to make the parish system work, and, on both highways and turnpikes, to make the traffic adapt itself to the roads, rather than provide better roads to meet the developing needs of the age. There is something almost grotesque in Parliament's persistent devotion to the cult of the ' broad wheel '. For, quite apart from the regularity with which the legislation prescribing the breadth of wheels was evaded or ignored, the conception behind it was radically at fault. Whereas the narrow-wheeled vehicles made deep ruts in the soft eighteenth-century roads, the broad-wheeled vehicles, so beloved of Parliament, were no less destructive in another way. With their heavy loads, they simply ground the loose road surface to powder ; and thereafter winds blew it away or the rains soon reduced it to a sodden pulp. What was needed in order to make the roads fit for heavy traffic was a better and stronger surface and, equally, improved drainage. This involved expert road engineering, which the statute labour system was quite incapable of providing. The Turnpike Trusts, able to engage skilled assistance, gave the opportunity for a new profession. John Metcalfe— ' Blind Jack of Knaresborough '—was the first of the great road engineers ; and after him came Thomas Telford and John Loudon McAdam, whose name is still alive in the new road surface which he devised. Metcalfe was the pioneer of road drainage, by making ditches along the sides and giving the roads a convex surface off which the water could run freely ; and he also insisted on the need for firm foundations. Telford, first noted as a bridge builder, began by improving the road between Glasgow and Carlisle, and later on was the engineer of the famous new road from London to Holyhead, which was put in hand in 1815 under a Board of Parliamentary Commissioners, empowered to replace the entire road, and to enforce conformity on the numerous small Turnpike Trusts along its route. Telford was notable for his insistence on really firm foundations and easy gradients ;

and the Holyhead road became the wonder of the great coaching age just before the railway age. McAdam, after road experience in Scotland, became the leading turnpike engineer in the west of England and later in London, where he and his sons succeeded in consolidating the London turnpike roads into something more like a unified system. He was less concerned than Telford with strong foundations, and more with a good convex surface, impervious to water and easily drained. Perhaps his greatest achievement in the eyes of his contemporaries was that his roads were a great deal cheaper to build than Telford's, and also cheaper to maintain. McAdam, in fact, was even more a cheapener than an improver of road construction and upkeep. He was able to show that what Telford had achieved at very high cost could be done much more cheaply by his own methods, which involved less weighty and expensive foundations, and depended more on really effective drainage than on any other factor.

These three men, and the host of lesser engineers who applied and developed their methods, revolutionised the art of road-making ; and the magnitude of their achievements caused contemporaries to look on the older roads as much worse than they had seemed only a little time before. The new standards set by the road improvers partly explain the spate of criticism of road surfaces wherever the road engineers had not made them new.

While these changes were being made in the roads, the vehicles upon them were changing too. These changes were in part closely connected with the development of the ' post '. The postmaster in each town in the eighteenth century was not primarily a deliverer of letters and packets, though that was part of his business. His primary function was to supply horses for those travellers who ' posted ' on horseback or in vehicles over the country. The traveller who went ' post ' changed his horses at each stage ; and it was the affair of the postmaster to have horses waiting at the ' relay ' posts. This system had been regulated by Proclamation in 1583, and again in 1603, when the postmasters, whose chief rivals were the innkeepers, were given a prior right in the supply of horses.

Up to about 1750 travellers who ' posted ' usually rode ; but thereafter there was a rapid increase in posting by wheel. In 1720 Ralph Allen, one of the leading citizens of Bath, had been given the contract for the cross-country delivery of letters by postboys on horseback. In 1784 John Palmer of Reading secured, in face of strong opposition from vested interests in the Post Office, the contract for carrying the mails by his new Mail Coaches, which speedily became the regular means of conveying passengers also along many of the principal roads.

' Posting ' by hired or private light vehicles gradually declined as public conveyances on the roads improved. From the middle of the eighteenth century the comforts and conveniences of coaching gradually advanced, not only as the roads became better, but also as progress was made in the design and springing of the vehicles. Up to about 1750 coaches, as well as stage waggons, were without springs ; but thereafter increasing attention was given to design, and many different types of coaches and chaises were put on the market. Coach-building, especially in London, came to be one of the most important trades. More and more public vehicles made their appearance on the roads ; and facilities for public carriage of goods were also multiplied fast.

To a great extent the provision of coaches fell into the hands of the innkeepers, who had long been the rivals of the postmasters in the posting business. In London there grew up big firms, owning whole fleets of coaches and many hundreds of horses ; and these firms often bought up provincial as well as London inns. It became possible to select between many alternative lines and routes for journeys between the principal towns ; and the choice involved a number of considerations. There were swift ' flying ' coaches planned for speed, reliable coaches travelling at a steadier pace, and, especially to Bath and other health resorts, invalid and family coaches which took twice as long over the journey as their ' flying ' competitors, but were guaranteed not to jolt or spill the passengers. The great coaching days described by Dickens in his novels had begun : the ' flying ' coach seemed to contemporaries the ultimate wonder of speed and mobility—until the railways came to end its dominance, and sadly to diminish the glory of the famous coaching inns, which are now climbing back to favour in the new era of travel by motor-car.

A few examples of the time taken in journeying from London to various parts of the country in 1750 and at certain later dates will serve to illustrate both the magnitude of the change in conditions of travel even before the coming of railways, and also its continuity. It must of course be borne in mind that there was in 1750 a substantial difference between summer and winter rates of travel, whereas this had largely disappeared well before 1830.

Until about 1750 the journey from London to Edinburgh usually took from ten to twelve days. By 1775 it could be done in four days and by 1800 in three. In 1822 the best time was under 51 hours, and by 1830 it was 46 hours. It took rather longer to get to Glasgow in 1750, because of the extreme badness of the western road north of Lancashire ; but it could be reached in four days by 1780, and in 47 hours by 1822. Holyhead took three days to reach in 1785, and only 27 hours in 1835, when the new road was finished. Leeds was a three-days' journey from London in 1760, and one of 26 hours in 1830. The times for Liverpool were about the same as for Leeds. Manchester also took three days in 1760 ; but by 1830 the fastest coaches got there in 17 or 18 hours. Newcastle-on-Tyne was six days' journey from London in 1750, and three days in 1775 ; but by

1830 it could be reached in 26 hours by the quickest route in summer. The time needed to reach Bath and Bristol fell from two days in 1750 to 12½ and 14 hours in 1822. The time taken in getting to Brighton came down from a full day to 5½ hours ; and the journey to Dover, which could not be reached in a day in 1750, took 10 hours round about 1820. Shrewsbury required four days to reach in summer in 1750, and only 16 hours in 1830.

The times here recorded are all the shortest available according to the published coaching tables. Many coaches went much more slowly ; and many travellers continued to prefer comfort to speed. There were still two-day coaches to Bath in the 1820's.

When a traveller did want to journey at speed the improvement was sufficiently remarkable. By 1830, on a rough average, the time taken in getting from one place to another by coach had been cut to something between one-third and one-fifth of the time needed in the middle of the eighteenth century. This change, however, was chiefly for the well-to-do ; for coaching was, and remained, expensive. The new flying coaches carried very few passengers—the mail coaches usually but four inside and none outside ; and even the somewhat slower coaches which carried outside passengers at lower rates than inside made charges which the poorer sections of the population could not hope to afford. The working classes did not travel by coach ; they continued to use the slow stage-waggons or the local carriers' carts—or to walk. Or rather, most of them stayed where they were, or ventured afield only when they belonged to skilled crafts, with ' houses of call ' or friendly arrangements between local Trade Clubs in different towns, or set out afoot to seek their fortune in the great metropolis or in one of the growing factory districts. The ' coaching age ' was much less democratic than the railway age which followed hard upon it. Despite all the road improvements of the early nineteenth century, it remained difficult, at least until the

1840's, for the ordinary workman to travel far afield.

Such was the revolution on the roads, of which about 22,000 miles, out of a total mileage of 127,000, had been turnpiked by 1838. The second revolution in transport affected goods much more than passengers. For the carriage of heavy goods England in 1750 depended chiefly on her navigable rivers. There were at that time five great systems of river navigation—those of the Humber, the Wash, the Thames, the Bristol Channel, and the Mersey estuary. Each of these systems embraced a number of rivers, navigable for the most part not by ships but by barges, and liable to serious interruptions at certain seasons owing to shortage of water, through silting-up, or through failure to keep the channel in good order. When a river is described as ' navigable ' it must not be assumed that it was so at all seasons, or in all years. Thus, the Dee was continually silting-up and having new channels cut in order to give access to Chester, and there were constant troubles over the upper reaches of the Wye and Severn, and over the Thames itself. There were, moreover, often strong local jealousies and obstructions. Each municipal corporation wanted its river, if it had one, to be navigable from the sea up to its own town, but often obstructed making it navigable any further, in order to shut out up-river competition, and in the hope of making itself the centre for the transhipment of goods from places further inland. Nottingham and Burton-on-Trent waged perpetual warfare over the Trent navigation ; and the Corporation and leading citizens of Nottingham spent large sums of money in trying to prevent the citizens of Burton and Derby from getting powers to improve the Trent and Derwent beyond their city.

It is worth while to describe briefly these five great navigations. With luck, barges could get up the Thames beyond Oxford as far as Cricklade ; and the Thames served most of Middlesex, Surrey, Hertfordshire, Buckinghamshire, Oxfordshire, and Berkshire. There were tributary navigations by the Wey to Guildford, by the Mole to Leatherhead, by the Roding to Ongar, by the Lea to Ware and Hertford, and by the Kennet to Reading and Newbury.

Apart from the Thames the south of England was poorly served with river navigation. The Medway was navigable as far as Maidstone, and the Kentish Stour as far as Fordwich, a few miles from Canterbury. There was a very little navigation on some of the Sussex rivers quite near their mouths, and on the Itchen past Southampton. The Avon in Wiltshire was navigable to quite near Salisbury, and the Exe as far as Exeter. But apart from these there was no navigation of importance along the whole of the South Coast.

The Bristol Channel group of rivers began in the south with the Parret, which was navigable as far as Bridgwater and Langport, and by way of the Tone to Taunton. Next came the Avon, navigable past Bristol to Bath. But the two chief rivers of this group were the Severn and the Wye. Barges could get up the Severn right past Shrewsbury, and sometimes as far as Welshpool ; and into the Severn ran the Warwickshire Avon, navigable to Stratford and Warwick, the Salwarpe navigable to Droitwich, and the Stour to Stourbridge, Stourbridge was of considerable importance as the nearest navigable water to Birmingham, and also as a terminal for local carriage from Cheshire and Staffordshire. The Wye could be navigated as far as Hereford, and barges could get by way of the Lug as far as Leominster. This river system did something to open up Central Wales and the Welsh Marches, and was of vital importance, especially before the rise of Liverpool, for communication with Bristol. Wales had no other river communications except in the West, where the Towy was navigable only as far as Carmarthen.

North Wales was served, where it was served at all, by land carriage to and from the Dee or the Mersey and its tributaries. The Dee was navigable only as far

113

as Chester, and that precariously because of the silt.
Nor was the Mersey itself open beyond Warrington ;
but it communicated, by way of the Irwell Navigation,
with Manchester, by the Weaver with Northwich and
Nantwich, and by the Dane with Middlewich, which
was an important terminal for trade with the interior,
including land cartage to the Trent system at Burton
or Derby. Further north, Wigan could be reached by
the Douglas, and the Ribble was navigable a little way
up to Preston. In Cumberland, Cockermouth as well
as Workington was served by the Derwent, and Carlisle
by the Eden. That completes the navigable rivers of the
West.

On the North-East vessels of small burthen could get
to Newcastle, but not beyond the bridge. Most of the
ships stopped in Shields Roads, and were served by
barges plying up and down the Tyne to and from Newcastle. Sunderland could be reached by the Wear;
but there was no other river navigation of importance
north of the Humber group of rivers—the most extensive river navigations in the whole country. In this
region, to the north, Beverley Brook could be navigated as far as Beverley, the Ouse to York, and the Yorkshire Derwent, which runs into the Ouse, right up to
New Malton, whence Scarborough was not far off across
the moors. The Aire and Calder Navigation, much improved just before the canal age, served Leeds and Wakefield, and the Don, Doncaster, Rotherham, and Sheffield.
But far more extensive was the Trent Navigation,
which, reaching only to Nottingham in the seventeenth
century, was extended up the river to Burton in the eighteenth despite the opposition of the Nottingham Corporation, and by way of the Derwent served Derby also.
Into the Trent ran the Idle, navigable to Bawtry and East
Retford ; and, to the east, the ancient artificial waterway called Foss Dyke connected the Trent with the
Witham, making a continuous route for barges from the
Humber to the Wash, by way of Lincoln and Boston.

The Witham, thus linked with the Trent, formed the northern arm of the Wash group of rivers. South of the Witham the Welland was navigable to Stamford, and the Nen, by its newer cut, to Wisbech and Peterborough and right on to Northampton. The Greater Ouse, reaching tidal water at King's Lynn, served St. Ives, Huntingdon, and Bedford, and had important tributaries—the Cam, navigable to Cambridge, the Lark to Mildenhall and Bury St. Edmunds, and the Little Ouse to Thetford.

There remain only the relatively short navigations of the Yare to Norwich, the Waveney to Beccles, the Orwell to Ipswich, the Suffolk Stour to Sudbury, and the Coln to Colchester. These complete the record of England's navigable waterways before the coming of the canals.

If we follow the navigable courses of these rivers on the map, we shall see that all Eastern England between Humber and Thames was well served with river-ways. On the other hand, the North-East and the counties along the South Coast had practically none. Wales was almost devoid of navigable rivers except the Severn, and Lancashire and the North-West had very little, except in the extreme south of Lancashire. Moreover, there was a large tract of Central England, including Birmingham and Stoke-on-Trent, and also Leicestershire, which had no available waterways at all. These facts, important in settling the location of people and industries in the eighteenth century, were also of vital significance in creating the demand for canals, and in making Birmingham the canal metropolis of England.

The canal age opened with the enterprises of Brindley and the Duke of Bridgewater in the neighbourhood of Manchester. A canal is essentially an artificial waterway, usually involving locks, as distinct from a mere ' cut ' designed to improve a natural river. There had been many ' cuts ' before the canal age. The Exeter ' Canal ' was finished in 1567, and the Worsley Brook Navigation was authorised in 1737. The Duke of Bridgewater's Sankey Brook Navigation, an embryonic canal, was begun in 1755. But the first real canal in the modern sense was the Bridgewater Canal from Runcorn to Manchester, engineered by Brindley—much to the annoyance of the proprietors of the older Irwell Navigation. Thereafter canals came speedily one after another. The Canal Age effectively begins with the completion of the Grand Trunk Canal, which opened up water communication right across England from west to east, and thus made it possible to transport European produce to Liverpool, and American produce to the Continental markets, without coastwise carriage right round the island. The Grand Trunk Canal, linking the Trent with the Mersey, was begun in 1766 and finished in 1777. It ran from the Bridgewater Canal near Runcorn into the Trent below Burton, opening up the rapidly developing Potteries round Stoke-on-Trent, and linking Liverpool with the Midlands as well as with continental Europe. From the Grand Trunk the Coventry Canal, begun in 1768, and the Oxford Canal, begun in 1769, gave by 1790 through communication by water from the Trent and the Mersey to the Thames. Thenceforward, goods could reach London from both Lancashire and Yorkshire without being carried by sea.

Another extensive canal, the Leeds and Liverpool, was begun in 1770. But in this case, owing to the lie of the land, there were formidable engineering difficulties, and it was found necessary to take a very roundabout route. The Leeds and Liverpool Canal was not open for all its length till 1816, but when it had been finished it linked the two terminals by way of Wigan, Blackburn, Colne, and Skipton, and thus opened up important coal and textile districts.

Meanwhile in the West Midlands Birmingham had become the centre of a maze of canals. One of these, joining the Coventry Canal, communicated with the Grand Trunk and the Oxford Canal, and thus linked

Birmingham to Liverpool and London. A second ran to Worcester, and thus directly joined Birmingham to the Severn group, and gave access to Bristol. A third ran by Warwick to a second junction with the Oxford Canal ; and a fourth, begun only in 1826, ran all the way to the Chester Canal, and thence provided a second link with Liverpool by way of the Grand Trunk. Off all these canals ran others, linking Birmingham by water with almost the entire industrial region of the Midlands and of Lancashire and Yorkshire.

Meanwhile, in the East Midlands and further south, the Grand Junction Canal, begun in 1793 and finished in 1805, ran from a point of communication with the Oxford Canal near Northampton direct to London, which was thus linked, independently of the precarious Thames navigation, with the entire Midland and Northern area. From the Grand Junction Canal at Northampton the Grand Union and Leicester Canals ran through Leicester-shire into Derbyshire, communicating by subsidiary canals with Derby and Grantham, and linking up again with the Trent Navigation. The Thames and Severn Canal (1783–9) joined the Thames to the Stroudwater, and so made a way from London to the Bristol Channel, while the Kennet and Avon Canal ran from the Thames by Reading to the Avon at Bath and thus provided an alternative route to the west coast and avoided the awkward reaches of the Thames between Reading and Cricklade. The Wiltshire and Berkshire Canal, running from a point on the Thames south of Oxford, went through Swindon to join the Kennet and Avon at Trow-bridge, affording yet another route of communication between London and the Bristol Channel.

In South Wales canals were developed chiefly as means of carrying coal from the inland collieries to the ports. The Brecon, Pontypool, Cardiff, and Swansea Canals opened up the steep valleys, and stimulated the rapid expansion of the coalfields. Mid-Wales, as far as Newtown, then a textile centre, was linked to the Mersey

117

by the Severn, Montgomery, and Ellesmere Canals. In Yorkshire many short canals were made, replacing or connecting the older river navigations, and opening up the industrial towns and coalfield districts of the West Riding, which was thus enabled to send its goods by water to either Liverpool or the Humber.

In Scotland an old aspiration was realised by the linking of the Forth and Clyde (1768–90); and the famous Caledonian Canal was begun in 1803, but not finished until 1822.

It would be possible greatly to prolong this list; but enough has been said to show how widespread and rapid was the growth of the canal system. Beginning about 1760, the great era of canal-building was over by about 1830; and by that time the railway era was well on its way.

Widespread as the canal movement was, it could not cover the entire country, even in conjunction with the improved river navigations which were being developed over the same period. In particular, the North of England —Northumberland, Durham, Cumberland, Westmorland, and most of Yorkshire north of Leeds and Bradford —remained, because of the hilly nature of the country, almost entirely without either canals or navigable rivers. That was one great reason why railway development began in the North—with the Stockton and Darlington Railway, which was chiefly designed to open up the inland coalfield of South Durham. The railways were needed to do for the extreme North of England what had been largely accomplished earlier for the centre of the country by the canals.

In effect, with the advent of the canals, England ceased to be hollow. There were no longer obstacles to the development of population and industry in the central area, between Birmingham and Stoke-on-Trent in the West, and Sheffield, Nottingham, and Leicester in the East. Staffordshire, Warwickshire, and the East Midlands began to fill up rapidly with industries and inhabitants. So did South Wales and the parts of Lancashire to the north of Manchester and Liverpool. Between 1801 and 1831 the population of Stoke-on-Trent rose from 23,000 to 52,000. Over the same period Birmingham rose from 71,000 to 144,000 inhabitants, Sheffield from 46,000 to 92,000, Wolverhampton from 31,000 to 68,000, Nottingham from 29,000 to 50,000, and Leicester from 17,000 to 41,000. A similar development occurred in a long list of Midland towns. In Lancashire Blackburn grew from 12,000 to 27,000 and Burnley from 4000 to 10,000. Staffordshire rose from tenth to seventh place for populousness among the English counties, and Warwickshire from fifteenth to eleventh place.

Thus, over most of the country, the canals seemed, right up to the advent of the railways, to be solving the problem of the carriage of heavy goods with almost miraculous efficiency. Together with the improved roads, they had revolutionised the conditions of internal transport and communication, and made possible the development of industry and mining on an unprecedented scale. But their reign was brief. Before the last of the great canals, the Birmingham and Liverpool, had been opened in 1834, the Manchester and Liverpool Railway, as well as the Stockton and Darlington, had proved its superior efficiency, and the canals were being challenged in the very area in which Brindley and the Duke of Bridgewater had inaugurated the canal era seventy years before.

A Study in Legal Repression
(1789–1834)

THE six men of Dorset who were sentenced to transportation in 1834 for the crime of 'administering unlawful oaths' have lived on in history under the name of the 'Tolpuddle Martyrs'. Their offence was indeed no more than that they had attempted in their remote Dorsetshire village to organise the agricultural labourers into a Trade Union, with the intention of joining the Grand National Consolidated Trades Union, to which, under Robert Owen's leadership and inspiration, half a million workers had rallied since its establishment in the previous year. In this there could be, on the face of the matter, no crime; for the laws against combination had been repealed three years before, and it was no longer 'criminal conspiracy' for workers to organise for the protection of their standards of living. Indeed, it is probable that, if the Tolpuddle Martyrs had been industrial workers, or had lived in a town, instead of being villagers working on the land, no one would have molested them; for no one did in fact molest—by legal prosecution, that is to say—the countless other bodies of workers who were doing, in 1834, exactly the same things as sufficed to send George Loveless and his fellow-labourers as convicts to the other end of the world.

It was, however, one thing for industrial workers in a town to form a Union, and quite another for a group of agricultural labourers—Dissenters at that—to defy the parson and the squire. And fortunately—or at least so thought the Dorset squires, the judge who tried the case, and the Whig Government of the day—there were means at hand for the repression of these audacious rebels. For in forming their little Union they, following a practice widespread among the trade and friendly societies of that time, had adopted a ritual borrowed in part at second or third hand from the Freemasons, and had administered to those who joined their society an oath pledging them to observe its laws and regulations, and to be secret and loyal one to another in the management of its affairs. For this offence—for ' administering unlawful oaths ' and not for forming a Trade Union— were the Dorchester labourers convicted and sentenced. But in practice it came to the same thing ; and the fears engendered by the Dorchester decision played an important part in breaking up Robert Owen's ambitious Trades Union before it had been in existence for as long as a single year.

The trial and condemnation of these six men came at the end of a long period of savagely repressive legislation directed against the efforts of the lower classes to combine for the redress of their political or economic grievances. It came as a surprise ; for most men had believed that with the passing of the Reform Act of 1832 the period of repression had been brought definitely to an end. No doubt, only a few years before, in 1830 and 1831, the Whigs had been ruthless in putting down what Mr. and Mrs. Hammond have called ' The Last Labourers' Revolt '—known to contemporaries as the ' Captain Swing Riots ', in the course of which the half-starved labourers had gone about the villages burning ricks, ducking unpopular overseers of the poor in the horse-ponds, and demanding higher wages and the remission of the hated tithes. But it had been assumed that the enactment of Reform had begun a new era ; and at any rate it was regarded as certain that, since the repeal of the Combination Acts, the mere forming of a Trade Union had ceased to be a punishable offence. That was why the Dorchester labourers, more than the hundreds who had been transported before them, were felt to be martyrs ; and that was why every section of the working-class movement heard of this conviction with astonishment and dismay.

For the Act under which these unfortunates were sentenced had been almost forgotten until it was invoked against them, and assuredly no one had expected that it would be put to such a use. When it was passed, thirty-seven years earlier, no one had such a case as this of the Dorchester labourers in mind. The Act against Unlawful Oaths (37 George III, c. 123) was the immediate outcome, not of Trade Union agitation, but of naval mutiny. It was the sequel to the Naval Mutinies of 1797, when, first at Spithead and then at the Nore, the sailors rose and displaced their officers, demanding redress for the under-feeding and under-payment, the harsh discipline of perpetual floggings, the tolerated corruption and peculation which befouled the Navy in those days of press-gangs and purchased commissions, of long spells at sea in crowded and insanitary quarters, and of new ideas of ' Liberty, Equality, and Fraternity ' which could not but reach the ears even of men so remote from politics as the seamen before the mast.

It does not appear to scholars who, in our own day, have studied dispassionately the events of the Naval Mutinies of 1797 that politics had much to do with them —even if they had anything at all. The sailors had grievances enough of their own to account for their conduct, without bringing in the vexed question of the Rights of Man. Doubtless, Robert Parker, who was chosen as leader by the Nore mutineers, had picked up a few revolutionary phrases—probably from Irish rather than French sources ; and one or two of these phrases found their way into the manifesto of the mutineers. But at Spithead there was not even a phrase to suggest that the trouble had any political significance ; and it seems certain that most of Parker's followers were equally innocent of any purpose beyond the improvement of their own conditions.

But the Government and Parliament thought otherwise ; for in 1797 the governing classes in England were in mortal fear. There was trouble brewing in Ireland ; and ever since the taking of the Bastille the nerves of the nobility and gentry had been on edge all over Europe. The Government and Parliament were fully convinced that the mutineers were revolutionaries and traitors, even if their own admirals assured them that this was not the case. Consequently, hard upon the suppression of the mutinies Parliament laid down that 'whereas divers wicked and evil disposed persons have of late attempted to seduce persons serving in his Majesty's forces by land and sea, and others of his Majesty's subjects, from their duty and allegiance to his Majesty, and to incite them to acts of mutiny and sedition, and have determined to give effect to their wicked and traitorous proceedings by imposing upon the persons whom they have attempted to seduce the pretended obligation of oaths unlawfully administered'—therefore it was necessary for Parliament to legislate against such dangerous proceedings, and accordingly the Act to which those phrases form the preamble provided penalties for such offences up to the maximum of transportation for seven years.

This repressive Act, under which the Tolpuddle Martyrs were to receive their sentence thirty-seven years later, formed part of a large body of punitive legislation enacted during the years which immediately followed the French Revolution. Indeed, the period of the French Wars and the troublous years which followed the return of peace were plentifully bespattered with laws designed to crush out every form of Radical agitation or potentially dangerous combination among the lower classes. Nor is this legislation of merely historical interest even to-day ; for, though a good deal of it has been swept away by the periodical laws for the repeal of obsolete statutes, a surprising number of these repressive measures of more than a century ago are still on the statute book, and might even to-day be invoked in an emergency against Radical agitators, quite as unexpectedly as they were called out of abeyance against the Dorchester labourers in 1834. Indeed, certain of them have actually been used in quite recent years, albeit no longer with the old severity, against Communists suspect of seditious propaganda or intent on holding meetings and demonstrations at times or places regarded as unsuitable by the police. There are other and older statutes than the Trade Unions Act of 1927 and the Sedition Act of 1934 which the Labour movement needs to get repealed if it is to enjoy that secure freedom of speech and organisation which Englishmen have often boasted of as their right.

In this essay, however, I am concerned not with the modern application of these laws, but with the laws themselves and the circumstances which called them into being. They fall, broadly, into two groups. The first of these includes the Acts passed between 1794 and 1800, in the years of political excitement and unrest following upon the French Revolution: the second consists of the further series of repressive measures with which Parliament attempted to stifle the hunger movements of the years of exceptional distress and unrest after the end of the Napoleonic Wars. Into the first group fall the ' Two Acts ' of 1797 (of which the Act against Unlawful Oaths was one), the Unlawful Societies Act of 1799, and the Combination Acts of 1799 and 1800, together with certain other statutes hereafter to be mentioned. To the second group belong Lord Sidmouth's ' Gagging Acts ' of 1817, and the notorious ' Six Acts ' of 1819, passed on the morrow of the ' Peterloo Massacre '. Between these two groups lie certain lesser repressive measures—notably the Act passed against the Luddites in 1812, which made the crime of machine-breaking punishable with death.

The circumstances which gave rise to the first of these outbursts of punitive legislation are well enough known. The events in France, especially after the Reign of Terror, had created a mood of undiscriminating panic among the governing classes in Great Britain ;

and under the influence of this panic every demand for even the most moderate and constitutional reforms was damned as treason and sedition, especially if it came from any section of the people which the ruling classes regarded as potentially dangerous or disaffected, and therefore as capable of imitating the French example unless it were kept down with a firm hand.

There is indeed no evidence, if we except Ireland, that in these troublous years the British Government was ever faced with any real threat of revolution. It does not appear that the leaders of any important Radical or working-class society in Great Britain at any time seriously contemplated revolutionary action, or made any preparations at all for a violent uprising. They sent, no doubt, fraternal addresses of greeting and sympathy to the French Assembly ; and some of them exchanged declamatory manifestoes with the Jacobin Clubs in France, as well as with the United Irishmen nearer home. But it seems clear that all the leading societies, at all events until they were driven underground by the repression of their normal activities, were seeking to engage in a wholly peaceable agitation for the reform of Parliament, and were often more disposed to appeal to the principles of the English ' Glorious Revolution ' of 1688 than to French notions. There were, of course, many shades of opinions among the British Radicals, who ranged from respectable Dissenting divines, such as Dr. Richard Price and Dr. Joseph Priestley, to mere working men. But there is no sign that any of them, at any rate until the Government had set out to suppress them all alike, had gone further than the expression of a determination to defend their liberties if they were subjected to attack.

It is true that, after the repression had closed the way to peaceful agitation, a few groups here and there began to dream of more violent courses. But this was only when the hand of the law had already been laid heavily upon them ; and it is significant that, even at this stage, the presence of Irishmen was usually needed to urge even a tiny group of Englishmen or Scotsmen to the point of revolutionary plotting. In face of Pitt's repression, most of the Radical societies either speedily perished or lost most of their following. The revolutionary societies which Parliament suppressed by name in 1799 were for the most part so obscure that historians can find out nothing about them, and are in some cases disposed to doubt if they had any real existence. Plotters no doubt there were; but they were a mere handful—a pitiable residue from the numerous bands of Reformers whose hearts had been uplifted, like those of Wordsworth and Coleridge, by the events of 1789.

Nor can we take such evidence as there is of revolutionary plotting entirely at its face value. It is pertinent to remember that the most circumstantial evidence of a revolutionary design—that of the Scottish 'Pike Plot' of 1793, came from an *agent provocateur*. Robert Watt, who both devised and exposed this useful conspiracy, had been a Government spy, but had found his services dispensed with. How far he became a revolutionary, or how far he instigated his plot in the hope of regaining the Government's favour by exposing it, we are unlikely ever to know : nor can the fact that he was not rewarded, but executed with ignominy as a traitor for his part in it, resolve our doubts. But we know enough to be able to say that no share in Watt's conspiracy was ever brought home to more than a handful even of the Scottish Reformers ; and in England the most searching enquiry by the parliamentary Committee of Secrecy in 1794 failed to bring to light even the smallest evidence of revolutionary designs. Spies, such as the notorious Castles, Oliver, and Edwards, were again to play an important part, as provocative agents, in the years of unrest after 1815, and to bring their hapless dupes to the scaffold. In this unsavoury business Watt seems to have been a pioneer : and undoubtedly his activities smoothed the way for the repressive policy which Pitt and his colleagues were already determined to follow. But, in spite of Watt, and of a few Irishmen in England who were really ready for anything, there was never for a moment, whatever the fears of the governing classes caused them to believe, the smallest prospect of a British Revolution on the French model.

The societies at which the Government launched its thunderbolts in 1793 and 1794 were in fact, with insignificant exceptions, engaged in an entirely pacific agitation for parliamentary reform and for the recognition of the ' Rights of man '. This was certainly true to the fullest extent of the two leading London societies. One of these, the society for Constitutional Information, headed by Major John Cartwright and John Horne Tooke, was a purely middle- and upper-class body of Radical politicians and respectable Dissenters. Its main purpose was the dissemination of informative propagandist pamphlets telling the people of their constitutional rights : it was about as likely to start fomenting violent revolution as the Corporation of the City of London, which in those days also counted usually on the Radical side. The second body, Thomas Hardy's London Corresponding Society, was indeed predominantly a working-class body, notable as the first such organisation known to have been created for a purely political purpose. But it was hardly more disposed to resort to revolution than its middle-class ally ; and its membership was in practice confined to skilled artisans, with a sprinkling of tradesmen and minor professional persons—in other words, to a stratum of society fully as far removed in culture and standard of living from the less skilled workers as from the *bon bourgeois* of Major Cartwright's Constitutional Society. It was formed as a separate body, not mainly because its members wished to draw a sharp distinction between the aspirations of the middle and working classes, but rather because artisans and tradesmen could not afford the guinea subscription of the Constitutional Society, or the dinners which served that body in lieu of meetings. It set out to work as closely as possible with Major Cartwright and his associates, but to adopt methods of organisation and propaganda better suited to the needs of those who were used to meeting in ale-houses or coffee-houses, and could only spare their penny or so a week.

Besides these London societies, there grew up many others in the leading provincial towns; and some of them—perhaps most—adopted the same dual system of organisation as found favour in London. In Manchester, for example, where the merchant, Thomas Walker, was the recognised Radical leader, and his house and ware-house the regular meeting-place, there were two societies —one of middle-class supporters, which met in his house, and a second of working men, which was allowed to hold its more numerous assemblies in his warehouse. Societies of these types—or sometimes single societies combining both elements—came into existence in the years after 1789 in almost every considerable town.

Doubtless these bodies enthusiastically welcomed the French Revolution, and most of them were prepared to send greetings to the French Jacobin Clubs. But it does not in the least follow that their members had in mind the making of an English Revolution. Their minds were set on reform, and they were well aware that the 'mob' was for the most part not on their side, but was a ' Church and State ' mob, such as had expressed itself a little earlier in the Gordon Riots, and was soon engaged, after the Revolution, in burning down the houses of Radical Dissenters, such as Dr. Joseph Priestley.

Undoubtedly the book which was above all others the gospel of these pioneering working-class political societies was Thomas Paine's *Rights of Man*. Paine himself was in France, but his trial in his absence in 1792 was the real opening of the campaign of repression. The attack on the Radicals developed next in Scotland, which had long been accustomed to an even more repressive form of government than England. The leading delegates to the

Scottish Reform Convention of 1793 were condemned and transported despite the protests of the English Radicals, some of whose leaders, sent as delegates to the Convention, were among the condemned ; and thereafter the Government launched early in 1794 its onslaught on the London Radical societies, arresting the leaders of both the Constitutional and the Corresponding Society, and placing them all on trial for high treason. At the same time arrests of local leaders were made all over the country. These wholesale arrests were immediately followed by the appointment by the House of Commons of a Committee of Secrecy to investigate and report upon the alleged revolutionary plot, and by the rapid passing of an Act of Parliament suspending the Habeas Corpus Act and enabling the Government to seize and hold persons in prison without trial. This suspension of Habeas Corpus lasted, with only a brief interval between 1795 and 1797, right up to the Peace of Amiens in 1802, and, as we shall see, was again invoked in the years of unrest after 1815.

' *Whereas a traitorous and detestable conspiracy has been formed for subverting the existing laws and constitution, and for introducing the system of anarchy and confusion which has so fatally prevailed in France* '—so the preamble of the suspending Act began, and the Act went on to confer upon the Government the power to keep in prison those whom it had already arrested without special powers and to add others to their number even without putting them on trial. Nevertheless, the Government was sufficiently satisfied with the evidence which it believed it had accumulated against the Radicals to place the London leaders whom it had arrested on trial for high treason ; and it is common knowledge how the London jury in 1794 acquitted the leaders of the Constitutional and Corresponding Societies, and thus administered to the Government a serious rebuff. It is not so well known that London was in this matter quite exceptional : London juries were notoriously independent ; but all over the provinces similar trials were being held, and practically the whole of those arrested outside London were condemned, though Thomas Walker, the substantial merchant who was the leader of the Radicals in Manchester, also escaped conviction. Despite the London acquittals, these prosecutions did much to break the strength of the young Radical movement, by frightening away its more timorous adherents ; and the Government, not content with the powers it had already taken, proceeded promptly to the enactment of further repressive laws.

Between 1795 and 1801, in addition to the repeated Acts suspending the Habeas Corpus Act for further periods and to the annual measures dealing with mutiny in general and marine mutiny in particular, there were no less than nine repressive laws designed to compass the destruction of Radical and working-class movements. The series opened with the Treason Act (36 George III, c. 7) of 1795, which extended the definition of treason to cover writings which had a tendency to incite the population to hatred or contempt of the Crown or Government. This Act was immediately followed by the Seditious Meetings and Assemblies Act of the same year (36 George III, c. 8), which imposed severe restrictions on the right of public meeting. Under this Act no meeting of more than fifty persons, except election meetings and certain types of meeting held under official auspices—it is interesting to note that there had to be a special clause exempting educational meetings held in the Universities—was allowed to be called except on a requisition by seven householders. The magistrates were, moreover, given wide powers to disperse even meetings called in accordance with the law if they attempted to discuss any matter regarded as subversive, and to arrest speakers at such meetings ; while refusal to disperse at the magistrate's orders was made a felony punishable with death. In addition, the Act laid severe regulations on all places at which meetings for political reading and discussion were held. All such places were to require licences from the magistrates, and these licences could be revoked at any time and the licence holders prosecuted if the magistrates considered that improper discussions were taking place. The magistrates were allowed to demand admittance to any house, licensed or unlicensed, in which they thought a meeting was being held. Under these conditions clearly public meetings were practically out of the question and even private meetings highly dangerous to hold, for the magistrates were by no means disposed to grant licences to known holders of Radical opinions.

In 1797, as the sequel to the Naval Mutinies, there came two further repressive laws, one (37 George III, c. 70) imposing the death penalty on anyone who was convicted of inciting soldiers or sailors to mutiny, and the other, mentioned at the opening of this essay, directed to the suppression of unlawful oaths (37 George III, c. 123). To these was added, in 1798, a further measure, the Newspaper Act (38 George III, c. 78), designed to counter written as well as spoken propaganda. This Act required all newspapers to be registered, with an affidavit by the printer, publisher, and proprietors. All copies of newspapers were to contain the names and addresses of their printers and publishers, and were to require stamps, the fees for which were placed at a high level in order to repress cheap publications. Special penalties were imposed, not only for the printing or publication of unauthorised newspapers or for the printing of seditious matter in authorised journals, but also for the mere possession of an unstamped paper. Thus began the great struggle for the freedom of the press, which extended over the next half-century.

In 1799, after the Irish Rebellion, two further Acts were passed. One of these (39 George III, c. 81) was the first of two general Combination Acts, making Trade Unions of every sort and kind criminal conspiracies by statute as at common law. The other, generally known as the Unlawful Societies Act (39 George III, c. 79) was concerned with the complete suppression of a number of the leading Radical societies, which had either survived the treason trials of 1793–4, or had been created (or were believed by the Government to have been created—for the very existence of one or two of them is a matter of doubt) since the collapse of a number of the societies which had been active at that time.

Five societies—the United Englishmen, the United Scotsmen, the United Britons, the United Irishmen, and the London Corresponding Society—were suppressed by name, on the ground that ' *a traitorous conspiracy has long been carried on in conjunction with persons from time to time exercising the powers of Government in France* ', and that the members of these societies ' *have taken unlawful oaths* '. In addition to the societies suppressed by name, the Act declared unlawful all societies whose members took oaths not required by law, or which possessed secret committees. Penalties were imposed on unlawful meetings of the societies suppressed under the Act, and provision was made for the closing of houses which had been used for unlawful meetings or lectures. A special provision, however, was made whereby any licensed ale-house was allowed to be licensed for political readings ; but power was given to revoke any ale-house's licence if seditious or immoral publications were read. The Newspaper Act was further strengthened by requiring that printers should hold a licence from a magistrate, and by extending the requirement that the name of the printer should appear from newspapers only to every type of printed paper or book. Power was also given to the justices to search any printing establishment and to seize papers, if they suspected that seditious or blasphemous matter was being put into circulation.

In the following year, came a second Combination Act (39 and 40 George III, c. 60) amending and strengthening the provisions against Trade Unions which had been enacted in the previous year. Finally, in 1801, a further Act was passed against seditious meetings (41 George III, c. 30) renewing and expanding the Act passed in 1795.

Thus from 1799 onwards all Trade Unions or forms of industrial combination among the workers were suppressed by law, and all Radical political activity was severely repressed under the other measures which have been outlined. It falls outside the scope of this essay to discuss in detail the effects of the two Combination Acts of 1799 and 1800. It is enough to say that these Acts placed in the hands of the Government and the magistrates an absolute power to suppress any Trade Union that they chose. This, however, did not make so much difference as appears at first sight, because there is little doubt that the judges already regarded Trade Unions as criminal conspiracies at common law, even apart from any special statute declaring them to be so.

The effect of the two Combination Acts was rather to encourage actual prosecutions and to provide a simpler procedure as an alternative to that which was already available at common law ; and, in fact, the majority of the known prosecutions which took place during the period while the Combination Acts remained in force appear to have been common law trials, though it is difficult to form an accurate judgment on this point in the absence of reports of many of the local cases. Neither the Combination Acts nor the common law did, however, achieve anything like a complete suppression of Trade Unionism, which lived on in spite of legal prohibition throughout the period between 1799 and the repeal of the Combination Laws under Francis Place's influence in 1824. What happened was that the local trade clubs of journeymen in the older crafts were left for the most part unmolested, and their leaders were convicted under the law only when they made themselves especially obnoxious to the employers. On the other hand, in the new factory districts the law was being constantly put into motion against every attempt to create effective Trade Unions, and one leader after another paid the penalty of imprisonment for his efforts on behalf of the exploited textile operatives and miners in the northern and midland counties. Nevertheless, even in these areas combinations persisted, and almost as soon as one Trade Union was suppressed a new one appeared. For there were desperate grievances crying out for remedy, and men were again and again found ready to take the risks of imprisonment and even transportation for violation of the law.

The reason for this difference in the treatment meted out to the Trade Clubs of the skilled urban artisans and to the combinations of the northern miners and textile workers is twofold. In the first place, whereas the skilled workers' Clubs were, and could in most cases, afford to remain, small and purely local, the miners and textile operatives could not hope to make their combinations effective without organising them over a fairly wide area. Whereas it would have been fantastic to suspect a little Club of a few dozen tailors or shoemakers of any revolutionary design, it seemed much more natural to regard with suspicion larger and more widespread combinations of half-starved miners or textile workers, whom desperation might impel to deeds of violence, even if they knew little or nothing of France or of the Rights of Man.

Secondly, the skilled men's Clubs were mostly in corporate towns, whereas the textile workers and miners were scattered over the country districts. There is ample evidence that the gentlemen justices of the county benches, urged on by the fear of revolution, were much more intent on breaking up working-class combinations than the small employers who dominated the urban benches, and had even sometimes some sympathy with Radical views. The main impulse towards enforcing the Combination Acts was, I believe, throughout much more a political than an economic impulse.

After 1801, there was a pause in the flood of repressive legislation, though most of the Acts which have been described still remained in force, to be invoked against Radicals and Trade Unionists as occasion required. There is, however, no doubt that after Pitt's death in 1806 the repression was for a time substantially relaxed ; and with one important exception there was no fresh repressive legislation between 1801 and the end of the Napoleonic Wars. This exception is the Act of 1812, directed against the Luddites, who had been active in the previous years chiefly in the hosiery districts in the midland counties, though there had also been outbreaks of Luddism, on somewhat different lines, in Yorkshire and Lancashire. This Act (52 George III, c. 104), which made the crime of machine-breaking punishable with death, stiffened up drastically the Act of 1797, against unlawful oaths ' *That every person who shall in any manner or form whatsover administer or cause to be administered, or be aiding or assisting at the administration of any oath or engagement purporting or intending to bind the person taking the same to commit any treason or murder or any felony punishable by law with death, shall be adjudged guilty of felony* '—so ran the new Act. Any such person was to suffer death, and any person who took any oath of the nature covered by the Act was also to be guilty of felony and to be subject on conviction to transportation for life. This savage measure was employed in the suppression of the Luddite disturbances of 1811 and the following years, which arose first in the midland textile districts over the introduction of new types of machinery into the framework knitting industry, and spread thence to Yorkshire, Lancashire, and other textile areas. This movement, and the part played in it by ' King Lud ', has been fully described by Mr. and Mrs. Hammond in their book *The Skilled Labourer*.

After 1812 no further repressive laws were enacted until the years immediately following the conclusion

of the Napoleonic Wars. The return of peace brought
with it a period of acute unemployment and distress
which extended to practically all industries and to every
part of the country. The unrest was most acute in the
northern textile and mining areas ; but it also affected
London, and it was in connection with the disturbed
condition of the Metropolis that the Government seems
chiefly to have taken fright. Once more Committees
of Secrecy were appointed by Parliament to investigate
the alleged attempts to bring about an armed rebellion
against the State, and this time the chief blame for these
activities was placed upon the tiny Society of Spencean
Philanthropists, consisting of the followers of the Radical
land reformer Thomas Spence. Spence himself was
already dead, but his followers, organised in the Society
of Spencean Philanthropists, were carrying on an active
agitation for the public ownership of the land, and were
regarded as the extreme left wing of the Radical movement. The Spencean Society organised the famous Spa
Fields meeting of 1816, which was followed by some
rioting in the City of London. Though there is no real
indication that the Spenceans had any considerable
following, or were engaged in laying plans for anything
in the nature of an armed insurrection, the occurrences
at the Spa Fields meeting gave the Government its excuse
for a fresh round of repressive laws, and in 1817 further
Acts were passed with the object of suppressing the
movement and of arming the Government with exceptional powers.

The first of these Acts (57 George III, c. 3) sus-
pended the Habeas Corpus Act, and this suspension
was renewed by a further Act later in the year.

' *Whereas a traitorous conspiracy has been formed for
the purpose of overthrowing by means of a general insurrection the established Government, Laws and Constitution of this Kingdom, and whereas designs and practices
of a treasonable and highly dangerous nature are now
carrying on in the metropolis and in many other parts of*

Great Britain '—so runs the preamble of 57 George III, c. 3, recalling closely in its phrases the repressive laws of the years immediately following the Revolution in France.

The next Act, the Treason Act of 1817 (57 George III, c. 6), re-created and made perpetual with minor modifications the Treason Act of 1795. At the same time there was passed, as in 1795, a further Act dealing with seditious meetings and assemblies (57 George III, c. 19). This Act for the most part practically repeated the phrases of the Seditious Meetings and Assemblies Act of 1795. Again, we have the prohibition of meetings of more than fifty persons except on a signed requisition of seven householders, the requirement that all places of meeting must be licensed by the magistrates, and that the magistrates may inspect such places of meeting and revoke the licences if they consider that any unlawful discussion is going on. But the Act of 1817 added further provisions. It suppressed by name all the Spencean Clubs and Societies, and all other clubs holding the same objects and doctrines. It further suppressed as unlawful combinations all Societies ' taking unlawful oaths or requiring declarations not required by law or electing delegates to confer with other clubs ', and it laid down that all persons who were members or induced others to become members of Societies of these types were guilty of unlawful combination under the Act of 1799 (39 George III, c. 79). There were penalties laid down against householders for allowing unlawful assemblies to take place on their premises, and provisions for forfeiting the licences of public houses where unlawful meetings were held. Moreover, there was the famous Clause 23 which prevented political meetings from being held within one mile of Westminster Hall save in connection with parliamentary elections.

These two measures (57 George III, c. 6 and c. 19) are commonly called Sidmouth's ' Gagging Acts ', or sometimes the ' Two Acts '. Drastic as they were, they were soon to be followed by the still more repressive ' Six Acts ' of 1819. For, after a brief recovery in 1818, in the following year, trade and employment again plunged into the abyss, and there were many disturbances all over the country, accompanied by a growing agitation for parliamentary reform. This was the year of the great reform meeting at St. Peter's Fields at Manchester, which ended in what is commonly known as the ' Massacre of Peterloo ', in which peaceful demonstrators were killed and trodden underfoot by yeomanry and soldiers sent to arrest ' Orator ' Hunt, who was the principal speaker at the meeting.

The Peterloo Massacre caused widespread indignation throughout the country, and many protest meetings were held not only by working-class bodies but even under the auspices of respectable Whig leaders. It was for his part in these protests that Earl Fitzwilliam was deprived of the Lord Lieutenancy of the West Riding of Yorkshire. The Government, however, so far from giving way before the Whig and Radical protests, proceeded, with the full support of the Prince Regent, to intensify its repressive activities and to imprison as many of the Radical leaders as it could bring within the reach of the law.

Of the Six Acts of 1819 the first (60 George III, c. 1) prohibited unlawful drilling or exercises of a military character, and laid down penalties against those organising such activities up to seven years' transportation, and for those taking part up to two years' imprisonment. The second Act (60 George III, c. 2) laid down penalties against the carrying of arms under suspicious circumstances, and enabled the magistrates to search private houses for arms, and to seize them when they thought fit. The third Act (60 George III, c. 4) was aimed at speeding up the administration of justice in cases of misdemeanour, in order to enable the courts to deal more promptly with Radical agitators. But these were all measures of secondary importance. The remaining three

Acts went very much further in arming the Government with exceptional powers to restrict the right of free speech and meeting.

The Seditious Meetings Act of 1819 (60 George III, c. 6) began by re-enacting broadly the opening sections of the Act of 1817, but in an even more stringent form. Under this Act meetings were to be allowed at all only in separate parishes or townships ; and only inhabitants of the area in which the meeting was held were to be allowed to attend, the penalty of imprisonment being proclaimed against anyone who attended contrary to the law. Justices of the Peace, accompanied by constables, were given the right to attend all meetings with power to arrest speakers ; and even a lawful meeting might be rendered unlawful if anything deemed seditious or blasphemous or in any way contrary to law was said during the discussion. Meetings in private rooms were, however, exempted from these provisions. Seven years' transportation was laid down as the maximum penalty for refusal of a meeting to disperse on the order of the magistrates, and two years' imprisonment for attending a meeting with arms or with flags or banners. There were also fresh provisions for the licensing and the revocation of licences of places where lectures could be held.

This Act was immediately followed by the Blasphemous and Seditious Libels Act (60 George III, c. 8), which made provision for the seizure of copies of printed matter alleged to be blasphemous or seditious, and laid down as a penalty for any second offence under the Act banishment for a term of years at the discretion of the court, with transportation up to fourteen years as the penalty for remaining in the country or returning to it after sentence of banishment had been passed.

Finally, under the last of the Six Acts (60 George III, c. 19) the heavy stamp duties already levied upon newspapers in order to prevent the growth of the popular press were extended to other types of publication.

' *Whereas pamphlets and printed papers containing observations upon public events and occurrences, tending to excite hatred and contempt of the Government and Constitution of these realms as by law established, and also vilifying our holy religion, have lately been published in great numbers and at very small prices* '—so runs the preamble to this Act—all such pamphlets and printed papers are to be made subject to the Newspaper Acts. This meant that even pamphlets and leaflets became subject to so high a rate of duty as to destroy all chance of popular circulation if the law were observed. The effect can be seen in that Cobbett was compelled to drop the twopenny edition of his *Political Register*, known as ' Twopenny Trash ', which had reached at one time a circulation of 60,000 copies a week, and to raise the price of his *Register* immediately to sixpence. Moreover, it was provided that nobody was to be allowed to print any newspaper or pamphlet of a political kind without entering into bonds and recognisances with the authorities ; and penalties were laid down not only for printing or publishing unlicensed publications, but also for selling them. This was the Act under which, after 1819, hundreds of Radicals went to gaol for the offence of printing, publishing, or selling cheap newspapers or pamphlets. Richard Carlile took the lead in the movement for defiance of the new law, and passed the years following its enactment mostly in gaol, where he was duly joined not only by his wife and sister, but by one after another of those who had volunteered to take his place in his shop or to sell the unstamped publications which he continued to edit even while he remained in prison.

Thereafter the leadership of the movement passed to Henry Hetherington, who is best known as the proprietor of the famous *Poor Man's Guardian*. It was in connection with the *Poor Man's Guardian*, over which Hetherington had been repeatedly prosecuted in earlier years, that Lord Lyndhurst delivered in 1834 his remarkable judgment, declaring that after all this could not be regarded as a newspaper falling under the ban imposed by the Newspaper Acts. But even thereafter the stamp duties remained, and the agitation against them was carried on until their repeal by stages in the eighteen-forties. After 1834, however, the active repression of unlicensed publications for the most part died away. The story of the newspaper duties and of the agitation against them has been fully told in two books—Mr. Wickwar's *The Struggle for a Free Press*, and Mr. C. D. Collet's *History of the Taxes upon Knowledge*. I have no space to tell it further here.

With this measure the long sequence of Acts directed to the repression of working-class and Radical movements comes to an end. Five years after the passing of the Six Acts the Combination Laws were repealed, thanks largely to the untiring activities of Francis Place, and Trade Unionism became lawful, though the Act of 1825, which replaced the more generous measure of 1824, still left open many possibilities of prosecution—as was clearly seen in the period between 1825 and the passing of the Trade Union Act of 1871. This story of the struggle of the Trade Unions with the law falls, however, outside the scope of this essay, which is designed only to describe the repressive laws which were passed during the thirty years following the Revolution in France, and invoked successfully in the prosecution of the Dorchester labourers in 1834, when most people had forgotten their existence, and certainly no one anticipated their use as a means of suppressing Trade Unionism after the Combination Acts had been repealed. It is only necessary, in conclusion, to emphasise once more the fact that many of the repressive powers conferred by these laws remain on the statute book even to-day,[1] and can at any time be invoked against the working-class movement. It would be a fitting tribute to the Tolpuddle Martyrs for the Trade Union movement to take up, one hundred

[1] 38 George III, c. 78 ; 55 George III, c. 80 ; 55 George III, c. 185 ; 56 George III, c. 56.

years after their martyrdom,[1] the task of sweeping away what is left of a body of law which was widely denounced as unjust and repressive when it was first enacted and has become ludicrously inappropriate to the recognised status of the Trade Union and Socialist movement of to-day.

[1] This essay was originally written in 1934, and published, in part, in the volume issued that year by the Trades Union Congress to celebrate the centenary of the Tolpuddle Martyrs.

William Cobbett
(1762–1835)

THERE are certain Englishmen who, being memorable for much besides, make one think, whenever they come into one's mind, of England. Not of England as a nation, much less a Great Power, or of England as a political unit, or of England with any other special qualification, but purely and simply of England. It is not merely that these men are ' so English ', though they are : it is that they have in some sort the quality of being England, and of expressing in whatever they do or say something as unmistakably English as the burr of an Oxfordshire (not, be it noted, an ' Oxford ') accent. They have an English burr ; and it goes without saying that, having this, they are none of your desiccated townsmen, remote from the life of field and village, but countrymen in mind, wherever they live. For the heart of our urbanised England is still in the country.

Cobbett was an Englishman in this very special sense. Carlyle called him ' the pattern John Bull of the century ' ; and the phrase sticks in the mind. Bluff, egotistical, shrewd, capable of meanness as well as of greatness, positive in all things and desperately wrong in some—but also devastatingly right in many more—no theorist till he could see with his own eyes the human stuff of which problems are made, quick to anger and indignation but also infinitely friendly ; didactical and often overbearing, and yet full of human sympathy ; very well satisfied with himself and ever ready to hold his own experience up as an example to others ; and therewith possessed of a singular power of identifying himself with the country he loved and the people for whom he fought —there, as nearly as I can paint it in a few words, you

143

have the portrait of this tall, gawky, florid, exuberant farmer, who looked like a farmer and did more than any other man to bring hope into dark places where hope was needed even more sorely than meat and drink.

Above all else, I think of Cobbett as the man who, at a wretched time in the history of the English people, put hope into their hearts, not by telling lies or painting fancy pictures, either of this world or of the next, but by good solid cursing that never degenerated into a whine or a mere vapouring of despair, but bade men gird up their loins and struggle for the right. No matter whether he was talking at the moment to a gathering of farmers in some country town on market day, or to a crowd of half-starved labourers assembled on some Hampshire heath, or to the journeymen and factory workers in one of the new industrial towns, he knew how to speak comfortable words, even if all he said was of men's wrongs and miseries, and nothing at all of their compensations. He had a wealth of righteous indignation always at command, not vamped up to suit his hearers, but coming naturally out of him—felt and swelling within him too strongly to be bottled up. There were so many things to arouse that indignation ; and, if he expended some of it on the wrong objects, that mattered very little, as long as his anger flowed like a sea over the inhumanity and injustice of the times.

Yet Cobbett was not only an angry man, finding everywhere he went ample cause for his anger. If he had been only that, his passion would have been far less compelling. He was angry, exceedingly angry ; but there was always love as well as anger in his words. He loved the people on whose behalf he made crusade ; and, equally with the people, he loved the land they lived in—the villages and churches, the great houses with their parks of orderly trees, the birds and beasts, the downs and valleys and rivers and streams, the crops that grew out of the earth and, last but not least, the earth itself. The smell and feel of the countryside were his tonic ; and, though much of his life was lived in towns, he had to be coming back always to the open country for refreshment and inspiration. In the town, he often seemed to be only guessing : in the country, he knew.

Not that Cobbett's love of the country was just like mine, or probably yours ; for I at any rate am a town-dweller, and not a countryman. The country is a place to which I go, not with the sense of going home. But to Cobbett the country was home, and his eye for it was the eye of a countryman. He wanted it to be useful, and not merely ornamental. The barren heath of Hindhead stirred no pleasure in him ; and the sight of a field full of thistles put him quite out of humour for a morning. Gentlemen's parks he could bear with, for he loved a good tree, above all if it was one of his favourite locusts. He had, moreover, a feeling for the old squire that never forsook him even when he was most roundly denouncing the squire's political opinions. The squire was a part of Old England : he had been there so long that, equally with the village church, he fitted into the scene. It was another matter when the park belonged to a stockbroker or an army contractor, or any of the new-fangled money-spinning class. Then indeed Cobbett had a good look at the man's park and house, very ready to find fault. But the old squire had, if not his agreement, at least his sympathy, extended the more readily because, in Cobbett's opinion, his chance of survival was poor enough in the bad new times.

For Cobbett was one of those evangelists who see the future by looking back to the past. Maybe the past they think they see is not quite what really was ; for they are as ready to pick out from it the things they love and value as to pick out what is bad in the present. That is nothing against them ; for every age needs men to tell it in good homespun language what is wrong with it, and a touch of exaggeration does not come amiss either for stirring the imaginations of the victims or for shaking the complacency of the smug. Nor is there any harm

in idealising the past, in the sense of seeing its virtues
more plainly than its faults; for that is one way of
giving men heart to set about mending present wrongs.
Or, if it be a fault not to see all things steadily and whole
and in the correct perspective, it may be a fault that is
inseparable from a certain sort of greatness. To be always cool may be a virtue; but to lose one's temper at
injustice may be a virtue too, even if loss of temper always distorts the vision.

The past that Cobbett saw in this idealised way was
sometimes nearer, and sometimes more remote. At
times, it was a past beyond the Reformation, when
monasteries recognised the obligation to care for the
poor, and the tithe was a charge on property for the
relief of the poor, and not itself a form of property.
Under the spell of that vision he produced his *History
of the Protestant Reformation*, which roused the Evan-
gelicals to the height of fury, as he fully meant it to do.
At other times the past was nearer, in the glorious days
before the Bank of England, founded to help Dutch
William's wars, had saddled the country with the
National Debt. Or again the past would draw nearer
still, to the days of his own childhood, before Pitt had
ruined the country with his villainous ' system ', or the
stock-jobbers enriched by the war had bought up the
old estates, or ' the Wen ', London, had been swollen
to its present monstrous size. Those were the days—
the days when Cobbett was a boy scaring crows in a
field, or weeding the garden paths at Waverley Abbey,
or watching the fine gentlemen—who could afford it
then—ride out to hounds. But now, he tells us again and
again, all that is gone—or going. The stock-jobbers are
putting up their ugly big houses all over the countryside, or shoving the old decaying gentry out of their
homes : the peasants, who used to be cheery souls, with
good healthy appetites and a healthy respect for the
State, are shivering in rags at the gang-work set by the
parish, or gone away to work long hours in the suffocat-

ing misery of the new factory towns. The old squires,
where they are left, wear long faces because of the rates
and taxes ; and they are thinning fast. It is their fault,
too, that they are being undone, because they backed
up Pitt and his ' system ' and never lifted a hand to
save the labourers from ruin. And they lived fine too,
when they couldn't afford it. There's Squire Ridge, ruined
with fox-hunting, and Squire Somebody-else, who tried
to hold up his head among a pack of stock-jobbers,
spending pound for pound. All the old glories fast de-
parting ; and in their places lords of the loom and steam
engine, brokers from Change Alley, and the pestilent
fellows who make the paper for the Bank to print its
filthy notes on.

You would get tired of this quite soon ; but suddenly,
in the middle of his tirade, Cobbett would see something
else in his mind's eye, and in a minute he'd be off after that.
Perhaps it was only the really excellent crop of Swedish
turnips he passed when he was riding past Mr. Acres'
farm to-day, or perhaps it was a pretty girl in a field with
whom he exchanged the glad eye. Whatever it was, you
hear about it, as soon as the picture comes into his
vision ; and then you are in the fields with him, in sun
or rain, seeing what the Swedish turnips looked like, or
giving the girl the glad eye yourself. Or perhaps what
comes up in his mind is a remembrance of his own life ;
and then too you hear about it. ' When I was a soldier
in New Brunswick ', ' when the swindling Americans
robbed me of five thousand dollars ', ' when Pitt offered
me one of the Government newspapers ', ' when I was in
Newgate gaol '—all vastly egotistical, all much to Cobbett's honour and glory, and for an example for all good
citizens in the middle way of life to follow, but withal
immensely vivid, racy, diverting, and altogether human.

In *Rural Rides* you get this expansive, discursive,
objurgatory, preaching, reminiscent, but above all
noticing William Cobbett at his best. Here is writing
dashed off quickly, often on the morrow of a long day's

ride over the country, while the impressions were fresh, and sent post-haste up to London to be printed in that most personal of all periodicals, Cobbett's *Political Register*. Their fascination lies a good deal in this impressionistic quality, or rather in their absolute naturalness and spontaneity. As you read them, you follow his racing thought and roving eye, never knowing what either will light on next. They are the perfection of political journalism, because they weave politics into the texture of normal living ; but they are also literature that has long survived our minding about many of the persons and controversies with which they deal. Cobbett rode over southern England, and as he rode he wrote ; and no book was ever written that was more England's own book, getting the smell and feel and look of the English country and the English country people down in print, so that the reader can smell and feel and see as well as Cobbett. Usually I set no store by first editions ; but my first edition of *Rural Rides* always seems to have a country smell. Perhaps that is only because it is a little mouldy.

Or take *Advice to Young Men—and Young Women*, for they are both on the title-page, though the book is generally spoken of discourteously without the young women. Here you get less of the vivid pictures of field and farm ; for here Cobbett is writing not a journal, but a sort of tract. You will probably not take Cobbett's advice ; for his standards and habits are not yours. You will hardly choose your wife by deciding that she is the very woman for you when, on a second meeting, you find her scrubbing out a washing-tub in the snow, in the half-light of very early morning, on a bitterly cold day, out of doors. Nor will you, probably, insist on doing your writing-work on a stone floor, or obey Cobbett's precepts about rising early and going early to bed. You will not, I think, agree fully with his views on education, or find your wife, when you get one, willing to be written about quite as Cobbett wrote about Anne Reid, though assuredly he never wrote anything about her that was not vastly complimentary as he meant it. But, though on many points you will not quite share Cobbett's views—for, whatever your opinion may be, it is pretty certain you have twentieth-century habits of mind—I think you will enjoy *Advice to Young Men—and Young Women*—above all else the bits that are about the author's own life. If you do not enjoy it, I am inclined to say that is your fault ; for it means you do not know and like racy, redolent English writing when you meet it.

Then there is the *Political Register*, which Cobbett conducted as a weekly for well over thirty years, writing the greater part of it himself, and basing its appeal practically to the exclusion of all else on his own personality. Others contribute to the *Register* now and then : there are screeds by the old prosy Radical, Major Cartwright, who was, for all his prosiness, the salt of the earth, and whole pages of reports of current events, or important documents reprinted, or extracts from parliamentary papers and debates. But no one bought the *Register* for the sake of these : men bought it to see what Cobbett was saying now, whom he had chosen to pillory this week, what particular feature of the iniquitous ' system ' he had chosen this time to denounce, or perhaps where he had been riding last, and what he had seen and thought by the way. The *Register* was *Cobbett's* Register —the weekly register of Cobbett's impressions, reactions, and ideas derived from what he had been seeing and hearing and doing during the past week. His leading articles were enormous : often they took up most of the paper. But they were read—read aloud by poor men at coffee-houses and ale-houses where other poor men gathered who could not read, or at least could not afford to buy, and read no less in rich men's clubs round Westminster ; for Cobbett's political opponents always wanted to know what he had to say this week. The *Political Register* was a power. Sometimes it barked up the wrong tree, but never up the wrong wood. And whether Cobbett chose the right or the wrong tree, men always attended to his barking. For a man cannot write like Cobbett, and not be attended to, even if he happen on occasion to be talking nonsense.

The *Political Register* went through strange metamorphoses. It was founded as an extreme patriotic journal, to back up Pitt and the French war policy, to denounce Jacobins and Radicals and to shout down the demagogues on the other side. Within a few years it was shouting down the very groups that had supported its establishment, and Cobbett was bellowing as loudly for Radical Reform as he had bellowed against it. He did not change sides again ; for he had found out by then where his allegiance really belonged. But the *Register* went through many queer changes after that. For two years Cobbett edited it from Newgate Gaol, where he had been sent for saying libellous things about the flogging of soldiers. For two more he edited it from the other side of the Atlantic—in days when there were no telegraphs or steamships, and letters could come only as fast as a sailing ship could travel. That was when he had fled to the United States partly from Lord Sidmouth's 'Gagging Acts' of 1817, but also from his creditors, who had become far too pressing in their attentions. At different times the *Register* was sold at the most varied prices—from a shilling or more down to twopence, according to the changing exigencies of the Stamp Duties—those 'taxes on knowledge' which were deliberately used to hamper the activities of Radical journalists. Its appeal was widely different from year to year. At one time it was full of appeals to the farmers, and plainly addressed to them as its principal audience. That was when Cobbett had gone a-crusading among the farmers to raise up support for an 'equitable adjustment' of the monstrous burden of the National Debt, as well as for Radical Parliamentary Reform. At other times, it was written to and for the agricultural labourers—victims of a Poor Law which condemned them to semi-starvation and to serf-labour under the

Speenhamland arrangement. Or again, it would be filled with *Addresses to the Journeymen and Labourers* of the towns, adjuring them to join manfully in the cry for Radical Reform, and painting a lurid picture of their exploitation by the financial power. Whatever the direction of the appeal might be, there in the *Register*, week after week, you had Cobbett talking about every conceivable sort of thing that wanted doing or undoing, in language that even the plainest readers could readily understand. Perhaps Cobbett's predilection for stone floors helped him to write fast. Assuredly he did write fast : so that no other journalist, save Daniel Defoe, has ever approached his output, and certainly none has ever sold a paper for more than thirty years, almost exclusively on the strength of his own personality. The circulation of the *Register* ebbed and flowed with changes in political interest or tension. But no other paper on the same side ever came near equalling the influence of Cobbett's weekly diatribe.

This account of the *Political Register* has taken me back to Cobbett's early days when, so far from upholding the cause of Radical Reform, he made his bow as the most violent of all the anti-Jacobin pamphleteers. Cobbett's first published work, unless we accept the view that he had a hand in an earlier pamphlet written to uphold the rights of the common soldier, was a violent diatribe against that estimable Radical Reformer, Dr. Joseph Priestley, whose house had been burnt down not long before by the Birmingham mob. Priestley, finding liberty at a discount in an England at war with France, had come to look for it in the brave New World that had so lately flung off the tyrant's yoke. He had landed in the free United States, to a salvo of congratulatory addresses from American Societies, whose members, fresh from singeing the King of England's beard, were eager to wish the Jacobins the same good hunting. Cobbett himself was in the United States because of a little disagreement with the powers that were in

England; for he had used his experience as sergeant-major in the British army to collect imposing evidence of corrupt practices on the part of his officers, and this excess of zeal had made England too hot to hold him. But Cobbett in exile was very much the Englishman ; and the revolutionary societies' addresses to Dr. Priestley were altogether too much for him. His *Observations on Dr. Priestley's Emigration* were neither polite nor profound ; but they were undoubtedly pungent, and the British diplomatic representatives in the United States were not long in seeking out so doughty a champion. During the remaining years of his sojourn in America Cobbett, not without encouragement from official quarters at home, laid about him with a will, defending the British cause through thick and thin, and lavishing upon the American people a wealth of home truths and home untruths that made them at all events sit up and take notice.

Philadelphia, where Cobbett was living, was then the capital of the young American Republic, and strongly pro-French. Cobbett opened a bookseller's shop there after a series of entertaining quarrels with the regular booksellers ; and, just to teach these rebel dogs their place, filled his shop-window with all the things most calculated to annoy the American public. Pictures of his Sovereign Lord the King, George III—not an American hero—a fine battle-piece of Lord Howe routing the American fleet, and so on. As Lewis Carroll said ' He only does it to annoy, because he knows it teases '. That was always apt to be Cobbett's way. His *History of the Protestant Reformation* was written in just that spirit.

That was not the end of Cobbett's American escapades. He accused Dr. Rush, who was not only a famous physician, but also a political figure, of bleeding George Washington to death ; and there were unpleasant consequences of the libel, especially as Cobbett went on to say just what he thought about the judge who tried the case and, in *The Rushlight*, to devote a whole periodical to further unpleasantness about Dr. Benjamin Rush. Cobbett had gone to America because he found England too hot to hold him : he returned to his native country because the American continent also blistered at his presence.

He came back, however, in the odour of political sanctity, to be greeted by Tory politicians in search of a journalist with enough punch to put the lousy Radicals in their place. The anti-Jacobins put up enough money to start the *Political Register* as an organ of the extreme right. It was to set about all Radical traitors in the same spirit as Cobbett had shown when he blackguarded Dr. Priestley or wrote his scurrilous life of the ' impious ' Tom Paine. The *Register* began in that spirit ; but, if the spirit lasted, the heroes and the villains soon exchanged rôles. Cobbett did indeed damn the Peace of Amiens up hill and down dale ; he had his windows broken for refusing to illuminate in celebration of the peace. But before long he was causing his backers serious anxiety ; and in a few.years they became well aware that they had received a serpent into their bosom. Cobbett began by taking a rooted dislike to Pitt, and probing inconveniently into the financial abuses of what he began to call ' the Pitt system '—the very last things which even Pitt's political opponents wished to have exposed. He was then still all for war with France ; but he wanted the war to be run cleanly, without pandering to stock-jobbers and handing out pensions and sinecures to the cousins and aunts of the important people. What a hope !

In 1806 Pitt died, leaving behind him an unresolved ambiguity about his dying words. Some say they referred to the fate of England, and others that they were about pork chops ; but there was no doubt that Pitt left behind him a fair microcosm of the National Debt in the form of private obligations of his own ; and these debts a grateful nation, eager to honour ' the pilot' who died without weathering the storm, elected to pay. Cobbett celebrated the occasion by some candid words about Pitt, following his own maxim ' *De mortuis nil nisi verum*—and then some '. But when his own friends, including William Windham, succeeded to office, there was at least a lull in hostilities. The Ministry of All the Talents—except Cobbett's—was to be given a chance. Cobbett only remarked that Fox was not quite such a scoundrel as he had hitherto always made him out to be, and offered a few simple proposals for the new Ministry's acceptance. For example, Windham, now at the War Office, might begin by cleaning up military corruption.

William Windham thought otherwise—for, like most politicians, he regarded public corruption as an ' act of God '. Cobbett admonished, expressed pained surprise, threatened, and finally fulminated. Of a truth, the new lot was as bad as the old. New minister was but old Pitt writ large ; and within a year of Pitt's death, Cobbett was decisively of the Opposition, clamouring for Radical Reform to end the ' Pitt system ', and, before long, as determined to end the war that bred corruption and national decay as he had been a while before to pursue it to the bitter end. The infidel Tom Paine had been right after all. Cobbett soon loved to quote his *Decline and Fall of the English System of Finance* against the transgressors. Soon, he was rubbing salt into the wounds of orthodoxy by quoting with approval irreligious pamphlets that followed up the ideas of Paine's *Age of Reason*. He did not abandon the Church ; but he loved to quote a refutation of orthodox Christianity, and fling out a challenge to the parsons about it. ' Answer that if you can, you lazy, tithe-eating dogs. What are you paid for, if not to answer ? '

This political Odyssey of Cobbett's needs a word of explanation. In his American exile, during the years that followed the Revolution in France, Cobbett was, as we have seen, the extremest of anti-Jacobins. How does that square with his later attitude ? I think the answer must be that, almost from a boy, he had seen little of England. Still a youth, he had fled from his incarceration in a lawyer's office to go for a soldier ; and his years of service in the army had been spent in Canada, largely among those ' Yankee Loyalists ' who had settled there after the War of Independence. From them he had doubtless learned to think of the Americans as a pack of rebels. His penchant for attacking corruption in high places and for defending the weak had been with him already ; and on his return to England he tried hard to bring the officers of his regiment to book for defrauding the soldiers. But while he was in England his ' case ' occupied all his time, except what he spent courting Anne Reid ; and though he had cause to find himself ' agin ' the Government over the court-martial proceedings, he saw nothing of the country, and found no reason to modify his general political outlook. Failing to get a fair chance of proving his case against his officers, he fled to France, then in the throes of Revolution, but not yet at war with England. But he did not go to France for politics, or to a part of the country where political excitements ran high ; and it seems likely that when, on the outbreak of war, he escaped from France to the United States, he carried with him no clear political convictions at all. He was not a man who theorised easily : it needed actual sights and experiences to stir his mind to thought.

In America, he found himself surrounded by anti-British feeling, strongly on the side of France. John-Bullishly, he revolted in exile against the abuse of his country, and became by reaction a fervent patriot. In his vigorous pamphlets denouncing and trouncing Priestley and Tom Paine, there is not a trace of political thinking. They are simple scurrility, carried off by the sheer vigour of the writing. Having found his trade, Cobbett stuck at it ; but he developed no new ideas except by reaction against his American surroundings. He came back at length to his own country, knowing nothing of it, except the Farnham of his youth.

Plunging at once into English journalism as a writer
on the patriotic side, he was kept hard at it in London for
some years, writing with plenty of vigour, but developing
few new ideas. Stuck in London and seeing nothing of the
countryside, which alone he thoroughly understood, he
found nothing to stir his imagination, or to make him
think, until his own friends came to office in 1806, in the
Ministry of All the Talents. Then he expected things to
begin to happen; and when they did not, he was in a
mood to look at the situation for himself, and form an
independent judgment. Moreover, after years cooped
up in town, he felt the longing for the country coming
upon him; and he began to go and look again at the
places he had known in his youth. He was shocked,
appalled. He saw everywhere signs of the intense misery
which high prices and economic change had wrought
upon the country people; and at once his reaction
against the 'Pitt system' turned into a full-blown
Radicalism. He rallied to the defence of his own people
against their oppressors, and learnt a new hatred of the
stock-jobbers and war financiers whose great houses he
found everywhere scarring the country. Their opulence
seemed to him to affront the misery of the starveling
labourers. His case against 'Pitt finance' became in an
instant not merely an intellectual case, but a belief
charged with intense emotion. These were the devils
who were responsible for the labourers' miseries: down
with them and all they stood for to the nethermost hell!

Thus Cobbett, converted, became the foremost of
Radical agitators—foremost, because he was so like in
mind to those on whose behalf he stood forward that the
poor people readily recognised him for their own, as no
merely intellectual leader of revolt could ever have been.
Cobbett was a luckier, cleverer, more forcible peasant,
who, thanks to his luck and brain and force of character,
was able to stand forward to present the poor men's case.
Knowing their own, they acclaimed him. Knowing that
the English poor had at last found a representative leader,

the wiser heads among the enemies of the poor were alarmed, and took counsel together against him.

It took but four years or so after Cobbett's full conversion to Radicalism to land him in Newgate Gaol. There, cooling his heels not uncomfortably, he had time to get ready for a fresh onslaught on the 'Thing'. For gaols in those days were not as gaols are now. A prisoner with money in his pocket could do well enough in gaol, living in a hired apartment of his own, much to the gaoler's profit, writing pamphlets and articles which he could send out and publish freely, having his family to stay with him in the prison, receiving visits of sympathy from one of His Majesty's judges, dressed in his full robes in order to mark his protest at the sentence, and last but not least entertaining his friends, whenever he chose, with steaks and porter within the precincts of the prison. It was not so bad to be gaoled in those days, provided only that you could afford to pay through the nose. Cobbett paid, and lived in Newgate like a fighting cock ; but his publishing business and his farm at Botley went to rack and ruin the while, and a few years later he paid the penalty with his bankruptcy.

The occasion of Cobbett's gaoling need not much concern us here. He had written in the *Political Register* an article about the flogging of English soldiers on which the Government was able to base a successful charge for sedition ; and for this he was put in prison, after a tangle of negotiations in the course of which he decided at one point to stop publishing the *Register* altogether, as the price of being let off. But the negotiations fell through, and the *Register* went on. Cobbett was able to write its main article regularly from prison, though he had to be careful not to provoke a further prosecution, which might have ruined him once and for all. To this circumstance, and to the opportunity for thinking things over that his term in prison afforded him, we owe his *Paper against Gold*—the first of his long series of books published in parts and, apart from the *Register*, the first of his

Radical writings of importance. From this time paper money is seldom long out of Cobbett's mind. It becomes for him the symbol of the ' system ', and by his denunciation of it he becomes the first of the long line of English popular monetary reformers, or shall we say ' currency cranks ' ?

The root idea of *Paper against Gold* Cobbett got from Tom Paine, whose pamphlet, *The Decline and Fall of the English System of Finance*, he never wearied of quoting with the strongest approval. A large part of the sorrows of the people was to be scored up against the wretched Bank of England ; for the foundation of the Bank had been also the origin at one and the same time of the accursed National Debt and of paper bank notes, the twin plagues that were dragging the country down. The Debt was piling up to such a height that it would be impossible ever to repay it, and ruinous even to meet the interest charge ; and as the Debt grew, the curse of paper money grew with it, for how else could the Debt grow ? These were the days of the famous Bullion Committee, which demonstrated plainly, despite the Government's denials, the depreciation of the Bank's paper in relation to gold, as a consequence of the attempt to finance the long war by borrowing instead of taxation. Pitt had chosen the easy way of inflation because he wanted to make the war popular among the swindling fraternity of stock-jobbers and speculators, who profited handsomely by the manipulation of government loans. The paper money had meant high prices, and starvation conditions for the unfortunate agricultural labourers, who were unable to raise their wages. It had meant temporary prosperity for the farmers, who had taken to new-fangled habits on the strength of it—buying pianos and educating their daughters to behave like gentlefolk. It had meant high rates for the landlords, but high taxes as well, as the burden of the poor rates increased, and as the long war had to be financed more out of taxes, even to meet the annual charges of the mounting debt. The landlords had profited for the time, like the farmers ; but both these classes were beginning to pay, and for both there was coming a real day of reckoning, when they would be called upon to meet the postponed costs of the war. Only the money-spinners were in clover, with their ceaseless jobbing of inflated money-values. Only they throve and multiplied as the mass of paper money grew greater and greater with each year.

Holding these views about the curse of paper money, Cobbett might have been expected to be found on the side of the ' sound money men ' when the war was over, and the sages were once more urging a return to the gold standard. But not a bit of it ! Cobbett, the arch-enemy of paper money, took the field as the strongest critic of the Bank Bill of 1819, under which the restoration of the gold standard was finally carried through. He did so without abating one word of his denunciations of the paper system, but arguing that it was manifestly unfair and ruinous to repay in gold a debt which had been contracted in inflated paper money, and that before a resumption of cash payments could properly be allowed steps ought to be taken to scale down the debt, and the interest on it, to a figure corresponding to the changed value of money. Cobbett demanded an ' equitable adjustment ', by which he meant a lowering of the interest burden of the debt, by means of a forced reduction in the rates of interest, as a necessary preliminary to putting back the gold standard.

To this struggle we owe Cobbett's famous ' gridiron ' prophecy. If he were wrong in predicting that a return to the gold standard without an ' equitable adjustment ' would mean collapse, he gave leave to Lord Castlereagh ' to put me on a gridiron and broil me alive, while Sidmouth stirs the fire, and Canning stands by making a jest of my groans '. Cobbett always claimed that his prophecies had come true, on the ground that, though the gold standard was put back, and the interest on the

Debt was not reduced, the events of the financial crisis of 1825, when the Bank was compelled to reissue the small notes withdrawn a few years earlier, justified what he had said. He held, in 1826, his ' Feast of the Gridiron ', to celebrate his rightness ; and he developed a habit of putting a gridiron as a sort of crest at the top of the front page of the *Political Register*. The ' gridiron ' became a recognised symbol among the Cobbettites : it turned up again in Chartist days as the motto of John Cleave's Cobbett Club. Cobbett himself lived long enough to offer strong opposition to Attwood's paper money projects when they were put forward by the Birmingham Political Union, and to conduct at Birmingham with Attwood one of those prodigious debates to which huge audiences seem to have been ready in those most enduring times to listen all day and most of the night. On this occasion Attwood spoke for four and a half hours, and his supporter, Charles Jones, for I forget how long, before Cobbett got a word in. Cobbett then went at it for two hours, and Attwood took two more to reply. There were giants in those days.

This discussion of Cobbett's views about currency has taken us far away from his enforced residence in Newgate from 1810 to 1812, when he was still only at the beginning of his career as a Radical leader. His great period as a leader did not come till the war was over, and the great wave of economic distress which followed the peace had swept over the industrial districts. Till then the *Register* had been read mainly by gentlemen and farmers : it hardly had reached the working class. But in 1816 Cobbett, conscious of the rumblings of unrest all over the new industrial areas, suddenly altered his appeal and began to talk directly to the working classes in the north of England. Knowing the country far better than the town, he had till then been more alive to agrarian than to industrial grievances and hardships ; but now, in his *Addresses to the Journeymen and Labourers*, he began to make a vigorous call to the miners and factory workers to rally to the cause of Radical Reform. In order to do this, he started producing off-prints from the *Register*, containing no news that would have subjected them to the Newspaper Tax, for sale at a penny and twopence a time ; and these special off-prints, started as purely occasional pamphlets, soon turned into a regular twopenny edition of the *Political Register* for popular consumption. The success of his vigorous appeals was immediate. It is said that, at the height of their popularity, Cobbett was selling sixty thousand copies a week. Undoubtedly Cobbett's cheap *Register*—called ' Twopenny Trash ' first by its enemies, though he joyfully adopted the name—had a great deal to do with bringing over the factory workers to the cause of Radical Reform of Parliament. ' At this time,' writes Bamford, the Lancashire weaver, ' the writings of William Cobbett suddenly became of great authority : they were read on nearly every cottage hearth in the manufacturing districts. . . .' Bamford attributed to Cobbett's influence the abandonment of rioting, and the creation instead of an organised Reform movement among the weavers. Whether that be true or not, certainly Cobbett leapt of a sudden to an outstanding position among the leaders of the working class.

He had soon to pay the penalty of his success. Sidmouth's ' Gagging Acts ' of 1817, followed up by the Six Acts of 1819, suppressed his cheap *Register*, by imposing upon it the high newspaper tax, and so making cheap publication impossible. Moreover, knowing the Acts of 1817 to be largely aimed at him, and having also serious private embarrassments of his own, Cobbett evaded the prison, which was the fate of most of the other working-class leaders, by flight. In 1817 he took ship secretly to the United States ; and there he stayed for the next two years. He was accused of cowardly desertion of his post in the hour of danger ; and there is no doubt that he did run away. Whether he should have stayed, to face gaol for debt, or sedition, or both, is a moot point. We at any rate can afford to be grateful for his flight ; for with it begins the sequence of books by which he is best remembered. Away from the constant battle of journalism and political agitation, Cobbett found leisure to sit down and write books—though, with his passion for the land, his first thought when he reached the United States was to get land to farm as well as a political asylum. For two years he farmed, and wrote ; and when, late in 1819, he came back to England to face the repression, just as the Six Acts were being passed into law, he brought back with him the stock of ideas that went to the making of a whole series of books that will not easily die.

Two of these books, *A Journal of a Year's Residence in the United States of America* and *A Grammar of the English Language*, appeared while he was still away from England. Cobbett's *Grammar* is, I think, still an admirable grammar, for the sort of person for whom Cobbett meant it. I have tried it on grown-up students to whom their teachers had omitted to teach their native language at school, and the results of using it have been excellent. Nor is it worse as a grammar for being at times a political tract as well. For just as in *Rural Rides* Cobbett mixed his politics with the affairs of the countryside, till the Swedish turnip became a political weapon, so in his *Grammar* he bombarded his political adversaries unmercifully with the parts of speech. ' The nominative is frequently a noun of multitude ; as *mob, parliament, gang.*' ' The gang of borough-tyrants *is* cruel, and *are* also notoriously as ignorant as brutes.' ' Amongst a select society of empty heads, " moderate reform " has long been a fashionable expression ; an expression which has been well criticised by asking the gentlemen who use it, how they would like to obtain *moderate justice* in a court of law, or to meet with *moderate chastity* in a wife.'

In 1819, despite the Six Acts, which intensified the repression, Cobbett came back to England, and resumed

his place among the outstanding Radical leaders. Thereafter his books followed one another in quick succession.
The American Gardener appeared in 1821 ; and in that
year he also began publishing his series of *Rural Rides*
in the *Political Register*. His *Sermons*, including one on
The Sin of Drunkenness, pointedly directed at George IV,
followed in 1821, in the midst of the Queen Caroline
case ; and *Cottage Economy* appeared the same year.
Part I of his *History of the Protestant Reformation*
followed in 1824 ; and a succession of lesser books led
up to *Advice to Young Men in* 1829, and the first collected
issue of *Rural Rides* in 1830. Cobbett's best books are
thus the work of late middle age. He was nearing sixty
when he began *Rural Rides*, and sixty-six when he
published *Advice to Young Men*. Like Defoe, who alone
can dispute his claim to be the greatest of English
journalists, he wrote all the better as he grew old.

All this time he was vigorously pursuing his political
campaigns. In 1820 and thereabouts he became absorbed
in the case of Queen Caroline—the best of all sticks for
beating a reactionary Ministry and a profligate King.
Cobbett, who was perhaps induced to espouse the
Queen's cause mainly for this reason, became Caroline's
most devout champion, writing her manifestoes for her in
most un-Carolinian prose, and building up behind her an
immense popular agitation throughout the country. When
the Queen's death knocked away the foundations of the
movement, Cobbett was ready for a new cause. During
the next few years he headed a revolt of the farmers
against high taxation, working up among them a big
movement in favour of Radical Reform. But returning
agricultural prosperity caused the tide of agrarian unrest
to ebb for a time ; and the circulation of the *Register* went
down till the country, now under milder and more
hesitant Ministers, began to warm up for the struggle
over the Reform Bill.

Into this struggle Cobbett put the whole of his energy.
He felt a profound distrust of the various groups of

parliamentary reformers—from Whigs bent on ' moderate reform ' to the ' feelosofical villains ' from north of the Border who were determined to transfer power to the middle classes in such a way as to leave their working-class allies out in the cold. Throughout the campaign he denounced the Whigs and Lord Brougham with impartial vigour, urging the working-class Radicals to get control of the Political Unions throughout the country, in order to press forward their own nominees to Parliament and so dish the Whigs. In this contest, Cobbett's followers were usually worsted, and the Whigs and ' feelosofers' between them captured most of the nominations. The Reformed Parliament of 1832, when it came at last, contained Cobbett, as member for Oldham. But he had only a handful of followers to face a powerful Whig majority with which the Tories were usually ready to make common cause when really Radical measures were at issue. It was said by his parliamentary contemporaries that old Cobbett did not make much of a politician, and never demeaned himself as a proper ' House of Commons man '. He has, however, apart from his violent attacks on Peel and on the Speaker, at any rate one very memorable House of Commons speech to his credit. He spoke it in the course of the debates on the Factory Bill of 1833. Though it has been quoted often, I feel I must quote it again—the one longish quotation from Cobbett's writings I have introduced into this essay :

Sir, I will make but one single observation upon this subject, and that is this : that this ' reformed ' House has this night made a discovery greater than all the discoveries that all former Houses of Commons have ever made, even if all their discoveries could have been put into one. Heretofore, we have sometimes been told that our ships, our mercantile traffic with foreign nations by means of these ships, together with our body of rich merchants—we have sometimes been told that these form the source of our wealth, power and security. At other times, the land has stepped forward, and bid us look to it, and its yeomanry, as the sure and solid foundation of our greatness and our safety. At other times the Bank has pushed forward with her claims, and has told us that, great as the others were, they were nothing without ' PUBLIC CREDIT ', upon which not only the prosperity and happiness, but the very independence of the country depend. But, sir, we have this night discovered, that the shipping, the land, and the Bank and its credit, are all worth nothing compared with the labour of three hundred thousand little girls in Lancashire ! Aye, when compared with only an eighth part of those three hundred thousand little girls, from whose labour if only we deduct two hours a day, away goes the wealth, away goes the capital, away go the resources, the power, and the glory of England ! With what pride and what pleasure, sir, will the right hon. gentlemen opposite, and the honourable member for Manchester behind me, go northward with the news of this discovery, and communicate it to that large portion of these little girls whom they have the honour and the happiness to represent !

Cobbett was not destined to have a long or distinguished parliamentary career. He was an old man when he was elected ; and, proud as he was of being there to represent the common people, the House of Commons was by no means his spiritual home. He sat assiduously through the debates, though the late hours did not suit him and he had very little respect for most of the proceedings of the ' honourable House '. But his letters show him pining for the country and for his farm ; and he was happiest when Parliament was in recess, and he could get back to his crops. For throughout his life, whatever he was doing—and that was usually a great deal—he was never really happy without a patch of land to look after. He made one farm after another—his Botley farm, on which he lavished many years of labour, only to be ousted as a result of his bankruptcy, his farm on Long Island during his two years' exile in the United States from 1817 to 1819, his seed farm at Kensington, his farm at Barn Elms, and in his last years Normandy Farm, Ash, near Aldershot. There he made his agricultural experiments, with acacia trees or locusts, as he called them, with Cobbett's corn, swedish turnips, straw plait, and a host of other things ; and he was always eager to pass on his knowledge to his fellow farmers and labourers. He wrote and edited agricultural manuals, from Jethro Tull's famous *Horse-hoeing Husbandry* to his own *English Gardener, The Woodlands*, and *A Treatise of Cobbett's Corn*. Farming and education were blended together in his mind. He must always be turning over land, and tilling the soil of other men's minds as well.

Yet for formal educational systems he had for the most part a great contempt. His references to Oxford are uniformly derogatory : he loved nothing better than to see a professor caught out ; and his most outrageous diatribes were poured out against the ' feelosofical villains ' like Brougham, who set out to teach the poor the blessings of the new industrial system. He had no use for the Society for the Diffusion of Useful Knowledge, Brougham's favourite, which Thomas Love Peacock aptly nicknamed ' The Steam Intellect Society '. The kind of education he believed in firmly was the sort he had got himself, and was ready at every opportunity to impart to others—the kind a man picked up not at school, but by sitting over Cobbett's *Grammar* or Cobbett's *History* or even Cobbett's *Register* before or after a hard day's work. If you read *Advice to Young Men* you will soon realise that the young men who set out to follow it were not in for an easy time. They had to be up early, and abed late. They were to live sparingly ; and plenty of hard work was recommended as a means to keeping fit. Beer they might have—especially home-brewed ; but they had better keep off other intoxicants, and certainly off such noxious brews as tea. Cobbett had learnt in a hard school ; and he was thoroughly well satisfied with the results. Let others go and do likewise, if they wanted to make their way in the world.

This egoism of Cobbett's is everywhere in his work. I can imagine that his contemporaries often found it offensive as well as laughable. Certainly they were always on the look-out for weak points in his armour, of which there were not a few. It is laughable still, because, of its *naïveté* ; but it is no longer a source of offence. For it is

only the prig, like Marcus Aurelius, whose self-satisfac-
faction continues to offend when the possessor is centuries dead and gone. Cobbett's self-satisfaction is not
priggish. It rests not on an interest in saving his own
soul, but on an assertion that he is as good a man as anyone else ; and it is preserved from self-centredness because he also made it an assertion of the rights and claims
of the common people from whose ranks he had come.
' Hate me, hate my class ', Cobbett seemed to be always
saying ; and it was to a great extent his egoism that enabled him to go on throughout his life thinking and feeling as one of the country folk among whom he had been
born, and thus able to speak to them, far more than any
of his contemporaries, as one of themselves. The common people of England have not had so many interpreters that they can afford to forget Cobbett.

When Cobbett died, in 1835, *The Times*—the 'bloody
old *Times* ', as he had often called it—said that he was an
' episode '. *The Times* meant that, with all his doing and
saying, he had never understood or formed part of the
main stream of the development of English life. He had
lived, battling against an unwelcome and unintelligible
present in the cause of a romanticised past. Therefore, it
was predicted, he was destined to have no successor.
On that last point *The Times* was right ; for Cobbett
was the last—and indeed also the first—articulate voice
of that English countryside, which, even in his own day,
the rising tide of industrialism was swiftly drowning.
He belonged to an age that was dying ; and, as he saw
the sufferings and injustices that the birth of the new
age brought upon his own people, it was natural for him
not only to revolt, but to look romantically at the ages
that had been swept away. This explains his attitude
to the old squires ; and it also explains his views about
the Protestant Reformation.

It was fitting that Cobbett's last crusade should be
made on behalf of the village labourers for whom he had
been fighting hard the best part of his life. In the agri-

cultural troubles of 1830–31, which Mr. and Mrs Hammond have called ' The Last Labourers' Revolt ', he stood up manfully on behalf of the unfortunates whom the Whig Government was putting down with so savage a severity. He was put on trial himself, on the charge of responsibility for fomenting the revolt ; and doubtless his speeches about the labourers' wrongs had helped to stir up the spirit of resistance in them, though Cobbett had certainly not incited them to actual rioting. He was acquitted, for the jury disagreed ; and his acquittal was regarded as a bad blow for the Whig Government. But the labourers, though they had behaved with a singular absence of violence, were put down ruthlessly ; for the Whigs were determined to show that, though they were parliamentary reformers, they were as devout upholders of law and order as the Duke of Wellington himself. Cobbett's hatred of the Whigs was greatly fanned by the events of 1831 ; and his last crusade was against a further Whig blow at the rights of the poor.

In 1834 the Poor Law Amendment Act was passed, to sweep away the ' Speenhamland ' system of poor relief in aid of wages in the rural areas, and to make an end of outdoor relief for the unemployed in the industrial regions. In the early months of 1835—he died in June 1835— Cobbett was trying to stir up the whole country to a revolt against the new Poor Law, which he had fought hard, with only a handful of supporters, while it was before the House of Commons. His last articles are a summons to this crusade to preserve the right of the poor to maintenance. But he died just as the new Poor Law Commissioners were beginning their work ; and in fact the agricultural labourers had been too heavily beaten down four years before to have strength left to respond to his appeal. The response came in 1837 among the industrial workers, when the ' Three Bashaws of Somerset House ', having completed the introduction of the new Poor Law into the agricultural areas, turned to applying it to the industrial districts. The outcome of that response was the Chartist Movement. But before the advent of Chartism Cobbett was dead ; and Feargus O'Connor was left to lead it.

Whether Cobbett was an ' episode ' or not, he was certainly an Englishman. I know of none so English, so much of that England which was not a nation of shop-keepers, but a nation of farmers and sailors and adven-turers over the face of the earth. Not that Cobbett scorned shopkeeping. He kept shop for many years, first in Philadelphia, and latterly bookselling in London. In the Strand and at Bolt Court he sold not only books and newspapers and pamphlets, but also seeds and trees, and even patent fire-grates of a type which he was trying to introduce from the United States. Cobbett kept shop ; and he had a very good idea of the value of making money though he never mastered the art of keeping it for long. But for him shopkeeping was an incident ; and the wares he sold were mostly of his own making. He de-lighted in making things, and was never happy unless he had plenty of work on hand. Whatever he was doing, his day was like a farmer's day. I have a diary of his, written at the end of his life, in which jottings about the crops and the weather appear all mixed up with notes about Parliament and politics and family affairs, and anything that happens to need noting down. Its jumble of activities gives an extraordinarily clear impression of the ceaseless round of doing and making that was Cobbett's life.

Much of that round I have left out—far more, indeed, than I have put in ; for this is an essay, and not a bio-graphy. But I have at least tried to suggest the sort of man William Cobbett was. If you want more, I have written a life of him. But, best of all, go to his own books, and of these, above all others, to *Rural Rides*. For there you will find Cobbett himself, talking about all manner of things as he rides over the country he loves and sees in it only too much to hate. *Rural Rides* is Cobbett; and it is also a not inconsiderable part of England.

Rural Rides

NINE out of ten readers, asked to name off-hand a work by William Cobbett, would answer *Rural Rides*. It is not that Cobbett wrote nothing else; his output, in millions of words, was probably greater than that of any other English writer of his ability. It is not that *Rural Rides* has been the most widely circulated of his books : *Advice to Young Men* has been reprinted at least as often, and Cobbett's *English Grammar* had a far greater circulation in his own day, and has continually reappeared in cheap editions ever since. It is not that Cobbett himself set most store by *Rural Rides* ; for, if he had been asked to name his best book, he would probably have chosen, according to his mood of the moment, *Paper against Gold*, or *The Poor Man's Friend*—neither of which anyone reads nowadays—or even that highly unhistorical squib, the *History of the Protestant Reformation*. But posterity has no doubts : purely as a writer, and apart from his importance as a political influence, Cobbett lives to-day mainly as the author of *Rural Rides*.

It is easy to see why. To begin with, *Rural Rides* contains some of the best, the most vivid and vigorous writing that has ever appeared in the English language. But there are many works of Cobbett's—such as *Advice to Young Men* and the *Letters to the Luddites*, to take only two examples—which are equally well written. The real reason is that in *Rural Rides*, as in no other work, the reader finds the whole of Cobbett, the whole of that vigorous, combative, prejudiced, but always interested and interesting personality, who for a number of years held a position among the English working classes almost equivalent to that of O'Connell among the Irish peasants. The literature which is compendiously called ' Anti-Cobbett ' takes up a pretty large space in the catalogue of the British Museum Library ; the reader of *Rural Rides* will find out what exactly it was that ' Anti-Cobbett ' was trying to combat.

Into *Rural Rides* Cobbett put the whole of himself— what he really loved as well as what he really hated. In a casual glance at the *Political Register*, or at almost any of his political writings, the hatreds are apt to bulk too large. The economist angrily shrugs his shoulders at Cobbett's somewhat *ad hoc* opinions on national finance; the historian gasps at his violent historical prejudices; the social student feels slightly bewildered at the comprehensive flinging of Castlereagh, Wilberforce, Mrs. Fry, Burdett, Owen, Brougham, and Oliver into the same circle of hell ; and all together wonder audibly, as Creevey did in his own day, that a man who was so absurd, so unreasonable, and so abusive, could be so worshipped. But all these prejudices are but knots and warts on his personality. Essential knots, no doubt ; for Cobbett would not have been Cobbett without his prejudices. But they were only part of the man himself ; and it is simply as a man, not as a philanthropist, like Owen, or a strategist, like Place, or even an agitator, like Henry Hunt, that Cobbett holds his place in working-class history.

The collection of travels through England known as *Rural Rides* is admirably fitted to express that personality. In the first place, the form exactly suited the writer, allowing him to break off at any moment into one of his characteristic digressions. In the second place, the date at which he began to write them was one of very great significance, both in Cobbett's personal career and in the history of the English working class. The first *Ride* was written in 1821, two years after Cobbett's return from America, and two years after ' Peel's Act ' had put an end to the period of war inflation. Everything that Cobbett saw around him seemed at this time to bear witness abounding to the truth of his predictions. The

' Pitt system ', which he had been denouncing for at least fifteen years, seemed at last on the point of collapse. Agriculture, industry, finance—all lay in ruins around him. Everywhere, popular discontents rumbled and resounded. Reform, which would sweep away the abuses and all the causes of distress, could not, he thought, be much longer delayed.

The evolution of Cobbett's Radicalism had, indeed, been a gradual process. From 1804 onwards, the reader of the *Political Register* will notice the beginning of the change in Cobbett from violent Anti-Jacobinism to a Radicalism no less aggressive. Until then, he had been an intransigeant supporter of war to the death against France ; he had attacked the Peace of Amiens, and fiercely exhorted his countrymen to renew the struggle. He was, even in those days, beginning to attack Pitt's system of war finance, and still more the rapidly developing system of places, pensions, and sinecures which Burke had denounced twenty years before. But, at this stage, he kept highly respectable political company. William Windham was his closest political associate ; and he looked to Windham and his friends, when they came into power, to end the abuses as well as to get on with the war. His awakening came soon, when Windham joined with Fox and Grenville in the Ministry of All the Talents. For the first, but by no means for the last time, Cobbett then discovered that politicians in opposition are apt to differ in outlook from the same politicians in power. Cobbett required of Windham and his friends that, immediately upon taking office, they should drastically reform the army, end the rule of placemen and pensioners, and stop the Pitt system of financing the war. And when—Grenville being himself not the least of the sinecurists—they did nothing of the sort, he passed instantly into opposition, and, after offering to stand himself, backed Lord Cochrane as Radical candidate for Honiton.

The *Political Register*, which had been hitherto a

strongly anti-reform journal, was soon definitely on the Radical side. But it was not yet a journal of overwhelming importance ; it was more like any opposition weekly of the present day (though somewhat better written) than the terrific power which it afterwards became. For that we have to wait another ten years. In the meantime, Cobbett gradually grew more and more extreme in his Radical opinions. Grenville's Ministry fell, and its place was taken by that Tory ascendancy which under the aegis successively of Portland, Perceval, Liverpool, Canning, Goderich, and Wellington, dominated England to the verge of the Reform Bill. The placemen and the sinecurists went on untroubled; to the scandal of Melville succeeded the scandal of Mrs. Clarke ; Old George Rose continued his profitable career ; Quintin Dick bought a seat from Castlereagh and was turned out of it for voting against the Government. More important for Cobbett's development was his growing consciousness of the oppression which was bound up with the corruptness of the system. In 1809 his indignant protest against the flogging of English militiamen under the guard of German mercenaries earned him two years in Newgate, and from 1811 onwards the protests of Luddites and others in the manufacturing towns began to be put down with increasing severity. At the same time, the agricultural labourers and cottagers, who were Cobbett's own people, driven off the land by the growing movement towards enclosure, saw their standard of life steadily lowered by the soaring prices of the foodstuffs which they produced, but which their wages were not enough to buy. It roused Cobbett's heartiest indignation that neither Government nor philanthropists had any proposals to help his poor chopsticks, though Wilberforce, the Frys, and others of their kin could whip up subscriptions and rouse public opinion to distribute bibles and tracts among them, or to mend the woes of felons and negroes ; and he was not soothed when he came across a group of ' feelosofical villains ' who explained that the

173

real reasons for the plight of the agricultural labourer were that he had too many children and ate too much white bread. Cobbett came on the scene rather after the famous campaign to EAT MORE SOUP which is so prominent a feature of the early years of the French wars ; in his day the advertised substitutes for bread were oatmeal and potatoes, and when, in after years, he is found attacking a public character with really disproportionate venom, it will frequently be found that the unfortunate offender has been an advocate either of potato-eating or of birth control.

Gradually all these things came together in Cobbett's mind to form a system of corruption and oppression against which it was his life work to fight. This conception was not completed all at once. Cobbett's mind was not one which dealt naturally in abstract ' systems ' : anyone less like a Marxian Socialist could hardly be imagined. In some ways his mind was curiously unsophisticated; for some time he was still disposed to believe that, certain things apart, the ruling powers were substantially in accordance with his notions of justice, and that, when he found an abuse, he had only to call attention to it loudly enough for it to be remedied. He regarded abuses as he might stones in his road—as obstacles which needed a kick, possibly two kicks, to remove them, but which were essentially removable. It was only when a long series of kicks, accompanied by the natural language of a full-blooded and indignant man, had failed to make the slightest impression on the obstacles, that it began to dawn on him that possibly what he had mistaken for casual stones were in reality parts of a monstrous erection which his former friends were acutely interested in preserving. Once he had grasped this idea, everything fell into place. The chopstick could not have his wages high and his food cheap— why ? Because his employer, the farmer, was so burdened by taxes levied to pay the pensioners and sinecurists, the fundholders and army contractors, that he could not afford wages enough to meet the high prices which war finance and paper money had brought about. Who benefited by the paper money ? The loanmongers and stock-jobbers, the Barings and Ricardos, who got rich by sucking the farmers, and who, with their financial power, propped up the governing class and enabled it to divide fat Government jobs among its sisters and its cousins and its aunts ; while the same governing class, through its control of the rotten boroughs, passed the laws which gave the stock-jobbers their privileged position. This, in brief, was the system which Cobbett called ' *the Thing* '—a *Thing* which seemed so vividly personal to him that one is tempted to believe he must have seen it in his dreams as something like Peer Gynt's Great Boyg, a vast immovable object which bore the face now of Pitt, now of Malthus, now of Baring, and now of Castlereagh. And the key to the Thing's power, he rapidly came to believe, lay in the rotten boroughs. A Parliament of placemen-stockjobbers who had bought their seats could not be expected to take any steps to put an end to the system which suited them so well, and unless the system was ended chopsticks could not have bread and meat and home-brewed beer. But once the rotten boroughs were destroyed, then the unrepresented people would rise and put an end to the scandal. So Cobbett became a Radical, an ally of Burdett, Cartwright, and Cochrane, though the road by which he had travelled to Radicalism was different from theirs.

He was in this state of mind when, in 1815, the war ended. Almost at once, with the stoppage of war production and the return of the soldiers, distress became general. Prices dropped sharply, and even the new Corn Law could not save the farmers. With distress, of course, went discontent, and a growing clamour for Reform, behind which now stood, not the little knot of intellectual Radicals who had made the movements of 1789, but all on whom the great economic changes had pressed hard, the depressed agricultural labourer, not a few of the farmers, and, with these, the craftsman menaced by machinery, and the power-driven factory worker in the new towns.

Almost by accident, Cobbett found himself the leader of this seething movement for Reform. In 1816 he began to issue a twopenny edition of the *Political Register*, which had steadily been gaining popularity among the working classes. His *Addresses to the Journeymen and Labourers* inaugurated the new régime, which was an immediate and startling success. Cobbett, as the only Radical who could write really well—one is sometimes tempted to say, the only Radical who could write at all— found his fame and his influence spreading into every town and village in the kingdom.

The Government's response was prompt. The ostensible reasons for Sidmouth's ' Gagging Bills ' of 1817 were the Spa Fields affair and the riots in the east and north ; but there is little doubt that Cobbett was right in saying they were in fact aimed largely at him and his ' Twopenny Trash '. As soon as the Bills were passed, he fled to America and remained there for two years.

It is amusing, in a way, to observe what a different America greeted Cobbett the Radical from that which Cobbett the Tory found when he went there at the time of the French Revolution. Then, America was a scandalous place, full of liars and thieves who ' break through and steal—five thousand dollars a time ' ; now, it is the Paradise of the working man and the yeoman farmer, the place where wages are high and land is cheap, and there is no standing army, no burden of taxation, no tithe-eating tribe of parson-justices, and no Wilberforces. The later picture is doubtless too rosy for strict accuracy, but the impression that it made on Cobbett filled him with righteous and still hopeful indignation when he turned back to consider the condition of the people of England. And Cobbett always wrote best when indignation pointed, and hope gilded, the shaft of his vehemence.

In 1819 he returned ; but not to quite the same

176

problems. The placemen and the stock-jobbers were flourishing as before ; and the political oppression had been intensified rather than lightened. Just before he left the States the news of Peterloo arrived, to be followed, immediately upon his return, by the famous Six Acts. But a new economic problem had arisen, which may shortly be designated ' Peel's Act and the Poor Law '.

Too much has been written of the ' Speenhamland system ' of poor relief and of its effects for any general account of it to be needed here. But it must be pointed out that its effects were certainly different, not only in different places, but at different times.

During the Napoleonic Wars there was no dearth of grumbling by landlords and farmers at the increasing burden of the poor rates. But, in face of the lag of rural wages behind rapidly rising prices, the agricultural interest could hardly help realising that it was collect-ively saving in wages at least as much as it was paying out in poor relief, and getting into the bargain a hold over the labourer which might be used to keep him in thorough and helpless subjection. Moreover, though landlord and farmer grumbled, they knew well enough that they had nothing to grumble at. Corn and meat were both scarce owing to war conditions, and prices— even in relation to the inflated currency—consequently high. As leases fell in, landlords were raising rents to heights undreamed of ; and yet farmers, after paying these rents, were making profits at a rate which enabled them to expand their scale of living and ape the manners of the gentlefolk. Under such conditions, there might be grumbling ; but the poor-rates were not really *felt* as a burden. The consumer—the insatiable, paper-money-fed, war-inflated consumer—paid for all.

After 1815 the position was very different. As soon as the war was over, prices fell sharply, and landlords and farmers had rapidly to readjust their ideas to a totally new set of conditions. They were given, indeed, a Corn Law to protect them ; but it could not save them from the effects either of the loss of the Allied Armies' demand for corn, or of the forces which brought about a fall in the price level without any equivalent reduction in the burdens of taxation. The further prices fell, the greater became the burden of the National Debt, which, contracted largely in depreciated paper, had now to be repaid with an increased quantity of actual goods and services. And then, on top of the misfortunes of the years immediately succeeding the war, came Peel's Act of 1819, under which cash payments were to be resumed by the Bank of England, and a complete return made to the gold standard abandoned in 1797. This meant, of course, a fresh contraction of the currency, and a further fall in prices, reacting sharply upon the agricultural interest, and, at least for the time, accentuating the distress. The sequel to Peel's Act was the Agricultural Committee of 1821, set up to consider the distresses of the rural community, and resulting in the proposed remedies of which Cobbett made short work in his *Letters to Landlords*, published in the *Political Register* during 1821.

These letters, and the report which provoked them, are undoubtedly the direct progenitors of *Rural Rides*. Cobbett made up his mind to see things for himself, and to enforce, by actual observation of rural conditions, the statements he had made in answer to the arguments of the landlords before the Agricultural Committee. The ' agriculturasses ', in brief, had demanded a prohibitive tariff on imported corn. George Webb Hall, ' that distracted creature ', to whom there are frequent derisive references in *Rural Rides*, had appeared before the Committee with a scheme for a fixed duty of 40s. on all imported wheat, irrespective of the home price, and similar preposterous duties on all agricultural products. And, as secretary to the semi-official Board of Agriculture, he had organised in support of his scheme a large body of agricultural opinion. County meetings were being everywhere held to press it upon the Govern-

ment ; ' Gaffer ' Gooch, the chairman of the Agricultural
Committee, and other county members, were hot in its
favour. Cobbett had torn Webb Hall's plan to tatters
in his pamphlet, *The Farmer's Friend*, making it clear
that a duty on imported wheat would do nothing to help
the farmer. The trouble was not that wheat was coming
in from abroad ; for it was not, and could not at the
prevailing prices, even under the existing law. The
trouble was that the home-grown wheat, even in the
absence of foreign competition, was not fetching a price
that enabled the farmer to meet his outgoings.

If Cobbett attacked Webb Hall, ' Gaffer ' Gooch, and
the rest of the ' agriculturasses ', he was equally hot
against the actual Report which the Agricultural Committee had presented to Parliament. The ' agriculturasses ', finding themselves in a minority, deserted the
sittings ; and it was left for their opponents, headed by
Huskisson and Ricardo, to draw up the Report. This was
actually done mainly by Huskisson ; and the Report
rejected, as emphatically as Cobbett had done, the proposals of the protectionists. It did not go to the length
of recommending free trade in corn, but put forward a
tentative plan for an open trade with a low fixed rate of
duty in substitution for the Corn Law's absolute prohibition of import as long as wheat stood at less than 80s. a
quarter. This, however, was not why Cobbett quarrelled
with it. He attacked Huskisson and Ricardo as fiercely as
Gooch and Webb Hall because their Report went out of
its way to deny that Peel's Bill and the consequent fall
in prices were among the principal causes of the distress,
and also denied that it could be largely attributed to the
burden of high taxation and the swollen war debt.

We see Cobbett then, in the earlier sections of *Rural
Rides*, dealing out his blows impartially at the agriculturasses, who seem to him more fools than knaves, and
at the economists, who seem far more knaves than fools.
Positively, he contends that the root of the trouble lies
neither in foreign competition nor in the inevitable dis-

turbance of equilibrium following on the long war, but in the deflation of the currency by Peel's Bill, in the colossal burden of the War Debt, and the standing charges for pensions, sinecures, the swollen army and navy, and the growing expenses of government. The remedy, therefore, is to be sought in domestic financial reform; and this in turn can be hoped for only through a Radical Reform of Parliament itself. Reform of Parliament is therefore the first thing ; and this Reform must come from outside, through the pressure of mass opinion.

In the ' Rustic Harangues ' which punctuate the early *Rides*, Cobbett is making his appeal chiefly to the farmers. He wants them to realise that the Corn Law is doing them no good, and that no Webb Hall amendment of it will remove their grievances. He appeals to them, with no small success, to turn Radical, and seek rather to reduce the burden of taxation than to raise the price of corn. To the landlords as well he appeals to realise that their interest is not truly at one with that of the fund-holders and stockjobbers of the great ' Wen '. The landlords may hold blocks of National Debt, and join therefore in the cry that the nation must ' keep faith with its creditors '. But this, Cobbett argues, will profit them little if the farmers are ruined. For ruined farmers mean vacant farms and no rents, and the passing of power in the land from the old aristocracy to the ' rag-rooks ', or paper-money men, who have grown fat through the ' Pitt system '. ' I told you so ', says Cobbett, not without satisfaction, whenever he records the sale of an old estate to one of the new gentry from the ' Wen '.

Such was the genesis of the first group of *Rural Rides* ; but the *Rides* themselves are very much more than the propagandist's tour which their origin suggests. Cobbett may have started out as a politician ; he may have turned into a politician as soon as he saw a jail, or a barracks, or even a man to whom he could talk about politics ; but he rode as a yeoman farmer, and still more as a passionate lover of England, the agricultural England of the South. It is impossible not to feel, as we go through England with Cobbett, that, though he had set out to find proof of the things he had been writing in London, what he really cared about was the condition of the crops, whether this helped his case or not, and the look and feel of the countryside. It matters very little, to the arguments on cash payments, whether or not Mr. Pym has a very fine crop of mangel-wurzels ; it matters even less that the water-meadows of Huntingdon are lovelier than those of Canterbury, Gloucester, Winchester, Hereford, etc. But this is the information that Cobbett is continually concerned to give us. Alexander Baring has spoilt Northington Down by planting his trees too big ; Mr. Hicks Beach has hares in a field as thick as sheep ; the Duke of Buckingham's turnip-hoers are very pretty girls ; there is the finest view in the world from Butser Hill in Hampshire ; Mr. Montague has got the most ridiculous sham-gothic estate that ever was seen ; and so on. None of these things has anything in the world to do with fundholders, or sinecurists, or rotten boroughs, or *Edinburgh Reviewers* ; but they are the things that remain with one after a reading of *Rural Rides*. There is nothing in English which gives better than this book the sensation of starting out on a fresh summer day in glorious country, healthy and full of vigour, to do work which really needs to be done.

It is, of course, true that on the page following one of these idyllic descriptions one finds, as often as not, a tirade, half as long again, against some ' lying reptile ', who may be a Minister, an economist, a parson, a philanthropist, a banker, a newspaper editor, or Sir Francis Burdett. But in *Rural Rides* these vigorous ebullitions fit into their proper place ; they are aroused by the sight of some object produced or caused by the ' lying reptile ' in question. Cobbett, like Dickens (whom he resembles in many other points beside his tremendous popularity), made up his mind about a thing when he came up against it. When he saw something he disliked, he said so there and then—and was often apt to forget it until he saw it again. He sees a martello tower—ugly thing—and at once remembers Pitt and Melville and the scandal of the taxpayers' money poured out on this ridiculous parody of a defence against Napoleon. His small boy innocently remarks on the pleasures of shooting, and is treated to a harangue about the evils of London sportsmen who buy land for shooting only, don't farm it properly, and demoralise the labourers. He visits Cheltenham, and finds it a horrid hole full of lazy pensioners. He passes near Gatton—GATTON! which once returned Wilberforce to Parliament—and his voice rises nearly to a scream as he meditates upon the scandal of the rotten boroughs. He sees a pauper on the roads, breaking stone while the corn stands unreaped, and he curses impartially McAdam who invented the road-metal which enables nasty stockbrokers to drive rapidly to places where no one wants them, and Sturges Bourne, whose Poor Law Acts—in essence an attempt to graft the principles of the New Poor Law on to the practice of the old—are rapidly driving the landless labourer to despair.

It was not, however, always upon abuses that Cobbett's eye fell. He was equally concerned to note pleasing and profitable devices, in particular any application of the farming principles of his hero, Jethro Tull, or of the new methods which he himself had advocated. During his stay in America, he had made three discoveries which he confidently expected would revolutionise English farming : maize, which he called Cobbett's Corn, the locust or acacia tree, and the making of straw plait from green grass. This last, in particular, he thought might be made a rural industry sufficient to rehabilitate the labourer. Previously, he had become very much interested in another crop, the Ruta Baga or ' Radical Swede ', as he called it, the name best indicating his view of its functions. Through the *Register* he had spread the knowledge of straw plait and the cultivation of swedes, maize, and locust trees to hundreds of farmers and villagers ; and at least one object of his *Rides* was to see how these pet crops of his were flourishing in different parts of the country.

During the years which followed the issue of the Agricultural Report of 1821 opinion in the countryside was profoundly stirred. If many of the farmers followed the agriculturasses in the demand for still more stringent protection, many more followed Cobbett, who built up behind his personality a really big Radical movement led by the farmers themselves. The friends he goes to visit in the shires—the Palmers in Herefordshire, the Clarkes in Norfolk, James Knowles at Thursley, William Budd at Burghclere, Joseph Blunt at Uphusband, and a host of others—are his lieutenants in this campaign. Its culminating point is the Norfolk movement of 1823, with its county petition, carried against the opposition of the local magnates, Coke of Norfolk and the Wode-houses, demanding Radical Reform and relief from taxation as the only means of curing the distress, and urging an ' equitable adjustment ' of the War Debt burden in accordance with the change in the value of money.

This movement came to a head in 1823. It was then swept back by the passing prosperity of 1824, only to revive in a new form in the course of the financial and commercial crisis of 1825. In its revival, however, it is no longer a purely agricultural movement, merging itself rather in the wider agitation which led up to the great Reform struggle of 1830 to 1832.

The first group of *Rural Rides*, from the beginning of the book down to the Ride from Dover to the Wen in the late summer of 1823, connect themselves naturally with the period of agricultural distress that has been described above. In 1824 Cobbett, busy on the instalments of his *History of the Protestant Reformation*, and occupied with his political concerns in London, did not ride at all. But the distresses of 1825 brought him forth again ; and in that and the following year he pushed further afield, re-traversing his familiar country in and near Hampshire, but also passing on into Wiltshire, Gloucestershire, Herefordshire, and Worcestershire. These *Rides* are full of the renewed controversies over the currency and the Corn Laws. When Peel's Act was passed in 1819, Cobbett had made his famous ' Gridiron ' prophecy that it could never be enforced without ruin. Thereafter, the Bank of England had, indeed, duly resumed cash payments, even before the appointed date ; but Cobbett had maintained that his prophecy was justified when, in 1822, the country banks were specially permitted to continue the issue of one-pound notes ; and he exulted again when, in the panic of 1825, the Bank of England had to have recourse to the old, withdrawn one-pound notes which were still lying in its cellars. In 1826, however, Parliament passed final sentence of death on the one-pound note ; and Cobbett found cause to reiterate his contention that the return to gold, without an ' equitable adjustment ' of the Debt, meant gross injustice to the farmers and to the labouring population. Equally, while he was against the Corn Law, he urged that it would be grossly unjust to repeal or modify it, as was then widely proposed, without relieving the farmer of the burden of high taxation. Huskisson, as the leading member of Canning's Government in its handling of home affairs, pleased him no better now than Huskisson as the draftsman of the Agricultural Report of 1821. These two groups of *Rides* are both part of a single period in Cobbett's life, though the emphasis varies slightly as between the two. But after 1826, there was a long period before he again went riding.

In 1827 he was busy with the move from his seed-farm at Kensington to his new farm at Barn Elms, where there was much land to be cleaned and put in order. In 1828, though he managed one solitary ride, he was occupied chiefly with his farm and with the writing of *Cobbett's Corn* and *Advice to Young Men*. Only in 1829, when these were done, did he set out on his third series of travels, riding out first into Sussex and then into Hertfordshire and the country north of London. And then, at the end of the year, he again broke new ground, visiting Yorkshire, the Eastern counties, and the Midlands in an extensive tour which included much speaking to great audiences in the towns as well as in the countryside.

These *Rides* of 1829–30 are, indeed, transitional. There is still much rural matter in them ; but Cobbett was beginning to go more among the artisans and tradesmen of the Northern and Midland towns, where his strongest political following now lay, than among the labourers of his own Southern counties. The reason is evident. By 1829, the year of the Catholic Emancipation Act, the great political movement which was to force the Reform Act upon a wavering House of Commons and a violently hostile House of Lords had already gathered force enough to be evidently on the point of success. Great changes were clearly inevitable ; but it was not yet clear what the nature of these changes was to be. Would the North follow the lead of the manufacturers and the ' feelosofical villains ' from over the border, and create a capitalist paradise of *laisser-faire* and the devil take the hindmost ? Or would the workers, who were the real backbone of the agitation, succeed in carrying through a Reform that would strike at capitalists as well as landlords, at the new rich as well as at the old ?

In the heat of this contest for leadership of the Reform movement, a new and not always welcome shrillness creeps into Cobbett's invective, which is more and more directed, not against the upholders of the old order, but against the rival prophets of the new. Brougham and Lord John Russell, the ' cotton-lords ' and the ' Manchester men ' and the tribe of *Edinburgh Reviewers*, become the chief objects of Cobbett's animosity, sharing the distinction with old Radicals turned moderate with years, such as Sir Francis Burdett, and rival claimants to the leadership of the extreme Radicals, such as ' Orator ' Hunt.

Radical doubts, however, still at that date centred round the question : Would Reform, when it came, be drastic enough ? Would it really destroy the rotten boroughs, which in Cobbett's eyes were still the cornerstone of the Thing ? Or would it merely throw a sop to the Reformers by removing a dozen or so of the worst cases, and giving their seats to Manchester and Birmingham ? Cobbett had not yet realised in the spring of 1830 that Reform, on its destructive side, might be as drastic as he wished, and yet fail to bring about any of the results which he had desired and promised. But before twelve months were out realisation was rudely thrust upon him. The Government of Lord Grey had hardly taken office before the ricks were blazing in the villages.

Mr. and Mrs. Hammond, in their book *The Village Labourer*, have described that last despairing revolt of the starving labourers too fully and vividly for any additional account to be needed here. There are few more pathetic stories in English working-class history than that of these agricultural labourers, whose wages and doles from the poor law had been year by year so remorselessly cut down, seeing, in the fall of Wellington, a new faint gleam of hope, and, stimulated possibly by the accounts Cobbett was weekly publishing of the triumphant French Revolution of July, venturing to demand of their masters that Reform might bring them at least their two shillings a day, that the salaried Bumbles of the parish might cease to oppress them, and that the threshing machines, which took away their last chance of earning an extra shilling, might be broken up and removed. Mr. and Mrs. Hammond's account, however, does not fully emphasise the extent of the riots. Their spectacular start in the South, and no less the spectacular way in which the southern landowners were revenged, has tended to concentrate the attention of both contemporary and later writers on Wiltshire, Hampshire,

186

Sussex, and Kent; but the newspapers of 1830 show plainly that from Wales to Yorkshire the countrymen were aroused, and hoping.

At the beginning, Cobbett seems to have in some measure shared their hopes. He disapproved of rick-burning as a means of agitation, and he was quite aware that, however much the labourers might seem to him to be justified, their choice of method would not endear them to the parsons and the landed gentry. He seems, however, to have thought at first that there was some chance that the Whigs would, for once, forget that they were landlords and remember that they were Reformers. ' They are not a fierce crew of hard lawyers,' he says, trying to reassure himself, ' such as we have seen in power before. The *chief* is a mild and kind man, very fond of his own family, and who is likely to make the case of the labourers his own. . . . Though Lord Melbourne did take part against us in 1817, he is not a ferocious fellow; he is a good-tempered man, and not inclined to be bloody. There is Lord Holland, who never gave his consent to an act of cruelty; and there is Lord Althorp, too, who has never dipped his hands in blood, nor crammed victims into the dungeon; and the Lord Chancellor [Brougham], with all his half-Scotch crotchets, has, at any rate, *no blood about him* '— and he goes on to say that he is sure he will not plead in vain before these men, as he pleaded in vain before Sidmouth and Castlereagh. He might have believed this the more because of the singular lack of violence among the rioters. Ricks were burnt, machines broken, and unpopular overseers in some places run out of the parish; but not a single life was taken by the labourers in the whole course of the revolt, and very little personal violence shown. The ' outrageous attack ', for which Henry Cook of Micheldever paid with his life, dealt Bingham Baring a thump on the head and seriously damaged his hat. Many of the farmers, conscious of the prevailing misery, which was doubly accentuated by the ferocity of the game laws, were openly sympathetic, and some, to their undoing, actually helped the labourers.

But, as everyone knows, Cobbett's confidence was misplaced. The Whig landowners were as scandalised as their Tory peers ; and the Government shook in its shoes at the very thought of seeming to sympathise with disaffection. Troops, sent to the areas of disturbance, soon scattered the unarmed village bands ; and in the wake of the soldiers came the Special Commissions. The indiscipline of the villagers was stamped out in blood ; and as Home Secretary that ' good-tempered man ', Melbourne, proved as inaccessible to pleas for mercy as ever Sidmouth could have been. Cook and Cooper were hanged ; there were wholesale transportations and imprisonments throughout the affected districts ; and Denman, the Attorney-General (whose Radical past ought to have caused him some misgivings), added insult to injury by making false statements about the condemned men in the House of Commons.

These labourers of the South were Cobbett's own people. Many of them came from the neighbourhood of Botley, and Hurstbourne Tarrant, and the centres in Surrey, Sussex, and Hampshire from which he had made his most famous *Rides*. He had lived for many years among them ; and he knew and had denounced again and again the misery which was the cause of their revolt. Here was reason enough for hating the Whigs ; but the Whigs then proceeded to fill the cup of his resentment by trying to make him a scapegoat for the risings. On the evidence of the famous ' confession ' of Thomas Goodman, procured under very dubious circumstances by a few Sussex magistrates, Cobbett was charged with being the instigator of the revolts. The prosecution was probably forced on the Government, which would have been well-advised to let it alone ; for Cobbett defended himself with so much vigour as virtually to turn the trial into an indictment of the Ministers ; and, in the end, the jury disagreed, and he was discharged. But, fiasco as it was, it was enough to make it impossible for Cobbett ever again to trust the authors of the Reform Bill. Not nine months had elapsed since his commendation of the new Cabinet which we have quoted above ; but already, in his defence, he is crying that if he is sent to ' a loathsome dungeon, I will with my last breath pray to God to bless my country and curse the Whigs, and I bequeath my revenge to the children and labourers of England '.

So ends the middle period of the *Rides*. There remain two groups : the *Tour in Scotland*, undertaken in 1832, just after the passing of the Reform Act, and the *Irish Tour* of 1834. The *Irish Tour* is a pleasant piece of work on a small scale ; the letters to Charles Marshall, Cobbett's employee, of which it consists, are mainly descriptive of the fearful condition of the Irish poor, a condition which was so much a matter of common knowledge that it could hardly rouse even Cobbett's political passions. There is, consequently, little ' extraneous matter ' in the *Irish Tour* ; the New Poor Law of England, which he was furiously opposing throughout that year, hardly finds a mention. The *Scottish Tour*, on the other hand, is brimful of politics and political abuse, so much so that Cobbett sometimes seems to forget that he is touring at all. Some readers may find the *Scottish Tour* disappointing : they may observe that the style is deteriorating, that the habit of shrill invective seems to be growing on the author, and is wearisome ; that there is far too little of that keen observation which made the earlier *Rides* a delight, and that no one could be entertained by long lists of signatories to ' welcoming addresses ' which all say much the same thing. To a certain extent, such criticisms would be justified. The *Scottish Tour* has these defects ; but they are easily explained.

For the bitterness, some cause has already been given ; but the causes had been increasing since 1830. After the Whigs had been shown up in their true colours, the one hope which remained to Cobbett was that the Reform

Bill would produce a total change in the personnel of Parliament, that the rotten boroughs would go, and the new constituencies send up streams of Radicals to break up the Thing. The rotten boroughs went ; but it was at once evident that the new constituencies would do nothing of the kind. The franchise was extended, not to the labourers and the factory workers, who had borne the burden and heat of the struggle, but to the middle classes; and the middle classes preferred Whigs to Radicals, unless they were extremely safe Radicals who were sound on the goose of property. In the struggle to secure nominations, Cobbett and Hunt and the extreme left were definitely worsted. Cobbett himself could indeed be fairly certain of a seat at Oldham as the colleague of Fielden, the Radical manufacturer. But at best he could hope for a very scanty following in the new Parliament. And at Manchester, which he was also contesting as the nominee of the working-class Radicals against the middle-class Radicals of the Potter group, his chances of success were poor.

It was at the height of this struggle that Cobbett went to Scotland ; and, under the circumstances, he had ample excuse for feeling that he, of all Radical politicians, was almost the only one who had not betrayed the men who fought for him. The persecutors of the agricultural labourers had once been his allies ; and now others of his allies—politicians, merchants, and journalists like ' Radical Dick ' Potter of Manchester, Edward Baines of Leeds, Macaulay and Poulett Thomson—were deliberately trying to shut the people out of Parliament. The new Parliament might not be a Parliament of placemen ; but it might easily be a Parliament of ' beastly Malthusians ', which pleased Cobbett no better. The manufacturing interest was not likely to make an ' equitable adjustment ' of the Debt, or to repeal Peel's Act. It might, indeed, amend the Poor Law ; but the amended Poor Law would be a Benthamite Poor Law, worse even than that of Sturges Bourne.

' They mean ', Cobbett had angrily prophesied in earlier years, ' that Lopez should sit there for ever '—Lopez being the rich Jew who was jailed for electoral corruption at Grampound. It seemed that the prophecy was coming true. In this mood of bitter disillusionment Cobbett went to Scotland.

His actual observations are less interesting than in earlier *Rides* for a very simple reason. In journeying to Scotland, his way lay, not through meadows and corn-lands, but through manufacturing towns ; and Cobbett knew nothing and cared less about manufacture. ' I never like to see machines,' he said, ' lest I should be tempted to endeavour to understand them.' He was not opposed to machinery—less so, perhaps, than he might have been had he understood it a little better. He looked upon machinery, when he thought about it at all, as a bene-ficent invention for producing goods with less labour ; and in that strain he had advised the journeymen in 1816 to let the machines alone. But of the problems which the factory machines brought in their train he had literally no idea ; he thought of himself as a semi-patriarchal farmer, and could not imagine an employer as anything but a semi-patriarchal master artisan. This lack of knowledge is very well brought out in his attitude to truck. He scoffed at Littleton's attempt to legislate against truck, explaining that of course the employer always had and always must pay his workers partly in kind ; he would not cheat them, because it was not in his interest to do so ; if he did cheat them, it was the fault of the vile paper-money which reduced his own re-sources ; nobody but a blind idiot would muzzle the ox that trod out the corn. He had no conception of the desperate scramble for capital, in the early days, which sent all the ox's gleanings, and often half his legitimate meals, back ' into the business '. When he did come across a case of factory tyranny, he attacked it promptly, but he attacked it as an exception to the ordinary re-lations between master and man, due to the emergence of the new classes of coal lords and cotton lords and their unfair competition with the ordinary employer. In reality, alongside of the system which Cobbett knew and called the Thing, there was now growing up another system, equally strong and equally oppressive. But Cobbett was not Marx, and he never saw it.

The same ' farmer's outlook ' colours his attitude to education, about which he had an amusing correspondence with one of his northern supporters. In education of a sort—the sort by which he had developed his own talents—he had a profound faith ; but he treated the whole middle-class movement for the education of the ' lower orders ' as a wicked device of Brougham's to infect the workers with Whig principles (in which he was partly right) ; and he could not see why honest Radicals should lend themselves to it. Self-education and education of one's own children he could understand, for he had experienced it ; but proposals for general schooling he regarded much as a modern man would receive a suggestion that his old nurse was useless without a course of Pelmanism. Cobbett's general views on industrial questions were based on his old-fashioned view of the normal relation between master and man ; and they were almost as inappropriate to the new problems of the industrial North as his attitude to education. If he were to be judged by the address to a carpenter on strike, which is printed in the *Register*, it would appear that the United Trades of Glasgow, who came to meet him with banners and addresses of welcome, can have got singularly little for their money.

But this, of course, was not why they came to meet him, or why the *Scottish Tour* is full of congratulatory addresses and speeches and votes of thanks. This part of the Tour is simply a triumphal procession. When Cobbett set out for the North, the London Whig journals, secure in the victory of middle-class reformism, raised a howl of scorn at the old failure going out to see a miserable handful of his adherents. The great gatherings at

Newcastle, at Glasgow, and at Edinburgh, are Cobbett's answer to the jeers ; and he was entitled to his triumph if any man ever was.

The United Trades did not pour out to hear Cobbett call 'Mr. Owen of Lanark' a 'beastly writer', or even to listen to his views on education or Trade Unionism ; they came to do honour to the man who, for close on thirty years of continuous agitation, had never ceased to uphold and defend the working-man, and whose influence, as all contemporaries bear witness, had been the one thing that reactionary Governments chiefly feared. If Mr Lansbury, who is Mr. Cobbett's nearest parallel among modern politicians, were to come into any town or village in the United Kingdom which contained any working men, it would not matter particularly what he talked about, or whether he stood on his head or his heels ; wherever it might be working men would turn out in a body to meet him. So, and still more so, it was with Cobbett. The politicians of Westminster had thrust him out, and his subjects, like O'Connell's in 1828, were still voteless ; but when he went on his Tour he came into his kingdom.

This *Scottish Tour* is of particular importance because it provides an answer to the question so frequently put : 'Was William Cobbett a failure ? ' On a superficial glance there is much that seems like failure in his career. He achieved very little of what he aimed at ; the Debt grew, the stock-jobbers waxed fatter and fatter, and England, after the Reform Act, plunged into a perfect orgy of Benthamism. Corruption in the Civil Service eventually ceased, but not until many years after his death ; the pensions paid to the heirs of Nelson continue to this day ; and the chopsticks, whom he loved best, descended further and further into want and had but little share in the mid-Victorian prosperity. He did, indeed, taste the Reform of Parliament, but only to find it turn to dust and ashes in his mouth. He was never, himself, a success in Parliament, partly because he was growing old and tired, but mainly because the Parliament of manufacturers and Free Traders was something very unlike the Parliament of his dreams. There are, it is true, splendid flashes of the old fire, as in his opposition to the New Poor Law—that triumph of the ' feelosofers '—and his speech on the first great Factory Bill ; but in the main it is a hobbled and disappointed Cobbett who speaks at Westminster.

The disappointment was inevitable, because what Cobbett wanted was something which in the nature of events he could not possibly have. He did not, like Owen and the Chartists, want a New Moral World ; he wanted his old world back again, his memory—idealised like most men's early memories—of the England which he had known and loved before the great wars and the great factories came. Like the dispossessed Highland crofter of whom Mr. Buchan has written in one of his books, he did not want compensation, he wanted restitution—of all things in the world the hardest to obtain. Had Cobbett lived in a Greek city-state, he would have been a far more successful politician, for what he desired can be almost entirely summed up in the programme of any Greek reformer, γῆς ἀναδασμὸς καὶ σεισάχθεια. He was really an agrarian tribune—the last of the line of Gracchus. But living in England of the Industrial Revolution, he was foredoomed to disappointment.

But is disappointment necessarily the same as failure ? The crowds who welcomed him in 1832 did not think so. They were not welcoming a failure, but a man who had succeeded, all through the time of oppression, in holding the working classes steadfastly to Reform, and in creating a movement of which the Governments—Whig as well as Tory—were really afraid. In the strictest possible sense of the word, Cobbett, through the dark years, *upheld* the working-class. At a time when those who professed most sympathy with the labourer vied with his open enemies in telling him that he was a poor creature whose whole duty was to restrain his natural impulses and to be obedient and grateful to all set in authority over him, Cobbett, almost alone, told him that he was a man, and that by holding up his head and bearing himself manfully he might gain a man's inheritance. No oppression enraged him so much as the insidious propaganda which hinted that the labourer was not capable of knowing his own mind or of thinking for himself. It is difficult for the twentieth-century reader, looking back on the Trade Union movement of the 'forties struggling into existence in holes and corners, and upon Social-Democratic leaders haranguing uninterested knots from soap-boxes, to realise what a huge working-class following Cobbett had. At its height, the unstamped *Register* had a sale of sixty thousand copies, and most of these copies were read, not by a single working man, but aloud in working-class houses, clubs, and branches throughout the country. If to have inspired sixty thousand groups of people in the battle for Reform, to have kept sixty thousand groups from despair when everything seemed combined to oppress them, is failure, then, and only then, Cobbett may be held to have failed.

Robert Owen and Owenism

ROBERT OWEN, shop-boy and manufacturer, factory reformer and educationist, Socialist and Co-operative pioneer, Trade Union leader and secularist, founder of ideal communities and practical man of business, was something of a puzzle to his own generation, and is no less a puzzle to posterity. Surely no man ever founded so many movements, and yet had so simple and unvarying a body of ideas. Surely no man was ever at once so practical and so visionary, so lovable and so impossible to work with, so laughed at and yet so influential. And there are few men who are so much talked about, and whose works are so little read.

There is a reason for this. Owen wrote voluminously, and often ill. He lived to be eighty-seven, and he was writing steadily up to the last weeks of his life. But of his later works, which make up the great bulk of his writings, by far the larger part is valueless. Owen said what he had to say in his earlier books ; his later works are merely more and more elaborate and prosy repetitions of his better writings. There is but one exception : his Life of himself, of which he completed only a first volume, is delightfully fresh and attractive—the best and most readable of all his books, though it was published in his eighty-sixth year. It can best be read as a companion volume to his expository writings ; for it gives Owen's own version of the circumstances which attended their issue.

With this one exception, all Owen's later works can be disregarded, except by the specialist. Indeed, one volume, even one slender volume, is enough to contain all the best of Owen's writings with the exception of his unfinished Autobiography. And all that need be included in such a volume was issued within a space of eight years. The opening essay of the *New View of Society* appeared in 1813, and the *Report to the County of Lanark* in 1821. In these eight years Robert Owen made his essential contribution to human knowledge. And, incidentally out of his work during these years arose in Great Britain the two great movements of Socialism and Co-operation.

In order to understand Owen's doctrines aright, it is necessary to know something both of the man himself and of the circumstances in which his ideas were developed. Owen was born in 1771, and the years of his manhood coincided with the most critical years of the great social change which we call the ' Industrial Revolution '. And his doctrines were above all designed as answers to the vast social and economic problems which the Industrial Revolution had raised up.

Let us begin with the man himself. Robert Owen was born in Newtown, Montgomeryshire, in Central Wales, on the Upper Severn. His father was a saddler and ironmonger, and also the local postmaster. Owen was a weakly boy, much given to introspection, but intelligent beyond his fellows. He was only seven years old when he became a sort of pupil-teacher in the local school. At nine, he left school and began work as shop-boy in a neighbour's shop. At ten, after a brief visit to London, he was apprenticed to a draper in good business at Stamford in Lincolnshire. There he remained three years, and then became assistant at a draper's in London. A year later he migrated to Manchester, and for four years was assistant there in a good drapery house. Then, at eighteen, his chance came, and the boy set up in business for himself.

Manchester, which was to be the scene of Owen's first considerable successes, was then at the height of a great and rapid industrial transformation. The great inventions of Hargreaves, Arkwright, and Crompton were in process of revolutionising the methods of cotton manufacture, and new factories for preparing, roving and spinning the cotton were springing up right and left. It was a time when great fortunes were to be made by the fortunate and the adventurous ; and young Owen seized his chance. He began business for himself, with a borrowed hundred pounds, in partnership with a mechanic who knew how to make certain of the new machines. Before long his partner left him, in search of a better-equipped colleague, and Owen was left on his own. No longer able to make machines, he set out to use those which remained in his hands. He succeeded ; but within a few months a better chance came his way. The position of manager to one of the largest and best-equipped spinning mills in Lancashire fell vacant, and Owen, still under twenty, was appointed, at a salary of three hundred a year—a handsome remuneration in those days. At twenty he found himself in full charge of a factory in which five hundred workers were employed.

Again Owen made good. The products of his factory became well known for excellence in the trade, not only in Manchester but as far away as Glasgow. His employer, a Mr. Drinkwater, offered him a partnership ; but difficulties arose, and instead Owen entered into partnership with two younger men who were starting a new company for the manufacture of yarn. He remained for some years in sole control of the new mill, and then on behalf of his company acquired from David Dale, whose daughter he soon afterwards married, the famous New Lanark Mills, the largest and best equipped spinning mills in Scotland.

This bald summary does far less than justice to the romance of Owen's early career. Every episode in it was an adventure, through which he climbed steadily to a further success. At twenty-eight, when he became managing partner in the New Lanark establishment, Owen was already a wealthy manufacturer according to the standards of the times, and bade fair to be before long very wealthy indeed.

Owen was by now well known as a successful business man ; but, beyond a small circle of friends, that was his only claim to distinction. He had, indeed, as a leading member of the Manchester Literary and Philosophic Society, given utterance to some peculiar opinions on the subject of religion and the formation of character; but these did not appear to possess any special significance in relation to his business. Only when he was established at New Lanark did it appear that he was aiming at something very much bigger than mere money-making or business success.

Owen remained at New Lanark for more than a quarter of a century. He made of it not only a most successful commercial establishment, but a show place which visitors came from all over the world to see. Through all the successive partnerships in which he was associated—and he quarrelled with each group of partners in turn because they would not give him full freedom to follow out his ideas—he aimed at making New Lanark, not merely an efficient factory, but a well-governed human community based on his ideals. The manufacturer of those days—especially when his factory stood in an isolated place—had a tremendous hold over his employees. The houses in which they lived, the shops at which they bought their provisions, the entire village as well as the factory belonged to the employer, who gathered together his force of labourers from far and near, and could rule over them as a benevolent or malevolent despot. Owen had a high idea of the duties which this vast power entailed. In his view, the employer had no right merely to treat his employees as a means to profit. It was his duty to ensure to them all the means of good living—to pay good wages, to avoid unreasonably long hours of work, to provide good houses and good food and clothing at reasonable prices, to make the factory village a sanitary and a pleasant place, and, above all, to ensure to the children, whether employed in the factory or not, the best education that sympathy and knowledge could place at their command. In his later partnerships, when he was in a position to make his own terms, Owen strictly limited the reward of capital to a fixed amount, and insisted that all surplus profits should be applied to the provision of communal services on the employees' behalf.

At New Lanark, Owen paid better wages, worked shorter hours, and gave infinitely better conditions than most of his competitors. He abolished all ' pauper apprentice ' labour immediately on assuming control, and refused to employ children at less than ten years of age when others were freely working them intolerably long hours at less than six years old. And yet he had no difficulty in making the factory pay, despite the large sums he was constantly spending on all manner of improvements and amenities. In short, he gave an astonishingly convincing demonstration of what later generations have called the ' economy of high wages ', at a time when appalling under-payment and over-work were almost everywhere regarded as the indispensable conditions of commercial success.

Owen's earlier writings, such as the *New View of Society* and the *Address to the Inhabitants of New Lanark* reflect this phase of his career. And they make it clear that there was already a quite definite theory behind his activities. He did what he did because he believed that in no other way could the foundations of a reasonable social order be truly laid. His main purpose, he insisted throughout, was educational. There was no way of making good citizens except by educating men and women so as to make them such. And there was no way of so educating them save by providing an environment in which their better natures would be encouraged to grow, and body and mind together be well cared for and trained in right habits and ways of living.

' Man's character is made for, and not by, him ', Owen was never weary of proclaiming ; and his whole system at New Lanark was based on this belief. What appalled him about the new 'manufacturing system' was not only its inhumanity, but also that it seemed to him to result in a perversion of the characters of those who were subjected to its rule. What chance had the child, forced into the factory at a tender age and there remorselessly compelled to labour under a rigid discipline for the profit of others, of becoming a good citizen? What sort of civic virtues was the rule of unlimited competition and 'devil take the hindmost' likely to breed up in both master and man? The child should not labour at all until it had been thoroughly grounded by education in right social principles. When it did go to work, the labour must be suited to its years, and animated by a social, instead of a competitive, motive. And education, while it must begin with the child, must not stop with the child: it must continue throughout life. Above all, a man's occupation has so strong an influence on his character that, if the factory is wrongly organised so as to appeal to the wrong motives in men, the whole of society will be poisoned by it.

It is important to understand exactly what Owen meant by his view of human character. He did not mean, as some people have supposed, that man's individuality has no real existence, or that the individual is merely the result of the circumstances in which he has been placed. On the contrary, he insisted strongly on the importance of individuality and on the large differences between one man and another, and made these differences in individuality an essential foundation of the system of education which he established at New Lanark. He held, however, that each individual would react in a different way according to the environment in which he was placed, and that, in particular, man's social and ethical ideas—what, in effect, he meant by their 'character'— were taken by them from the environment and the social and economic institutions under which they lived. Accordingly, he held that the evils which existed in the world of his own day, the competition between man and man which he regarded as the root of social antagonisms, and the competition between country and country which prevented concerted effort to develop the resources of the whole world in the common interests of its inhabitants, were the result of evil social institutions, including wrong traditional doctrines, and could be eradicated by a change in these institutions, including a change in men's beliefs. In particular he thought that the doctrine of individual responsibility, preached by the Churches, was a powerful influence in perpetuating social evils, because it led men to impute social misfortunes to individual sinfulness rather than to faulty social arrangements. This was the basis of his famous denunciation of all existing religions and of his attempt to create a new rational religion based on the denial of man's individual responsibility and the recognition that men's characters are formed for them and not by them. On this foundation too, he built up his system of education at New Lanark, and on the same principle the Owenites founded at a later period the numerous educational experiments which they carried on throughout the country in their Halls of Science.

Owen, then, set out to find a new basis for society in place of the existing competitive system, with the idea of establishing a set of social institutions on the basis of which men and nations would be brought to live in harmony one with another, and taught from infancy the moral doctrine of social co-operation. This was for him the significance of the Villages of Co-operation which, largely on the model of his own experiment at New Lanark, he proposed everywhere to establish. For he held that, if the basic unit of society came to be a small co-operative group working not for individual profit but for common service, this would effect a fundamental change in men's character and remove all danger of class rivalries within communities, or of war and competition between one community and another.

Although Owen ranks as the pioneer of the Co-operative Movement, he had little interest in consumers' co-operation as such. Indeed, at the outset the consumer's co-operative stores which grew up under the influence of his ideas, such as the famous Toad Lane Store of the Rochdale Pioneers of 1844, did not regard the retailing of goods on a non-profit-making basis as an end in itself, but only as a preparatory step towards the building-up among the members of a system of co-operative production and self-employment which would get rid of competition and the need for a separate employing class. The declared object, for example, of the Rochdale Pioneers, when they founded their store, was not shopkeeping on a mutual basis, but the building-up of a collective fund which could be subsequently used for co-operative production and ultimately for the establishment of an Owenite Co-operative Community.

These ideas of Owen's bear certain marked resemblances to the theory on which the Communists of the Soviet Union have been working of late in their plans of industrialisation, and above all in their intensive efforts to bring about the socialisation of agriculture. For the Russian experiment is not only, or even at bottom mainly, an attempt to raise the material standard of living of the Russian people, but far more an attempt to change the basis of men's thought by bringing them under the influence of a different social and economic environment. The Russians want, as Owen wanted, gradually to abolish the difference between town and country and the difference between industrial and agricultural conditions. They want to industrialise and collectivise agriculture because they believe that only by causing the peasants, as well as the industrial workers, to live in an environment of collective institutions based on co-operative rather than competitive principles can they hope to bring into existence a mental condition consistent with the successful functioning of a Communist community. In other words, they, like Owen, believe that man's ' character ', in the Owenite sense, is made for him and not by him, as the product of his social and economic environment. This doctrine, commonly regarded as distinctively Marxian, is in effect Owenite, and it is impossible to doubt that Marx, though he regarded Owen as a ' Utopian ' Socialist, owed far more to him in the formulation of the Materialist Conception of History than has generally been admitted. Owen, in this as in other respects, deserves much more credit than he has ever received as the true progenitor of modern Socialist ideas.

It can, no doubt, be urged that this root idea of Owenism concerning the influence of environment upon character was not original, and that Owen himself may have derived it largely from Godwin, who in turn was influenced by such eighteenth-century rationalists as d'Holbach and Helvetius. This is doubtless true, but the fact remains that Owen was the first person definitely to link up this doctrine of social determinism with economic conditions, and particularly with the new industrial system which was coming into existence in his day, and that he anticipated Marx in urging that the problems of the new industrialism demanded a co-operative rather than a competitive solution and accordingly a radical change from competition to co-operation as the basis of social institutions.

Owen lived on until 1858, and in his last years when his powers were failing became involved in spiritualist experiments. He had in fact finished his constructive work long before these later mental meanderings set in. His real importance to history is that, as an employer, he was the first man to demonstrate clearly the advantages of good wages and conditions and a pleasant hygienic factory environment ; that, as an educationist, he was in many respects a pioneer of new methods which are only now beginning to find substantial recognition, especially in his insistence on the inadequacy of mere book teaching and the necessity of an appeal to the eye and ear of the child and on the immense formative importance of the

earliest years of life ; and, finally, that, as a Socialist and
Co-operative thinker, he was the first person to formulate
in the light of the new industrialism a doctrine plainly
relating the possibilities of social and economic improvement to the material and mental environment in which
men had to live, and to urge the necessity of a complete transformation of the social system based on the
essentially co-operative character of modern large-scale
processes of production.

We may think that, in the *New View of Society*,
Owen pushed his view of the effect of environment on
character too far. But it can hardly be disputed that, in
the circumstances of his own time, his insistence on it
was wholly salutary. Owen's contemporaries were for the
most part acting on very different principles—treating
the acquisition of wealth as the highest good, and justify-
ing the most ruthless exploitation of labour by an appeal
to that standard. By insisting that the acquisition of
wealth on such terms might mean the destruction of men,
Owen put forward a different ideal, and became the
pioneer of new views both of education and of factory
management.

By common consent, the schools at New Lanark were
pronounced the outstanding success of that astonishing
factory. Both in ideas of education and in their practical
working out Owen was far ahead of his time. He saw at
once the inadequacy of Lancaster's monitorial system,
and insisted that the first aim of education must be not
to cram the memory but to equip the mind. He realised
the limitations of books, especially in their appeal to the
younger children, and the place of dancing, of physical
exercises, of appeals to eye and ear in any sensible
system of education. He trained his own teachers in his
own methods, and raised up a host of disciples to his
faith. And, above all, he realised that a tired mind cannot
learn, and that long hours of toil are incompatible with
the making of good citizens.

In all his work at New Lanark, Owen was doubtless

very much the benevolent autocrat, whose word all men in his village were bound to obey. And, as he came to wish to apply his doctrines over a sphere wider than his own factory, he began to visualise a world made in the image of New Lanark. He had done wonders. Why should not others do as much ? His employees were orderly, prosperous and happy. Why should other employers complain of the turbulence, laziness, drunkenness of their workers ? Why should there be so much misery in the world ? Need there be any misery at all, if the world would but follow his example ?

So Owen became gradually the leader of a crusade. For more than twelve years after his coming to New Lanark he worked away quietly, testing his theories and gradually proving their soundness. Then he set to work to convert others. His *New View of Society* was his first effort at propaganda of his views. For it seemed to him that if he could but convince the world of his doctrine concerning the formation of character, everything else would follow as a matter of course. If the world knew that ' man's character is formed for, and not by, him ', it would cease to blame the poor for being what they were, and would set out to provide an environment in which they would speedily become, as the workers at New Lanark were becoming under his guidance, industrious, prosperous, good, and happy. It would cease to blame the poor for their condition, and would take the obvious steps necessary to improve it.

Side by side with this wider crusade, Owen set on foot another. He began to work hard for a Factory Act which would prohibit the labour of young children, regulate hours of work, and set up a State system of factory inspection. Owen was the great pioneer of the movement for factory reform. Principally to his initiative the first Factory Act—that of 1819—was due, though he repudiated it as falling far short of what he held to be both just and expedient.

Owen was engaged in this double crusade when the

ending of the Napoleonic wars ushered in a period of intense unemployment and economic crisis. ' On the day the peace was signed ', he wrote, ' the great customer of the producers died '. Everywhere trade stagnated, thousands were flung out of work, wages came tumbling down. Soon there were throughout the country mutterings of discontent from the starving operatives ; and before long the mutterings swelled to a mighty clamour. The workers were driven in masses to the Poor Law for support ; and the parishes, appalled at the heavy rates, barely kept them from sheer mass starvation. The workers cried out for the Reform of Parliament as a means to the redress of their grievances ; the Government, fearing revolution, retaliated with the ' Peterloo ' massacre, the Six Acts of 1819, and a general campaign of repression.

To Owen, meanwhile, it seemed as if the world had gone mad. He had no belief in political reform as a means to the remedying of economic grievances ; but the repression of the workers seemed to him utterly beside the point. The thing to do was to remove the causes of distress, instead of tinkering with its effects. As early as 1816 he developed, with this end in view, the first outline of his famous 'Plan ', the germ of Socialism and of Co-operation, but in its first inception essentially a practical scheme for relieving the economic distress of the years immediately after the war.

The gist of Owen's plan can be very shortly stated. He proposed that, instead of paying out doles, the Government should employ the poor in ' Villages of Co-operation ' modelled on his own establishment at New Lanark and, like it, essentially centres of social life and rational education as well as of productive activity. These ' Villages ', Owen suggested, should be in the main self-supporting. They should be agricultural as well as industrial, and should raise the produce needed for their own consumption, exchanging their surplus products of different kinds one with another. As they would be based on rational principles of education, they would not compete but co-operate one with another, and their aim would be as much to train good citizens as to relieve the necessities of the poor. If this were done, Owen argued, the need for poor rates would speedily disappear, and, by the same token, the foundations of a new and better social order for the whole community would speedily be laid.

This is the ' Plan ' which, with minor variations, is expounded in many of Owen's writings, but most fully and maturely in the *Report to the County of Lanark*. As Owen expounded it, the conception of it broadened out in his mind. He began by preaching it as a cure for unemployment ; but soon he was putting it forward as a complete and immediately practicable social Utopia, destined speedily to sweep away capitalism and the competitive system, and to inaugurate for all the world a new era of peace and brotherhood based on a rational idea of the formation and development of human character under the influence of environment. ' Any character, from the best to the worst, from the most ignorant to the most enlightened, may be given to any community, even to the world at large, by applying certain means, which are to a great extent at the command, and under the control, or easily made so, of those who possess the government of nations.' So Owen had written in his *New View of Society* ; and in his ' Plan ' he was proposing the actual means by which the great change might be brought about.

There was, at the outset, nothing ' Radical ' or democratic in Owen's conception. He appealed for its execution to the Tory Government and the Unreformed Parliament. He enlisted for a time the respectful interest of Lord Sidmouth, the Tory Home Secretary and noted persecutor of Radicals. His projects were blessed by the Archbishop of Canterbury, and supported by the Duke of Kent. David Ricardo and other noted economists sat on a committee pledged to further his ' Plan '. As the famous and successful manufacturer of

New Lanark, he received a respectful hearing in high quarters. But it was one thing to listen, and another to act ; and, as the cries of distress and anger among the poor grew louder, the Government and the Parliament turned more and more from considering ways of relieving distress to taking measures for the suppression of disturbance and riot. Owen found himself less and less respectfully received ; he made up his mind to appeal from the Government to the general public.

This wider appeal is embodied in the Addresses and Manifestoes which Owen poured out one after another during the troublous years after 1815. In one of them occurs Owen's famous denunciation of all established religions as inveterate foes to the progress of mankind. There was nothing particularly novel in this declaration, save its outspokenness. All the religions, Owen held, treated man as a responsible agent—responsible for his own misdoings, whereas his faults of character and his sins were really the products of his environment, and could be washed away by a better moral and physical education. Owen had been preaching this doctrine for years, though he had never before declared so plainly his hostility to the Churches. But it was largely as a stick wherewith to beat his growingly unpopular social doctrines that the remark was seized upon, and quoted against him in every accent of horrified surprise. Owen ceased suddenly to be respectable ; and, though some of his highly placed friends stood by him for a time, yet from the date of this declaration his main appeal was made in effect to the working class.

Indeed, it became clear within a few years that a section of the workers was almost alone in taking Owen seriously. For a time he had still a following among the middle and professional classes, and produced for their consumption successive elaborations of his ' Plan ', culminating in the famous *Report to the County of Lanark*. But gradually, in despair of seeing any practical outcome of his labours in Great Britain, he conceived the idea of trying out his schemes in the more congenial, because less contaminated, air of the New World. In 1824 Owen left for the United States, and there, the following year, he founded the Co-operative Community of New Harmony.

The story of that failure has been often told. How the settlers, a motley band of enthusiasts and adventurers of every sort, fell out among themselves, how the parent community broke into several lesser communities, how finally the communal basis of settlement was given up, and New Harmony relapsed into a successful pioneer town based on individual tenure, and how Owen, having sunk his whole fortune in the venture, emerged poor but not discouraged from its collapse, cannot here be described. It is enough to say that in 1829 Owen returned to Great Britain to find that the face of the world had greatly changed in his absence.

For now Owenism had attracted a new body of disciples, and these were chiefly found among the most intelligent leaders of the working class. The Combination Acts had been repealed in 1824, and a rapid growth of Trade Unionism had immediately followed. The great political uprising which culminated in the Reform Act of 1832 was nearing its height ; but the workers were organising for industrial protection as well as for political agitation. There had begun too among the workers a growth of little Co-operative Societies and stores for mutual trading, explicitly based on Owen's teaching, and regarding themselves as forerunners of purely working-class ' Villages of Co-operation ' to be founded when the surplus funds accumulated through mutual trade grew large enough for so ambitious a venture.

After a momentary hesitation, Owen, who had by this time severed his connection with New Lanark and ceased to be an employer of labour, put himself at the head of the movement. All over the country his disciples set to work to bring the Trade Unions and other working-class bodies over to their way of thinking. John Doherty, the great Trade Union leader of the North and secretary of the Spinners, was a convinced Owenite. One after another, the Unions were converted : there was a rapid growth of Co-operative Stores, and many Unions set on foot Producers' Co-operative Societies of their own.

The Operative Builders' Union, the most powerful of the new Trade Unions which had sprung up during the excitements of the preceding years, went over completely to Owenism after Owen himself had addressed its national conference, ambitiously styled the 'Builders' Parliament'. Plans were made for basing on the Union a Grand National Guild of Builders, which was to dispense altogether with employers and new-fangled ' building contractors ', and to take the entire industry into its own hands. Moreover, in order to provide a market for the rapidly growing number of Producers' Co-operative Societies, or ' Union Shops ', Owen founded in 1832 his National Equitable Labour Exchange, of which branches were speedily opened in Birmingham, Liverpool, and Glasgow, as well as London. In these Exchanges, Owen's principle of ' labour value ', as expounded in his *Report to the County of Lanark*, was to be put into practice, and goods were to be exchanged for goods between the various groups of producers by means of ' labour notes ' standing for definite amounts of ' labour time ' embodied in each commodity.

Till the end of 1832 the preoccupation of the main body of the workers with the Reform struggle had delayed the growth of the movement. But thereafter disillusionment with the fruits of the political agitation, which had enfranchised the middle classes and left the workers voteless, had brought fresh recruits thronging into the Trade Unions and Owenite Societies. Political means having failed, the workers were minded to try Trade Unionism and Co-operation as the roads to social emancipation. By 1833 Owen found himself at the head of a huge working-class movement eagerly demanding a lead.

It was at this stage that most of the numerous Trade Unions which had come into being were organised under Owen's leadership into a Grand National Consolidated Trades Union with an Owenite programme. A little later, in the North, the Owenites, through the National Regeneration Society, placed themselves at the head of a movement for factory reform and the eight-hour day, which they set out to secure not by legislation but by industrial action. The Grand National Consolidated Trades Union at the height of its influence in 1834 is said to have had over half a million members, and another half million are said to have been enrolled in Unions, such as the Builders' Union, which were working in association with it.

The Grand National Consolidated Trades Union— known to its contemporaries as *the Trades Union*, speedily came to be feared as a vast and potentially revolutionary uprising of the working class. For a while Owen dreamed great dreams. In 1816 it had seemed to him that, if only his 'Plan' were adopted, the whole face of the world could be at once changed. The failure of New Harmony had not taught him to moderate his hopes ; he had become steadily more Utopian and millennial as he grew older. Now, he proclaimed to the workers that by their might and rationality there should come speedily a great change by which all misery and poverty would at once be swept away.

How rapidly this great movement crumbled students of the history of the Trade Union movement are well aware. The Owenites had projected a General Strike, to be followed by the sudden and complete institution of the new Co-operative system which Owen had preached. But in fact the 'Trades Union', as it was commonly called, soon found itself involved in a large number of sectional disputes, mostly lock-outs declared by employers who refused to employ anyone who admitted membership of the 'Trades Union'. Moreover, the trial and transportation for the administration of unlawful oaths of the Dorchester labourers who had formed a branch of the ' Trades Union ' indicated the readiness of the Government to go to all lengths in repressing the new movement. Under these blows the ' Trades Union ' rapidly crumbled away, and in the summer of 1834 Owen, realising its failure, decreed its dissolution. Thereafter Owen played little direct part in the fortunes of the organised working-class movement. For the rest of his life he devoted the whole of his energies to a social propaganda which became more and more ethical and rationalistic rather than directly political and industrial.

Within a year of its formation, the great Trades Union was shattered into a thousand fragments, and Owen had ceased to be the leader of the British working class. Within two years more, a new political agitation—the Chartist Movement—was arising, and the great Trade Union struggle of 1834 was no more than a memory.

Owenism, however, did not die. From one stream of Owenite influence sprang the modern Co-operative Movement ; another went on to give birth to the Secularist agitation. Owen himself, turning more and more from reformer to prophet, became the apostle of a ' Rational Religion ' which was the forerunner of the modern Ethical movement. For more than twenty years longer he poured out books, pamphlets and magazines in an endless stream, and a body of faithful disciples continued to spread his gospel. But he was already an old man when the great Trades Union collapsed ; and his later work was no more than a repetition of his earlier writings. The new Co-operative Colony, Queenwood, or Harmony Hall, which he founded in Hampshire in 1839, only repeated the failure of New Harmony in the 'twenties. Owen's real work was over in 1834.

I began by calling Robert Owen something of a puzzle. Leslie Stephen called him ' one of those bores who are the salt of the earth '. He was essentially a man of one idea, which he preached tirelessly, in and out of season, through the whole of his public life. In pursuit of this idea, practical business man though he had been, he lost all sense of the difference between conception and accomplishment. The millennium seemed to him always just round the next corner ; he was endlessly and fatuously hopeful and sure of success. He aimed constantly at the impossible, and was never in the least deterred by failure from aiming at it again. Consequently, he became, despite his early and outstanding successes, an exceedingly bad leader of men. He was, moreover, more than a little autocratic in his ways—a habit bred in him by his position of unquestioned command at New Lanark, and confirmed by his unswerving and absolute assurance of being on all occasions perfectly right.

This sounds an unlovable picture ; and yet, by the general testimony of those who knew him, Owen was a most lovable man. He was utterly without taint of self-seeking, a real and feeling lover of his fellow men, an unfailing favourite with children. His own children loved him very dearly, and were ardent disciples of his doctrine. Perhaps the easiest answer to the riddle of his personality is that he was a little mad.

If there are grave faults to be found with Owen's practical qualities of leadership, and many failures to his record, few men of the nineteenth century have more solid achievements to their credit. It was a very great thing to have demonstrated, as he did in the worst days of the Industrial Revolution, that low wages, long hours, and bad conditions of labour were not the indispensable foundations of Britain's greatness. It was a fine thing to have realised the need for a liberalising education as the basis of a rational citizenship at a time when the Lancasterian monitorial system was regarded as the last word in progressive education for the poor. And it was a fine thing to have spoken, even for the time in vain, a word of hope and promise to the unfortunate victims of the Industrial Revolution, and to have set them building up their Trade Unions and their Co-operative Societies with a new vision of self-government and freedom before

their eyes. Long before Carlyle or Ruskin, Owen looked
upon the new world which the ' Manchester School '
was making, and called it ' evil '; and his calling it so was
the more remarkable because he was himself one of the
most successful learners in that school. But Owen was
greatest because he not only revolted against the horrors
of the Industrial Revolution, but also sought a constructive way of escape. His Co-operative Colonies and
his great Trades Union alike failed ; but he laid the
foundations on which a later generation was better able
to build. Few men have exerted a wider or more bene-
ficent influence ; and none has been more whole-
hearted in the service of his faith.

Rousseau's ' Social Contract '

FOR the study of the great writers and thinkers of the past, historical imagination is the first necessity. Without mentally referring to the environment in which they lived, we cannot hope to penetrate below the inessential and temporary to the absolute and permanent value of their thought. Theory, no less than action, is subject to these necessities ; the form in which men cast their speculations, no less than the ways in which they behave, are the result of the habits of thought and action which they find around them. Great men make, indeed, individual contributions to the knowledge of their times ; but they can never transcend the age in which they live. The questions they try to answer will always be those their contemporaries are asking ; their statement of fundamental problems will always be relative to the traditional statements that have been handed down to them. When they are stating what is most startlingly new, they will be most likely to put it in an old-fashioned form, and to use the inadequate ideas and formulae of tradition to express the deeper truths towards which they are feeling their way. They will be most the children of their age, when they are rising most above it.

Rousseau has suffered as much as anyone from critics without a sense of history. He has been cried up and cried down by democrats and oppressors with an equal lack of understanding and imagination. His name, a hundred and seventy-five years after the publication of the *Social Contract*, is still a controversial watchword and a party cry. He is accepted as one of the greatest writers France has produced ; but even now men are inclined, as political bias prompts them, to accept or reject his political doctrines as a whole, without sifting them or attempting to understand and discriminate. He is still revered or hated as the author who, above all others, inspired the French Revolution.

At the present day, his works possess a double significance. They are important historically, alike as giving us an insight into the mind of the eighteenth century, and for the actual influence they have had on the course of events in Europe. Certainly no other writer of the time has exercised such an influence as his. He may fairly be called the parent of the romantic movement in art, letters and life ; he affected profoundly the German romantics and Goethe himself ; he set the fashion of a new introspection which permeated nineteenth-century literature ; he began modern educational theory ; and, finally, in political thought he represents the passage from traditional theory rooted in the Middle Ages to the modern idealist philosophy of the State. His influence on Kant's moral philosophy and on Hegel's philosophy of Right are two sides of the same fundamental contribution to modern thought. He is, in fact, for good and ill, the great forerunner of German and English Idealism.

It would not be possible, in the course of a short essay, to deal both with the positive content of Rousseau's thought and with the actual influence he has had on practical affairs. The statesmen of the French Revolution, from Robespierre downwards, were throughout profoundly affected by the study of his works. Though they seem often to have misunderstood him, they had on the whole studied him with the attention he demands. In the nineteenth century, men continued to appeal to Rousseau, without, as a rule, knowing him well or penetrating deeply into his meaning. ' The *Social Contract* ', says M. Dreyfus-Brisac, ' is the book of all books that is most talked of and least read.' But with the great revival of interest in political theory in the twentieth century there came a desire for the better understanding of Rousseau's work. He was again studied more as a thinker and less as an ally or an opponent ; there was more eagerness to sift the true from the false, and to seek in the *Social Contract* the ' principles of political right ', rather than the great revolutionary's *ipse dixit* in favour of some view about circumstances which he could never have contemplated.

The *Social Contract*, then, may be regarded either as a document of the French Revolution, or as one of the greatest books dealing with political philosophy. It is in the second capacity, as a work of permanent value containing truth, that it finds a place among the world's great books. It is in that capacity also that it will be treated in this essay. Taking it in this aspect, we have no less need of historical insight than if we came to it as historians pure and simple. To understand its value we must grasp its limitations. When the questions it answers seem unnaturally put, we must not conclude that they are meaningless ; we must see if the answer still holds when the question is put in a form more appropriate to our own times.

First, then, we must always remember that Rousseau was writing in the eighteenth century, and for the most part in France. Neither the French monarchy nor the Genevese aristocracy loved outspoken criticism, and Rousseau had always to be very careful what he said. This may seem a curious statement to make about a man who suffered continual persecution on account of his subversive doctrines ; but, although Rousseau was one of the most daring writers of his time, he was forced continually to moderate his language and, as a rule, to confine himself to generalisations instead of attacking particular abuses. Rousseau's theory has often been decried as too abstract and metaphysical. This is in many ways its great strength ; but where it is excessively so, the accident of time is largely to blame. In the eighteenth century it was, broadly speaking, safe to generalise and unsafe to particularise. Scepticism and discontent were the prevailing temper of the intellectual classes, and a short-sighted despotism held that, as long as they were confined to these, they would do little harm. Subversive doctrines were only regarded as dangerous when they were so put as to appeal to the masses ; philosophy was regarded as impotent. The intellectuals of the eighteenth century therefore generalised to their hearts' content, and as a rule suffered little for their *lèse-majesté* : Voltaire is the typical example of such generalisation. The spirit of the age favoured these methods, and it was natural for Rousseau to pursue them. But his general remarks had such a way of bearing very obvious particular applications, and were so obviously inspired by a particular attitude towards the government of his day, that even philosophy became in his hands unsafe, and he was attacked for what men read between the lines of his works. It is owing to this faculty of giving his generalisations practical content and actuality that Rousseau has become the father of modern political philosophy. He uses the method of his time only to transcend it ; out of the abstract and general he creates the concrete and universal.

Secondly, we must not forget that Rousseau's theories are to be studied in a wider historical environment. If he is the first of modern political theorists, he is also the last of a long line of Renaissance theorists, who in turn inherited and transformed the concepts of medieval thought. So many critics have spent so much wasted time in proving that Rousseau was not original only because they began by identifying originality with isolation : they studied first the *Social Contract* by itself, out of relation to earlier works, and then, having discovered that these earlier works resembled it, decided that everything it had to say was borrowed. Had they begun their study in a truly historical spirit, they would have seen that Rousseau's importance lies just in the new use he makes of old ideas, in the transition he makes from old to new in the general conceptions of politics. No mere innovator could have exercised such an influence or hit on so much truth. Theory makes no great leaps ; it pro-

ceeds to new concepts by the adjustment and renovation
of old ones. Just as theological writers on politics, from
Hooker to Bossuet, made use of Biblical terminology and
ideas ; just as nineteenth-century writers, from Hegel to
Herbert Spencer, made use of the concept of evolution,
Rousseau used the ideas and terms of the Social Contract
theory. We should feel, throughout his work, his struggle
to free himself from what is lifeless and outworn in that
theory, while he develops out of it fruitful conceptions
that go beyond its scope. A too rigid literalism in the
interpretation of Rousseau's thought may easily reduce
it to the possession of a merely ' historical interest ' :
if we approach it in a truly historical spirit, we shall be
able to appreciate at once its temporary and its lasting
value, to see how it served his contemporaries, and at the
same time to disentangle from it what may be serviceable
to us and for all time.

Of Rousseau's chief political works, the *Social Contract*,
by far the most significant, is the latest in date. It
represents the maturity of his thought, while his other
best-known political writings only illustrate his development. Born in 1712, he issued no work of importance
till 1750 ; but he tells us, in the *Confessions*, that in 1743,
when he was attached to the Embassy at Venice, he had
already conceived the idea of a great work on *Political
Institutions*, ' which was to put the seal on his reputation '. He seems, however, to have made little progress
with this work until in 1749 he happened to light on the
announcement of a prize offered by the Academy of
Dijon for an answer to the question, ' Has the progress
of the arts and sciences tended to the purification or to
the corruption of morality ? ' His old ideas came thronging back, and sick at heart of the life he had been leading
among the Paris *lumières*, he composed a violent and
rhetorical diatribe against civilisation generally. In the
following year, this work, having been awarded the prize
by the Academy, was published by its author. His success
was instantaneous ; he became at once a famous man,

the 'lion' of Parisian literary circles. Refutations of his work were issued by professors, scribblers, outraged theologians, and even by the King of Poland. Rousseau endeavoured to answer them all, and in the course of argument his thought developed. From 1750 to the publication of the *Social Contract* and *Émile* in 1762 he gradually matured his views : in those twelve years he made his unique contribution to political thought.

The *Discourse on the Arts and Sciences*, the earliest of his political writings, is not in itself of very great importance. Rousseau has given his opinion of it in the *Confessions*. ' Full of warmth and force, it is wholly without logic or order ; of all my works it is the weakest in argument and the least harmonious. But whatever gifts a man may be born with, he cannot learn the art of writing in a moment.' This criticism is just. The first Discourse neither is, nor attempts to be, a reasoned or a balanced production. It is the speech of an advocate, wholly one-sided and arbitrary, but so obviously and naïvely one-sided that it is difficult for us to believe in its entire seriousness. At the most, it is only a rather brilliant but flimsy rhetorical effort, a sophistical improvisation, and not a serious contribution to thought. Yet it is certain that this declamation made Rousseau's name, and established his position as a great writer in Parisian circles. D'Alembert even devoted the preface of the *Encyclopaedia* to a refutation. The plan of the first Discourse is essentially simple : it sets out from the badness, immorality, and misery of modern nations, traces all these ills to the departure from a ' natural ' state, and then credits the progress of the arts and sciences with being the cause of that departure. In it, Rousseau is already in possession of his idea of ' nature ' as an ideal ; but he has at present made no attempt to discriminate, in what is unnatural, between good and bad. He is merely using a single idea, putting it as strongly as he can, and neglecting all its limitations. The first Discourse is important not for any positive doctrine it contains, but as a key to the development of Rousseau's mind. Here we see him at the beginning of the long journey which was to lead on at last to the theory of the *Social Contract*.

In 1755 appeared the *Discourse on the Origin and Foundation of Inequality among Men*, which is the first of his major contributions to political thought. With this essay, Rousseau had unsuccessfully competed in 1753 for a second prize offered by the Academy of Dijon, and he now issued it prefaced by a long Dedication to the Republic of Geneva. In this work, which Voltaire, in thanking him for a presentation copy, termed his ' second book against the human race ', his style and his ideas have made a great advance ; he is no longer content merely to push a single idea to extremes : while preserving the broad opposition between the state of nature and the state of society, which runs through all his work, he is concerned to present a rational justification of his views and to admit that a little at any rate may be said on the other side. Moreover, the idea of ' nature ' has already undergone a great development ; it is no longer an empty opposition to the evils of society ; it possesses a positive content. Thus half the *Discourse on Inequality* is occupied by an imaginary description of the state of nature, in which man is shown with ideas limited within the narrowest range, with little need of his fellows, and little care beyond provision for the necessities of the moment. Rousseau declares explicitly that he does not suppose the ' state of nature ' ever to have existed : it is a pure ' idea of reason ', a working concept reached by abstraction from the ' state of society '. The ' natural man ', as opposed to ' man's man ', is man stripped of all that society confers upon him, a creature formed by a process of abstraction, and never intended for a historical portrait. The conclusion of the Discourse favours not this purely abstract being, but a state of ' savagery ' intermediate between the ' natural ' and the ' social ' conditions, in which men may preserve the simplicity and the advantages of nature and at the same time secure the rude comforts and assurances of early society. In one of the long notes appended to the Discourse, Rousseau further explains his position. He does not wish, he says, that modern corrupt society should return to a state of nature : corruption has gone too far for that ; he only desires now that men should palliate, by wiser use of the fatal arts, the mistake of their introduction. He recognises society as inevitable and is already feeling his way towards a justification of it. The second Discourse represents a second stage in his political thought : the opposition between the state of nature and the state of society is still presented in naked contrast ; but the picture of the former has already been filled out, and it only remains for Rousseau to take a nearer view of the fundamental implications of the state of society for his thought to reach maturity.

Rousseau is often blamed, by modern critics, for pursuing in the Discourses a method apparently that of history, but in reality wholly unhistorical. But it must be remembered that he himself lays no stress on the historical aspect of his work ; he gives himself out as constructing a purely ideal picture, and not as depicting any actual stages in human history. The use of false historical concepts is characteristic of the seventeenth and eighteenth centuries, and Rousseau is more to be congratulated on having escaped from giving them too much importance than criticised for employing them at all.

It is doubtful whether the *Discourse on Political Economy*, first printed in the great *Encyclopaedia* in 1755, was composed before or after the *Discourse on Inequality*. At first sight the former seems to be far more in the manner of the *Social Contract* and to contain views belonging essentially to Rousseau's constructive period. It would not, however, be safe to conclude from this that its date is really later. The *Discourse on Inequality* still has about it much of the rhetorical looseness of the prize essay ; it aims not so much at close reasoning as at effective and popular presentation of a case. But, by reading between the lines, an attentive student can detect in it a great deal of the positive doctrine afterwards incorporated in the *Social Contract*. Especially in the closing section, which lays down the plan of a general treatment of the fundamental questions of politics, we are already to some extent in the atmosphere of the author's later works. It is indeed almost certain that Rousseau never attempted to put into either of the first two Discourses any of the positive content of his political theory. They were intended, not as final expositions of his point of view, but as partial and preliminary studies, in which his aim was far more destructive than constructive. It is clear that, in first conceiving the plan of a work on *Political Institutions*, Rousseau cannot have meant to regard all society as in essence bad. It is indeed evident that he meant, from the first, to study human society and institutions in their rational aspect, and that he was rather diverted from his main purpose by the Academy of Dijon's competition than first induced by it to think about political questions. It need, therefore, cause no surprise that a work probably written before the *Discourse on Inequality* should contain the germs of the theory given in full in the *Social Contract*. The essay on *Political Economy* is important as giving the first sketch of the theory of the ' General Will '.

It will readily be seen that Rousseau does not mean by ' political economy ' exactly what we mean nowadays. He begins with a discussion of the fundamental nature of the State, and the possibility of reconciling its existence with human liberty, and goes on with an admirable short study of the principles of taxation. He is thinking throughout of ' political ' in the sense of ' public ' economy, of the State as the public financier, and not of the conditions governing production and exchange. He conceives of the State as a body aiming at the well-being of all its members and subordinates all his views of taxation to that end. He who has only necessaries should not be taxed at all ; superfluities should be supertaxed ; there should be heavy imposts on every sort of luxury. The first part of the article is still more interesting. Rousseau begins by demolishing the exaggerated parallel so often drawn between the State and the family ; he shows that the State is not, and cannot be, patriarchal in nature, and goes on to lay down his view that its real being consists in the General Will of its members. The essential features of the *Social Contract* are present in this Discourse almost as if they were commonplaces, certainly not as if they were new discoveries on which the author had just hit by some happy inspiration. There is every temptation, after reading the *Political Economy*, to suppose that Rousseau's political ideas really reached maturity far earlier than has generally been allowed.

The *Social Contract* finally appeared in 1762, in the same year as *Émile*. This year, therefore, represents in every respect the culmination of. Rousseau's career. Henceforth, he was to write only controversial and confessional works ; his theories were now developed, and, simultaneously, he gave to the world his views on the fundamental problems of politics and education. It is now time to ask what Rousseau's system, in its maturity, finally amounted to. The *Social Contract* contains practically the whole of his constructive political theory ; it requires to be read, for full understanding, in connection with his other works, especially *Émile* and the *Letters on the Mount* (1764), but in the main it is self-contained and complete. The title sufficiently defines its scope. It is called *The Social Contract, or Principles of Political Right*, and the second title explains the first. Rousseau's object is not to deal, in a general way, like Montesquieu, with the actual institutions of existing States, but to lay down the essential principles which, he holds, must form the basis of every legitimate society. Rousseau himself, in the fifth book of *Émile*, has stated the difference quite clearly. ' Montesquieu ', he says, ' did not intend to treat of the principles of political right ; he was content to treat of the positive right (or law) of established governments ; and no two studies could be more different than these.' Rousseau, then, conceives his object as being something very different from that of the *Spirit of the Laws*, and it is a wilful error to misconstrue his purpose. When he remarks that ' the facts ', the actual history of political societies, ' do not concern him ', he is not contemptuous of facts ; he is merely asserting the principle that a fact can in no case give rise to a right. His desire is to establish society on a basis of pure right, so as at once to disprove his attack on society generally and to reinforce his criticism of existing societies.

Round this point centres the whole dispute about the methods proper to political theory. There are, broadly speaking, two schools of political theorists, if we set aside the psychologists. One school, by collecting facts, aims at reaching broad generalisations about what actually happens in human societies ; the other tries to penetrate to universal principles which should be at the root of all human combination. For the latter purpose facts may be useful, but in themselves they can prove nothing. The question is not one of fact, but one of right.

Rousseau belongs essentially to this philosophical school. He is not, as his less philosophical critics seem to suppose, a purely abstract thinker generalising from imaginary historical instances ; he is a concrete thinker trying to get beyond the inessential and changing to the permanent and invariable basis of human society. Like Green, he is in search of the principle of political obligation, and beside this quest all others fall into their place as secondary and derivative. It is required ' to find a form of association able to defend and protect with the whole common force the person and goods of every associate, and of such a nature that each, uniting himself with all, may still obey only himself, and remain as free as before. This is the fundamental problem of which the

Social Contract provides the solution.' The problem of political obligation is seen as including all other political problems, which fall into place in a system based upon it. How, Rousseau asks, can the will of the State help being for me a merely external will, imposing itself upon my own ? How can the existence of the State be reconciled with human freedom ? How can man, who is born free, rightly come to be everywhere in chains ?

No one could help understanding the central problem of the *Social Contract* immediately, were it not that its doctrines often seem to be strangely formulated. We have seen that this strangeness is largely due to Rousseau's historical position, to his use of the political concepts current in his own age, and to his natural tendency to build on the foundations laid by his predecessors. There are a great many people whose idea of Rousseau consists solely of the first words of the opening chapter of the *Social Contract*, ' Man is born free, and everywhere he is in chains.' But, they tell you, man is not born free, even if he is everywhere in chains. Thus at the very outset we are faced with the great difficulty in appreciating Rousseau. When we should naturally say ' man ought to be free ', or perhaps ' man is born for freedom ', he prefers to say ' man is born free ', by which he means exactly the same thing. There is doubtless, in his way of putting it, an appeal to a ' golden age ' ; but this golden age is admittedly as imaginary as the freedom to which men are born is bound, for most of them, to be. Elsewhere Rousseau puts the point much as we might put it ourselves. ' Nothing is more certain than that every man born in slavery is born for slavery. . . . But if there are slaves by nature, it is because there have been slaves against nature ' (*Social Contract*, Book I, chap. ii).

We have seen that the contrast between the ' state of nature ' and the ' state of society ' runs through all Rousseau's work. His *Émile* is a plea for ' natural ' education ; the Discourses are a plea for a ' naturalisation ' of society ; the *New Héloïse* is the romantic's appeal for more ' nature ' in human relationships. What then is the position of this contrast in Rousseau's mature political thought ? It is clear that the position is not merely that of the Discourses. In them, he envisaged only the faults of actual societies ; now, he is concerned with the possibility of a rational society. His aim is to justify the change from ' nature ' to ' society ', although it has left men in chains. He is in search of the true society, which can leave men ' as free as before '. Altogether, the space occupied by the idea of nature in the *Social Contract* is very small. It is used of necessity in the controversial chapters, in which Rousseau is refuting false theories of social obligation ; but when once he has brushed aside the false prophets, he lets the idea of nature go with them, and concerns himself solely with giving society the rational sanction he has promised. It becomes clear that, in political matters at any rate, the ' state of nature ' is for him only a term of controversy. He has in effect abandoned, in so far as he ever held it, the theory of a human golden age ; and where, as in *Émile*, he makes use of the idea of nature, it is broadened and deepened out of all recognition. Despite many passages, in which the old terminology cleaves to him, he means by ' nature ' in this period not the original state of a thing, nor even its reduction to the simplest terms : he is passing over to the conception of ' nature ' as identical with the full development of capacity, with the higher idea of human freedom. This view may be seen in germ even in the *Discourse on Inequality*, where, distinguishing self-respect (*amour de soi*) from egoism (*amour-propre*), Rousseau makes the former, the property of the ' natural ' man, consist not in the desire for self-aggrandisement, but in the seeking of satisfaction for reasonable desires accompanied by benevolence ; whereas egoism is the preference of our own interests to those of others, self-respect merely puts us on an equal footing with our fellows. It is true that in the Discourse Rousseau is pleading against the development of many human faculties ; but he is equally advocating the fullest development of those he regards as 'natural', by which he means neither more nor less than 'good'. The 'state of society', as envisaged in the *Social Contract*, is no longer in contradiction to the ' state of nature ' upheld in *Émile*, where indeed the social environment is of the greatest importance, and, though the pupil is screened from it, he is none the less being trained for it. Indeed the views given in the *Social Contract* are summarised in the fifth book of *Émile*, and by this summary the essential unity of Rousseau's system is emphasised.

Rousseau's object, then, in the first words of the *Social Contract*, 'is to inquire if, in the civil order, there can be any sure and certain rule of administration, taking men as they are and laws as they might be '. Montesquieu took laws as they were, and saw what sort of men they made : Rousseau, founding his whole system on human freedom, takes man as the basis, and regards him as giving himself what laws he pleases. He takes his stand on the nature of human freedom : on this he bases his whole system, making the will of the members the sole basis of every society.

In working out his theory, Rousseau makes use throughout of three general and, to some extent, alternative conceptions. These are the Social Contract, Sovereignty, and the General Will. We shall now have to examine each of these in turn.

The Social Contract theory is as old as the sophists of Greece (see Plato, *Republic*, Book II, and the *Gorgias*), and as elusive. It has been adapted to the most opposite points of view, and used, in different forms, on both sides of every question to which it could conceivably be applied. It is frequent in medieval writers, a commonplace with the theorists of the Renaissance, and in the eighteenth century already nearing its fall before a wider conception. It would be a long, as well as a thankless, task to trace its history over again : it may be followed best in D. G. Ritchie's admirable essay on it in *Darwin and Hegel and Other Studies.* For us, it is important only to regard it in its most general aspect, before studying the special use made of it by Rousseau. Obviously, in one form or another, it is a theory very easily arrived at. Wherever any form of government apart from the merest tyranny exists, reflection on the basis of the State cannot but lead to the notion that, in one sense or another, it is based on the consent, tacit or expressed, past or present, of at any rate some of its members. In this alone, the greater part of the Social Contract theory is already latent. Add the desire to find actual justification for a theory in facts, and, especially in an age possessed only of the haziest historical sense, this doctrine of consent will inevitably be given a historical setting. If in addition there is a tendency to regard society as something unnatural to humanity, the tendency will become irresistible. By writers of almost all schools, the State will be represented as having arisen, in some remote age, out of a compact or, in more legal phrase, contract between two or more parties. The only writers who will be able to resist the doctrine are those who maintain the divine right of kings, and hold that all existing governments were imposed on the people by the direct interposition of God. All who are not prepared to maintain this will be partisans of some form or other of the Social Contract theory.

It is, therefore, not surprising that we find among its advocates writers of the most opposite points of view. Barely stated, it is a mere formula, which may be filled in with any content from absolutism to pure republicanism. And, in the hands of some at least of its supporters, it turns out to be a weapon that cuts both ways. We shall be in a better position to judge of its usefulness when we have seen its chief varieties at work.

All Social Contract theories that are at all definite fall under one or other of two heads. They represent society as based on an original contract either between the people and the government, or among all the individuals composing the State. Historically, modern theory passes from the first to the second of these forms.

The doctrine that society is founded on a contract between the people and the government is of medieval origin. It was often supported by references to the Old Testament, which contains a similar view in an unreflective form. It is found in most of the great political writers of the sixteenth century ; in Buchanan, and in the writings of James I : it persists into the seventeenth in the works of Grotius and Pufendorf. Grotius is sometimes held to have stated the theory so as to admit both forms of contract ; but it is clear he is only thinking of the first form as admitting democratic as well as monarchical government. We find it put very clearly by the Convention Parliament of 1688, which accuses James II of having ' endeavoured to subvert the constitution of the kingdom by breaking the original contract between king and people '. While Hobbes, on the side of the royalists, is maintaining the contract theory in its second form, the Parliamentarian Algernon Sidney adheres to the idea of a contract between the people and the government.

In this form, the theory clearly admits of opposite interpretations. It may be held that the people, having given itself up once for all to its rulers, has nothing more to ask of them, and is bound to submit to any usage they may choose to inflict. This, however, is not the implication most usually drawn from it. The theory, in this form, originated with theologians who were also lawyers. Their view of a contract implied mutual obligations ; they regarded the ruler as bound, by its terms, to govern constitutionally. The old idea that a king must not violate the sacred customs of the realm passes easily into the doctrine that he must not violate the terms of the original contract between himself and his people. Just as in the days of the Norman kings, every appeal on the part of the people for more liberties was couched in the form of a demand that the customs of the ' good old times ' of Edward the Confessor should be respected, so in the seventeenth century every act of popular assertion or resistance was stated as an appeal to the king not to violate the contract. The demand was a good popular cry, and it seemed to have the theorists behind it. Rousseau gives his refutation of this view, which he had, in the *Discourse on Inequality*, maintained in passing, in the sixteenth chapter of the third book of the *Social Contract*. (See also Book I, chap. iv, init.) His attack is really concerned also with the theory of Hobbes, which in some respects resembles, as we shall see, this first view ; but, in form at least, it is directed against this type of contract. It will be possible to examine it more closely, when the second view has been considered.

The second view, which may be called the Social Contract theory proper, regards society as originating in, or based on, an agreement among the individuals composing it. It seems to be found first, rather vaguely, in Richard Hooker's *Ecclesiastical Polity*, from which Locke largely borrowed : and it reappears, in varying forms, in Milton's *Tenure of Kings and Magistrates*, in Hobbes's *Leviathan*, in Locke's *Treatises on Civil Government*, and in Rousseau. The best-known instance of its actual use is by the Pilgrim Fathers on the *Mayflower* in 1620, in whose declaration occurs the phrase, ' We do solemnly and mutually, in the presence of God and of one another, covenant and combine ourselves together into a civil body politic '. The natural implication of this view would seem to be the corollary of complete popular Sovereignty which Rousseau draws. But before Rousseau's time it had been used to support views as diverse as those which rested on the first form. We saw that, in Grotius's great work, *De Jure Belli et Pacis*, it was already possible to doubt which of the two theories was being advocated. The first theory was, historically, a means of popular protest against royal aggression. As soon as popular government was taken into account, the act of contract between people and government became in effect merely a contract among the individuals composing the society, and readily passed over into the second form.

The second theory, in its ordinary form, expresses only the view that the people is everywhere Sovereign, and that, in the phrase of Milton's treatise, ' the power of kings and magistrates is only derivative '. Before, however, this view had been worked up into a philosophical theory, it had already been used by Hobbes to support precisely opposite principles. Hobbes agrees that the original contract is one between all the individuals composing the State, and that the government is no party to it ; but he regards the people as agreeing, not merely to form a State, but to invest a certain person or certain persons with the government of it. He agrees that the people is naturally supreme, but regards it as alienating its Sovereignty by the contract itself, and delegating its power, wholly and for ever, to the government. As soon, therefore, as the State is set up, the government becomes for Hobbes the Sovereign ; there is no more question of popular Sovereignty, but only of passive obedience : the people is bound, by the contract, to obey its ruler, no matter whether he governs well or ill. It has alienated all its rights to the Sovereign, who is, therefore, absolute master. Hobbes, living in a time of civil wars, regards the worst government as better than anarchy, and is, therefore, at pains to find arguments in support of any form of absolutism. It is easy to pick holes in this system, and to see into what difficulties a conscientious Hobbist might be led by a revolution. For as soon as the revolutionaries get the upper hand, he will have to sacrifice one of his principles : he will have to side against either the actual or the legitimate Sovereign. It is easy also to see that alienation of liberty, even if possible for an individual, which Rousseau denies, cannot bind his posterity. But, with all its faults, the view of Hobbes, when once his premises are granted, is on the whole admirably, if ruthlessly, logical, and to it Rousseau owes a great deal.

The special shape given to the second form of the Social Contract theory by Hobbes looks, at first sight, much like a combination, into a single act, of both the contracts. This, however, is not the view he adopts. The theory of a contract between government and people had, as we have seen, been used mainly as a support for popular liberties, a means of assertion against the government. Hobbes, whose whole aim is to make his government Sovereign, can only do this by leaving the government outside the contract : he thus avoids the necessity of submitting it to any obligation whatsoever, and leaves it absolute and irresponsible. He secures, in fact, not merely a State which has unbounded rights against the individual, but a determinate authority with the right to enforce those rights. His theory is not merely Statism (*étatisme*) ; it is pure despotism.

It is clear that, if such a theory is to be upheld, it can stand only by the view, which Hobbes shares with Grotius, that a man can alienate not merely his own liberty, but also that of his descendants, and that, consequently, a people as a whole can do the same. This is the point at which both Locke and Rousseau attack it. Locke, whose aim is largely to justify the principles which underlay the Revolution of 1688, makes government depend, not merely at its institution, but always, on the consent of the governed, and regards all rulers as liable to be displaced if they govern tyrannically. He omits, however, to provide any machinery short of revolution for the expression of popular opinion, and, on the whole, seems to regard the popular consent as something essentially tacit and assumed. He regards the State as existing mainly to protect life and property, and is, in all his assertions of popular rights, so cautious as to reduce them almost to nothing. It is not till we come to Rousseau that the second form of the contract theory is stated in its purest and most logical form.

Rousseau sees clearly the necessity, if popular consent in government is to be more than a name, of giving it some constitutional means of expression. For Locke's theory of tacit consent he substitutes an active agreement periodically renewed. He looks back with admiration to the city-states of ancient Greece and, in his own day, reserves his admiration for the Swiss free cities, Berne and, above all, Geneva, his native place. Seeing in the Europe of his day no case in which representative government was working at all democratically, he was unable to conceive that means might be found of giving effect to this active agreement in a nation-state ; he therefore held that real self-government was impossible except for a city. He would have liked to break up the nation-states of Europe, and create instead federative leagues of independent city-states.

It matters, however, comparatively little, for the appreciation of Rousseau's political theory in general, that he failed to become the theorist of the modern State. By taking the State, which must have, in essentials, everywhere the same basis, at its simplest, he was able, far better than his predecessors, to bring out the real nature of the ' social tie ', an alternative name which he often uses for the Social Contract. His doctrine of the underlying principle of political obligation is like that of all the modern idealist writers, from Kant to Bosanquet. This close resemblance has been obscured only because critics have failed to put the Social Contract theory in its proper place in Rousseau's system.

This theory was, we have seen, a commonplace. The amount of historical authenticity assigned to the contract —which was almost universally presupposed—varied enormously. Generally, the weaker a writer's rational basis, the more he appealed to history—and invented it. It was, therefore, almost inevitable that Rousseau should cast his theory into the contractual form. There were, indeed, writers of his time who laughed at the contract, but they were not writers who constructed a general system of political philosophy. From Cromwell to Montesquieu and Bentham, it was the practically minded man, impatient of unactual hypotheses, who refused to accept the idea of contract. The theorists were as unanimous in its favour as the Victorians were in favour of their ' organic ' theory. But we, criticising them in the light of later events, are in a better position for estimating the position the Social Contract really took in their political systems. We see that Locke's doctrine of tacit consent made popular control so unreal that he was forced, if the State was to have any hold, to make his contract in effect historical and actual, binding posterity for all time, and that he was also led to admit a quasi-contract between people and government, as a second vindication of popular liberties. Rousseau, on the other hand, bases no vital argument on the historical nature of the contract, in which, indeed, he clearly does not believe. ' How ', he asks, ' did this change [from nature to society] come about ? ' And he answers that he does not know. Moreover, his aim is to find ' a sure and legitimate rule of administration, taking men as they are and laws as they might be ' ; that is to say, his Social Contract is something which will be found at work in every legitimate society, but which will be in abeyance in all forms of despotism. He clearly means by it no more and no less than the fundamental principle of political association, the basis of the unity which enables men, in the State, to realise political liberty by giving up lawlessness and license. The presentation of this doctrine in the quasi-historical form of the Social Contract theory is due to the accident of the time and place in which Rousseau wrote. At the same time, the importance of the conception is best to be seen in the hard death it dies. Though no one, for a hundred years or so, has thought of regarding it as historical, it has been found so hard to secure any other phrase explaining as well or better the basis of political union that, to this day, the phraseology of the contract theory often persists. A conception so vital cannot have been barren.

It is indeed, in Rousseau's own thought, only one of the three different ways in which the basis of political union is stated, according to the preoccupation of his mind. When he is thinking quasi-historically he describes his doctrine as that of the Social Contract. Modern anthropology, in its attempts to explain the complex by means of the simple, often strays further from the straight paths of history and reason. In a semi-legal aspect, using the terminology, if not the standpoint, of jurisprudence, he restates· the same doctrine in the form of popular Sovereignty. This use tends continually to pass over into the more philosophical form which comes third. ' Sovereignty is the exercise of the general will.' Philosophically, Rousseau's doctrine finds its expression in the view that the State is based not on any original convention, not on any determinate power, but on the living and sustaining rational will of its members. We have now to examine first Sovereignty and then the General Will, which is ultimately Rousseau's guiding conception.

Sovereignty is, first and foremost, a legal term, and it has often been held that its use in political philosophy merely leads to confusion. In jurisprudence, we are told, it has the perfectly plain meaning given to it in Austin's famous definition. The Sovereign is ' a *determinate* human superior, *not* in a habit of obedience to a like superior, but receiving *habitual* obedience from the *bulk* of a given society '. Where Sovereignty is placed is, on this view, a question purely of fact, and never of right. We have only to seek out the determinate human superior in a given society, and we shall have the Sovereign. In answer to this theory, it is not enough, though it is a valuable point, to show that such a determinate superior is rarely to be found. Where, for instance, is the Sovereign of England or of the British Empire ? Is it the King, who is called the Sovereign ? Or is it the Parliament, which is the legislature (for Austin's Sovereign is regarded as the source of law) ? Or is it the electorate, or the whole mass of the population, with or without the right of voting ? Clearly all these exercise a certain influence in the making of laws. Or finally, is it now the

Cabinet ? For Austin, one of these bodies would be ruled out as indeterminate (the mass of the population) and an ther as responsible (the Cabinet). But are we to regard the House of Commons or those who elect it as forming part of the Sovereign ? The notion of a determinate Sovereign may be a valuable legal conception ; but it has evidently nothing to do with political philosophy. And in practice it is apt to resemble the search in a haystack for a needle that is not there.

It is therefore essential to distinguish between the legal Sovereign of jurisprudence, and the political Sovereign of political science and philosophy. Even so, it does not at once become clear what this political Sovereign may be. Is it the body or bodies of persons in whom political power in a State actually resides ? Is it merely the complex of actual institutions regarded as embodying the will of the society ? This would leave us still in the realm of mere fact, outside both right and philosophy. The Sovereign, in the philosophical sense, is neither the nominal Sovereign, nor the legal Sovereign, nor the political Sovereign of fact and common sense : it is the consequence of the fundamental bond of union, the restatement of the doctrine of Social Contract, the foreshadowing of that of General Will. The Sovereign, in Rousseau's sense, is that body in the State in which political *power ought* always to reside, and in which the *right* to such power *does* always reside.

The idea at the back of this philosophical conception of Sovereignty is, therefore, essentially the same as that we found to underlie the Social Contract theory. It is the view that the people, whether it can alienate its right or not, is the ultimate director of its own destinies, the final power from which there is no appeal. In a sense, this is recognised even by Hobbes, who makes the power of his absolute Sovereign, the predecessor of Austin's ' determinate human superior ', issue first of all from the Social Contract, which is essentially a popular act. The difference between Hobbes and Rousseau on this point is solely that Rousseau regards as inalienable a supreme power which Hobbes makes the people alienate in its first corporate act. That is to say, Hobbes accepts the theory of popular supremacy in name only to destroy it in fact ; Rousseau asserts the theory in its only logical form, and is under no temptation to evade it by means of false historical assumptions. In Locke, a distinction is already drawn between the legal and the actual Sovereign, which Locke calls ' supreme power ' ; Rousseau unites the absolute Sovereignty of Hobbes and the ' popular consent ' of Locke into the philosophic doctrine of popular Sovereignty, which has since been the established form of the theory. His final view represents a return from the perversions of Hobbes to a doctrine already familiar to medieval and Renaissance writers ; but it is not merely a return. In its passage the view has fallen into its place in a complete system of political philosophy.

In a second important respect Rousseau differentiates himself from Hobbes. For Hobbes, the Sovereign is identical with the government. Hobbes is hot for absolutism largely because he regards revolution, the overthrow of the existing government, as at the same time the dissolution of the body politic, and a return to complete anarchy or to the ' state of nature '. Rousseau and, to some extent, Locke meet this view by means of a sharp division between the supreme power and the government. For Rousseau, they are so clearly distinct that even a completely democratic government is not at the same time the Sovereign ; its members are sovereign only in different capacity and as a different corporate body, just as two different societies may exist for different purposes with exactly the same members. Pure democracy, however, the government of the State by all the people in every detail, is not, as Rousseau says, a possible human institution. All governments are really *mixed* in character ; and what we call a democracy is only a more or less democratic government. Government, therefore, will always be to some extent in the hands of selected persons. Sovereignty, on the other hand, is in his view absolute, inalienable, indivisible, and indestructible. It cannot be limited, abandoned, shared or destroyed. It is an essential part of all social life that the right to control the destinies of the State belongs in the last resort to the whole people. There clearly must in the end be somewhere in the society an ultimate court of appeal, whether determinate or not; but, unless Sovereignty is distinguished from government, the government, passing under the name of Sovereign, will inevitably be regarded as absolute. The only way to avoid the conclusions of Hobbes is, therefore, to establish a clear separation between Sovereignty and government.

Rousseau tries to do this by an adaptation of the doctrine of the ' three powers '. But instead of three independent powers sharing the supreme authority, he gives only two, and makes one of these wholly dependent on the other. He substitutes for the co-ordination of the legislative, the executive, and the judicial authorities, a system in which the legislative power, or Sovereign, is always supreme, the executive, or government, always secondary and derivative, and the judicial power merely a function of government. This division he makes, naturally, one of *will* and *power*. The government is merely to carry out the decrees, or acts of will, of the sovereign people. Just as the human will transfers a command to its members for execution, so the body politic may give its decisions force by setting up an authority which, like the brain, may command the members. In delegating the power necessary for the execution of its will, it is abandoning none of its supreme authority. It remains sovereign, and can at any moment recall the grants it has made. Government, therefore, exists only at the Sovereign's pleasure, and is always revocable by the sovereign will.

It will be seen, when we come to discuss the nature of the General Will, that this doctrine really contains the most valuable part of Rousseau's theory. Here, we are concerned rather with its limitations. The distinction between legislative and executive functions is in practice very hard to draw. In Rousseau's case, it is further complicated by the presence of a second distinction. The legislative power, the Sovereign, is concerned only with what is general, the executive only with what is particular. This distinction, the full force of which can only be seen in connection with the General Will, means roughly that a matter is general when it concerns the whole community equally, and has no differential reference to any particular class or group or person ; as soon as it refers specially to any class or group or person, it becomes particular, and can no longer form the subject matter of an act of Sovereignty. However just this distinction may seem in the abstract, it is clear that its practical effect is to place all the power normally in the hands of the executive : current legislation is almost always concerned with particular classes and interests. It is not, therefore, a long step from the view of Rousseau to the modern theory of democratic government, in which the people has little power beyond that of threatening its rulers with removal if they displease it. As long, however, as we confine our view to the city-states of which Rousseau is thinking, his distinction is capable of preserving for the people a greater actual exercise of will. A city can often generalise where a nation must particularise.

It is in the third book of the *Social Contract*, where Rousseau is discussing the problem of government, that it is most essential to remember that his discussion has in view mainly the city-state and not the nation. Broadly put, his principle of government is that democracy is possible only in small States, aristocracy in those of medium extent, and monarchy in great States (Book III, chap. iii). In considering this view, we have to take into account two things. First, he rejects representation as a possible instrument for the exercise of the sovereign function ; will being, in his theory, inalienable, representative Sovereignty is impossible. But, as he regards all general acts as functions of Sovereignty, this means that no general act can be within the competence of a representative assembly. In judging this theory, we must take into account all the circumstances of Rousseau's time. France, Geneva, and England were the three States he took most into account. In France, representative government was practically non-existent; in Geneva, it was only partially necessary; in England, it was a mockery, used to support a corrupt oligarchy against a debased monarchy. Rousseau may well be pardoned for not taking the nineteenth-century view of it. Nor indeed is it, even in the modern world, so satisfactory an instrument of the popular will that we can afford wholly to discard his criticism. It is one of the problems of democracy to find some means of securing effective popular control over elected Parliaments and despotic Cabinets. We have witnessed, in the twentieth century, strange perversions of the process of parliamentary election.

The second factor is the immense development of local government. It seemed to Rousseau that, in the nation-state, all authority must necessarily pass, as it had passed in France, to the central power. Devolution was hardly dreamed of; and he saw the only means of securing effective popular government in a federal system, starting from the small unit as Sovereign. The nineteenth century proved the falsehood of much of his theory of government; but there are still many wise comments and fruitful suggestions to be found in the third book of the *Social Contract* and in the treatise on the *Government of Poland*, as well as in his adaptation and criticism of the *Polysynodie* of the Abbé de Saint-Pierre, a scheme of local government for France, born out of its due time.

The point in Rousseau's theory of Sovereignty that offers most difficulty is his view (Book II, chap. vii) that, for every State, a *Legislator* is necessary. We shall understand this section only by realising that the legislator is, in fact, in Rousseau's system, the spirit of institutions personified; his place, in a developed society, is taken by the whole complex of social custom, organisation and tradition that has grown up within the State. This is made clearer by the fact that the legislator is not to exercise legislative power ; he is merely to submit his suggestions for popular approval. Thus Rousseau recognises that, in the case of institutions and traditions as elsewhere, will, and not force, is the proper basis of the legitimate State.

This may be seen in his treatment of law as a whole (Book II, chap. vi), a treatment which deserves very careful attention. He defines laws as ' acts of the general will ', and, agreeing with Montesquieu in making law the ' condition of civil association ', goes beyond him only in tracing it more definitely to its origin in an act of will. The Social Contract renders law necessary, and at the same time makes it quite clear that laws can proceed only from the body of citizens who have constituted the State. ' Doubtless ', says Rousseau, ' there is a universal justice emanating from reason alone ; but this justice, to be admitted among us, must be mutual. Humbly speaking, in default of natural sanctions, the laws of justice are ineffective among men.' Of the law which set up among men this reign of mutual justice the General Will is the source.

We thus come at last to the General Will, the most disputed, and certainly the most fundamental, of all Rousseau's political concepts. No critic of the *Social Contract* has found it easy to say either what precisely its author meant by it, or what is its final value for political philosophy. The difficulty is increased because Rousseau himself sometimes halts in the sense which he assigns to it, and even seems to suggest by it two different ideas. Of its broad meaning, however, there can be no doubt. The effect of the Social Contract, according to Rousseau, is the creation of a new individual. When it has taken place, ' at once, in place of the individual personality of each contracting party, the act of association creates a moral and collective body, composed of as

many members as the assembly contains voters, and
receiving from the act its unity, its common identity
(*moi commun*), its life and its will ' (Book I, chap. vi).
The same doctrine had been stated earlier, in the *Political
Economy*, without the historical setting. ' The body
politic is also a moral being, possessed of a will, and this
general will, which tends always to the preservation and
welfare of the whole and of every part, and is the source
of the laws, constitutes for all the members of the State,
in their relations to one another and to it, the rule of
what is just or unjust.' It will be seen at once that the
second statement, which could easily be fortified by
others from the *Social Contract*, says more than the first.
It is not apparent that the common will, created by the
institution of society, need ' tend always to the welfare
of the whole '. Is not the common will at least as fallible
as the will of a single individual ? May it not equally be
led away from its true interests to the pursuit of something which is really harmful to it ? And, if the whole
society may vote what conduces to the momentary
pleasure of all the members and at the same time to the
lasting damage of the people as a whole, is it not still
more likely that some of the members will try to secure
their private interests in opposition to those of the whole
and of others ? All these questions, and others like them,
have been asked by critics of the conception of the
General Will.

Two main points are involved, to one of which
Rousseau gives a clear and definite answer. ' There is
often ', he says, ' a great deal of difference between the
will of all and the *general will* ; the latter takes account
only of the common interest, while the former takes
private interest into account, and is no more than a sum
of particular wills.' 'The agreement of all interests is
formed by opposition to that of each ' (Book II, chap.
iii). It is indeed possible for a citizen, when an issue is
presented to him, to vote not for the good of the State,
but for his own good ; but, in such a case, his vote, from

the point of view of the General Will, is merely negligible. But ' does it follow that the general will is exterminated or corrupted ? Not at all : it is always constant, unalterable, and pure ; but it is subordinated to other wills which encroach upon its sphere. . . . The fault [each man] commits [in detaching his interest from the common interest] is that of changing the state of the question, and answering something different from what he is asked. Instead of saying by his vote " It is to the advantage of the State ", he says, " It is to the advantage of this or that man or party that this or that view should prevail ". Thus the law of public order in assemblies is not so much to maintain in them the general will as to secure that the question be always put to it, and the answer always given by it ' (Book IV, chap. i). These passages, with many others that may be found in the text of the *Social Contract*, make it quite clear that by the General Will, Rousseau meant something quite distinct from the Will of All, with which he insisted that it should never be confused. The only excuse for such confusion lies in his view that when, *in a city-state*, all particular associations are avoided, votes guided by individual self-interest will always cancel one another out, so that majority voting will always result in the General Will. This is clearly not the case, and in this respect he may be charged with pushing the democratic argument absurdly too far. The point, however, can be better dealt with at a later stage. Rousseau makes no pretence that the mere voice of a majority is infallible ; he only says, at the most, that, given his ideal conditions, it would be so.

The second main point raised by critics of the General Will is whether in defining it as a will directed solely to the common interest, Rousseau means to exclude acts of public immorality and short-sightedness. He answers the question in different ways. First, an act of public immorality would be merely an instance of corporate selfishness, different in no particular from similar acts

less unanimous, and therefore forming no part of a
General Will. Secondly, a mere ignorance of our own
and the State's good, entirely unprompted by selfish
desires, does not make our will anti-social or individual.
' The general will is always right and tends to the public
advantage ; but it does not follow that the deliberations
of the people are always equally correct. Our will is
always for our own good, but we do not always see what
that is : the people is never corrupted, but it is often
deceived, and on such occasions only does it seem to
will what is bad ' (Book II, chap. iii). It is impossible to
acquit Rousseau in some of the passages in which he
treats of the General Will, of something worse than
obscurity—positive contradiction. It is probable, indeed,
that he never quite succeeded in getting his view clear in
his own mind ; there is nearly always, in his treatment of
it, a certain amount of muddle and fluctuation. These
difficulties the student must be left to worry out for
himself ; it is only possible to present, in outline, what
Rousseau meant to convey.

The treatment of the General Will in the *Political
Economy* is brief and lucid, and furnishes the best guide
to his meaning. The definition of it in this work, which
has already been quoted, is followed by a short account
of the nature of *general wills* as a whole. ' Every political
society is composed of other smaller societies of various
kinds, each of which has its interest and rules of conduct ;
but those societies which everybody perceives, because
they have an external or authorised form, are not the
only ones that actually exist in the State : all individuals
who are united by a common interest compose as many
others, either temporary or permanent, whose influence
is none the less real because it is less apparent. . . . The
influence of all these tacit or formal associations causes
by the influence of their will as many modifications of
the public will. The will of these particular societies has
always two relations ; for the members of the association,
it is a general will ; for the great society, it is a particular

will ; and it is often right with regard to the first object and wrong as to the second. The most general will is always the most just, and the voice of the people is, in fact, the voice of God.'

The General Will, Rousseau continues in substance, is always for the common good ; but it is sometimes divided into smaller general wills, which are wrong in relation to it. The supremacy of the great General Will is ' the first principle of public economy and the fundamental rule of government '.

In this passage, which differs only in clearness and simplicity from others in the *Social Contract* itself, it is easy to see how far Rousseau had in his mind a perfectly definite idea. Every association of several persons creates a new common will ; every association of a permanent character has already a ' personality ' of its own, and in consequence a ' general ' will ; the State, the highest known form of association, is a fully developed moral and collective being with a common will which is, in the highest sense yet known to us, general. All collective wills are general only for the members of the associations which exercise them ; for outsiders, and also for other associations, they are purely particular wills. This applies even to the State ; ' for, in relation to what is outside it, the State becomes a simple being, an individual ' (*Social Contract*, Book I, chap. vii). In certain passages in the *Social Contract*, in his criticism of the Abbé de Saint-Pierre's *Project of Perpetual Peace*, and in the second chapter of the original draft of the *Social Contract*, Rousseau takes into account the possibility of a still higher individual, ' the federation of the world '. In the *Political Economy*, thinking of the nation-state, he affirms what in the *Social Contract* (Book II, chap. iii) he denies of the city, and recognises that the life of a nation is made up of the whole complex of its institutions and that the existence of lesser general wills is not necessarily a menace to the General Will of the State. In the *Social Contract*, he treats of these lesser wills only in relation to the government, which, he shows, has a will of its own, general for its members, but particular for the State as a whole (Book III, chap. ii). This governmental will he there prefers to call *corporate will*, and by this name it will be convenient to distinguish the lesser general wills from the General Will of the State that is over them all.

So far, there is no great difficulty ; but in discussing the infallibility of the General Will we are on more dangerous ground. Rousseau's treatment here clearly oscillates between regarding it as a purely ideal conception, to which human institutions can only approximate, and holding it to be realised actually in every republican State, *i.e.* wherever the people is the Sovereign in fact as well as of right. In Book IV, chap. ii, is the most startling passage expressing the latter view. 'When a law is proposed in the popular assembly, what the people is asked is not exactly whether it accepts or rejects the proposal, but whether it is in conformity with the general will, which is its will. . . . When, therefore, the opinion that is contrary to my own prevails, this proves neither more nor less than that I was mistaken, and that what I thought to be the general will was not so.' On his own principles laid down elsewhere, Rousseau would have to admit that it proves nothing of the sort, except in so far as the other voters have been guided by the general interest. Though he sometimes affirms the opposite, there is no security on his principles that the will of the majority will be the General Will. At the most it can only be said that there is a greater chance of its being general than of the will of any selected class of persons not being led away by corporate interests. The justification of democracy is not that it is always right, even in intention, but that it is less likely to be perverted to the service of sectional interests than any other kind of supreme power.

Fundamentally, however, the doctrine of the General Will is independent of these contradictions. Apart from Kant's narrow and rigid logic, it is essentially one with the Kantian doctrine of the autonomy of the will. Kant takes Rousseau's political theory, and applies it to ethics as a whole. The germ of this application is already found in Rousseau's own work ; for he protests more than once against attempts to treat moral and political philosophy apart, as distinct studies, and asserts their absolute unity. This is brought out clearly in the *Social Contract* (Book I, chap. viii), where he is speaking of the change brought about by the establishment of society. ' The passage from the state of nature to the civil state produces a very remarkable change in man, by substituting justice for instinct in his conduct, and giving his actions the morality they had hitherto lacked. . . . What man loses by the Social Contract is his natural liberty and an unlimited right to everything he tries to get and succeeds in getting ; what he gains is civil liberty . . . which is limited by the general will. . . . We might, over and above all this, add to what man acquires in the civil state *moral liberty, which alone makes him truly master of himself ; for the mere impulse of appetite is slavery, while obedience to a law which we prescribe to ourselves is liberty.*'

This one chapter contains the gist of the Kantian moral philosophy, and makes it quite clear that Rousseau perceived its application to ethics as well as to politics. The morality of our acts consists in their being directed in accordance with universal law ; acts in which we are guided merely by our passions are not moral. Further, man can only possess freedom when his whole being is unified in the pursuit of a single end ; and, as his whole being can be unified only in pursuit of a rational end, which alone excludes contradiction, only moral acts, only men directing their lives by universal law, are free. In Kantian language, the will is autonomous (*i.e.* pre-scribes to itself its own law) only when it is directed to a universal end ; when it is guided by selfish passions, or particular considerations, it is heteronomous (*i.e.* receives its law from something external to itself), and in bondage. Rousseau, as he says (Book I, chap. viii), was not directly

concerned with the ethical sense of the word ' liberty ',
and Kant was, therefore, left to develop the doctrine
into a system ; but the phrases of this chapter prove
false the view that the doctrine of a Real Will arises first
in connection with politics, and is only transferred
thence to moral philosophy. Rousseau bases his political
doctrine throughout on his view of human freedom ; it
is because man is a free agent capable of being determined
by a universal law prescribed by himself that the State
is in like manner capable of realising the General Will,
that is, of prescribing to itself and its members a similar
universal law.

The General Will, then, is the application of human
freedom to political institutions. Before the value of this
conception can be determined, there is a criticism to be
met. The freedom which is realised in the General Will,
we are told, is the freedom of the State *as a whole*; but
the State exists to secure *individual* freedom for its
members. A free State may be tyrannical; a despot may
allow his subjects every freedom. What guarantee is there
that the State, in freeing itself, will not enslave its
members ? This criticism has been made with such
regularity that it has to be answered in some detail.

' The problem is to find a form of association which
will defend and protect with the whole common force
the person and goods of each associate, and in which
each, while uniting himself with all, may still obey himself alone, and remain as free as before.' ' The clauses
of the contract . . . are everywhere the same and everywhere tacitly admitted and recognised. . . . These clauses,
properly understood, may be reduced to one—the total
alienation of each associate, together with all his rights,
to the whole community . . . for, if the individuals
retained certain rights, as there would be no common
superior to decide between them and the public, each,
being on one point his own judge, would ask to be so on
all, and the state of nature would continue ' (Book I,
chap. vi). Rousseau holds firmly that it is impossible to

place any limits upon the power of the State ; when the people combine into a State, they must, he says, in the last resort submit to be guided in all things by the will of the effective majority. Limited Sovereignty is a contradiction in terms ; the Sovereign has a right to all that reason allows it, and as soon as reason demands that the State shall interfere, no appeal to individual rights can be made. What is best for the State must be suffered by the individual. This, however, is very far from meaning that the ruling power ought, or has the moral right, to interfere in every particular case. Rousseau has been subjected to much mistaken criticism because, after upholding the State's absolute supremacy, he goes on (Book II, chap. iv) to speak of ' the limits of the Sovereign power'. There is no contradiction whatsoever. Wherever State intervention is for the best, he holds that the State has a right to intervene ; but it has no moral right, though it cannot be denied a legal right, to intervene where intervention is not for the best. The General Will, being always in the right, will decree intervention only when intervention is proper. ' The Sovereign ', therefore, ' cannot impose upon its subjects any fetters that are useless to the community, nor can it even wish to do so.' As, however, the infallibility of the General Will is not enough to make the State infallible, there still remains an objection. Since the General Will cannot always be arrived at, who is to judge whether an act of intervention is justified ? Rousseau's answer fails to satisfy many of his critics. ' Each man alienates, I admit, by the social compact, only such part of his powers, goods and liberty as it is important for the community to control ; but it must also be granted that the Sovereign is sole judge of what is important.' This, we are told, is mere State tyranny over again. But how is it possible for Rousseau to avoid such a conclusion ? He has already given his reasons for objecting to a limited Sovereignty (Book I, chap. vi) : it follows absolutely that men must take the best machinery they can find for the execution of the

State's functions. No doubt the machinery will be imperfect ; but men can only try to get as near the General Will as possible, without hoping to realise it fully.

Rousseau's answer, therefore, to the critics who hold that, in securing civil liberty he has sacrificed the individual may be put after this fashion. Liberty is not a merely negative conception ; it does not consist solely in the absence of restraint. The purest individualist, Herbert Spencer for example, would grant that a certain amount of State interference is necessary to *secure* liberty ; but as soon as this idea of securing liberty is admitted in the smallest degree, the whole idea has undergone profound modification. It can no longer be claimed that every interference on the part of the State lessens the liberty of the individual ; the ' liberty-fund ' theory is as untenable as that of the ' wages-fund ' : the members of a State may be more free when all are restrained from doing one another mutual damage than when any one is left ' free ' to enslave another or be himself enslaved. This principle once admitted, the precise amount of State interference that is necessary to secure freedom will be always a matter for particular discussion ; every case must be decided on its own merits, and, in right, the Sovereign will be subject only to the law of reason and not to any constitutional limitation of its powers or functions.

It has often been held that Rousseau cannot really have inspired the French Revolution because this view is totally inconsistent with the ' rights of man ', which the revolutionaries so fervently proclaimed. If every right is alienated in the Social Contract, what sense can there be in talking of ' natural rights ' afterwards ? This, however, is to misrepresent Rousseau's position. The rights of man, as they are preached by the individualist, are not the rights of which Rousseau and the revolutionaries who followed him were thinking. We have seen that the theory of the *Social Contract* is founded on human freedom : this freedom carries with it, in Rousseau's view, the guarantee of its own permanence ; it is inalienable and indestructible. When, therefore, government becomes despotic, it has no more right over its subjects than the master has over his slave (Book I, chap. iv) ; the question is then purely one of might. In such cases, appeal may be made either to the terms of the Social Contract, or, putting the same idea another way, to the ' natural right ' of human freedom. This natural right is in no sense inconsistent with the complete alienation supposed in the Contract ; for the Contract itself reposes on it and guarantees its maintenance. The Sovereign must, therefore, treat all its members alike and in accordance with the rule of reason ; and so long as it does this, its right remains unlimited. But if it leaves the general for the particular, and treats one man better than another, it ceases to be Sovereign ; for equality is already presupposed in the terms of the Contract. And, if it departs from the rule of reason, it ceases to be Sovereign.

It is more profitable to attack Rousseau for his facile indentification of the interests of each of the citizens with those of all ; but here, too, most of the critics have abused their opportunity. He does not maintain that there can be no opposition between a man's particular interests and the General Will as present in him ; on the contrary, he explicitly and consistently affirms the presence of such opposition (Book I, chap. vii). What he asserts is, first, that the Sovereign, as such, cannot have any interest contrary to the interest of the citizens as a whole—that is obvious ; and, secondly, that it cannot have an interest contrary to that of any individual. The second point Rousseau seeks to prove by showing that the omnipotence of the Sovereign is essential to the preservation of society, which in turn is necessary for the individual. His argument, however, really rests on the fundamental character of the General Will. He would admit that, in any actual State, the apparent interest of the many might often conflict with that of the few ; but we would contend that the *real* interest of State and individual alike, being subject to universal law, could not be such as to conflict with any other *real* interest. The interest of the State, in as far as it is directed by the General Will, must be the interest of every individual, in as far as he is guided by his *real* will, that is, in as far as he is acting universally, rationally, and autonomously.

Thus the justification of Rousseau's theory of liberty returns to the point from which it set out—the omnipotence of the *real will* in State and individual. It is in this sense that he speaks of man in the State as ' forced to be free ' by the General Will, much as Kant might speak of a man's lower nature as forced to be free by the universal mandate of his higher, more real and more rational will. It is in this recognition of the State as a moral being, with powers of determination similar to the powers of the individual mind, that the significance of the General Will ultimately lies. Even, however, among those who have recognised its meaning, there are some who deny its value as a conception of political philosophy. If, they say, the General Will is not the Will of All, if it cannot be arrived at by a majority vote or by any system of voting whatsoever, then it is nothing ; it is a mere abstraction, neither general, nor a will. This is, of course, precisely the criticism to which Kant's notion of ' real will ' has often been subjected. Clearly, it must be granted at once that the General Will does not form the whole actual content of the will of every citizen. Regarded as actual, it must always be qualified by ' in as far as ' or its equivalent. This, however, is so far from destroying the value of the conception that herein lies its whole value. In seeking the universal basis of society, Rousseau is not seeking anything that is wholly actualised in any State, though he must be seeking something which can exist, more or less perfectly, in every State.

The point of the Social Contract theory, as Rousseau states it, is that legitimate society exists by the consent of the people, and acts by popular will. Active will, and not force or even mere consent, is the basis of the 'republican' State, which can only possess this character because individual wills are not really self-sufficient and separate, but complementary and interdependent. The answer to the question 'Why ought I to obey the General Will ? ' is that the General Will exists in me and not outside me. I am ' obeying only myself ', as Rousseau says. The State, he is saying, is not a mere accident of human history, a mere device for the protection of life and property ; it responds to a fundamental need of human nature, and is rooted in the character of the individuals who compose it. The whole complex of human institutions is not a mere artificial structure ; it is the expression of the mutual dependence and fellowship of men. If it means anything, the theory of the General Will means that the State is natural, and the ' state of nature ' an abstraction. Without this basis of will and natural need, no society could for a moment subsist ; the State exists and claims men's obedience because it is a natural extension of their personality.

The problem, however, still remains of making the General Will, in any particular State, active and conscious. It is clear that there are States in which visible and recognised institutions hardly answer in any respect to its requirements. Even in such States, however, there is a limit to tyranny ; deep down, in immemorial customs with which the despot dare not interfere, the General Will is still active and important. It does not reside merely in the outward and visible organisation of social institutions, in that complex of formal associations which we may call the State ; its roots go deeper and its branches spread further. It is realised, in greater or less degree, in the whole life of the community, in the entire complex of private and public relations which, in the widest sense, may be called Society. It may be recognised not only in a Parliament, a Church, a University or a Trade Union, but also in the most intimate human relationships, and the most trivial, as well as the most vital, social customs.

But, if all these things go to the making of the General Will in every community, the General Will has, for politics, primarily a narrower sense. The problem here is to secure its supremacy in the official institutions and public councils of the nation. This is the question to which Rousseau chiefly addressed himself. Here, too, we shall find the notion of the General Will a strikingly original conception for the guidance of political endeavour. For the General Will is realised not when that is done which is best for the community, but when, in addition, the community as a whole has willed the doing of it. The General Will demands not only good government, but also self-government—not only rational conduct, but good-will. This is what some of Rousseau's admirers are apt to forget when they use his argument, as he himself was sometimes inclined to use it, in support of pure aristocracy. Rousseau said that aristocracy was the best of all governments, but he said also that it was the worst of all usurpers of Sovereignty. Nor must it be forgotten that he expressly specified elective aristocracy. *There is no effective General Will unless the people wills the good.* General Will may be embodied in one man willing universally ; but it can only be embodied in the State when the mass of the citizens so wills. The will must be ' general ' in two senses : in the sense in which Rousseau used the word, it must be general in its object, *i.e.* universal ; but it must also be generally held, *i.e.* common to all or to the majority.[1]

Rousseau's General Will is, then, above all a universal and, in the Kantian sense, a ' rational ' will. It would be possible to find in Rousseau many more anticipations of the views of Kant ; but it is better here to confine comment to an important difference between them. It is surprising to find in Kant, the originator of modern

[1] The term ' general will ' means, in Rousseau, not so much ' will held by several persons ', as will having a general (universal) object. This is often misunderstood ; but the mistake matters the less, because the General Will must, in fact, be both.

'intellectualism', and in Rousseau, the great apostle of 'sentiment', an essentially similar view on the nature and function of the will. Their views, however, present a difference; for, whereas the moving force of Kant's moral imperative is purely 'rational', Rousseau finds the sanction of his General Will in human feeling itself. As we can see from a passage in the original draft of the *Social Contract*, the General Will remains purely rational. 'No one will dispute that the General Will is in each individual a pure act of the understanding, which reasons while the passions are silent on what a man may demand of his neighbour and on what his neighbour has a right to demand of him.' The will itself remains purely rational, but Rousseau feels that it needs an external motive power. 'If natural law', he writes 'were written only on the tablets of human reason it would be incapable of guiding the greater part of our actions; but it is also graven on the heart of man in characters that cannot be effaced, and it is there it speaks to him more strongly than all the precepts of the philosophers' (from an unfinished essay on *The State of War*). The nature of this guiding sentiment is explained in the *Discourse on Inequality* (p. 197, note 2), where egoism (*amour-propre*) is contrasted with self-respect (*amour de soi*). Naturally, Rousseau holds, man does not want everything for himself, and nothing for others. 'Egoism' and 'altruism' are both one-sided qualities arising out of the perversion of man's 'natural goodness'. 'Man is born good'; that is, man's nature really makes him desire only to be treated as one among others, to share equally. This natural love of equality (*amour de soi*) includes love of others as well as love of self, and egoism, loving one's self at the expense of others, is an unnatural and perverted condition. The 'rational' precepts of the General Will, therefore, find an echo in the heart of the 'natural' man, and, if we can only secure the human being against perversion by existing societies, the General Will can be made actual.

This is the meeting-point of Rousseau's educational with his political theory. His view as a whole can be studied only by taking together the *Social Contract* and *Émile* as explained by the *Letters on the Mount* and his other works. The fundamental dogma of the natural goodness of man finds no place directly in the *Social Contract* ; but it lurks behind the whole of his political theory, and is indeed, throughout, his master-conception. However often he may contradict himself in detail, his educational, his religious, his political, and his ethical ideas are all inspired by this single consistent attitude. Here we have been attending only to his political theory ; and accordingly his ideas have been presented only from one angle and in a partial way. His political works, however, can be read separately, and the *Social Contract* itself is still by far the best of all text-books of idealist political philosophy. As new generations and new classes of men come to the study of his work, his conceptions, often hazy and undeveloped, but nearly always of lasting importance, form the basis of new political philosophies, in which they are taken up and transformed.

For good and for evil each generation reinterprets Rousseau in its own way. In our own, for example, he is invoked both by democrats insistent on the ultimate right of the common people and by Fascists who see in his notion of Sovereignty the theoretical justification of the Corporative State. For, where one man will find in his writings an unanswerable case for subordinating all particular wills to the omnipotent will of the Sovereign State, others, penetrating more deeply, I think, into the spirit of his thought, will insist that what matters most in his doctrine is the insistence that, as every government tends to substitute its own will for the will of the people (Book III, chap. x), the essential foundation for all good government is the lively and continuous assertion by the whole body of citizens of their claim to Sovereignty, and the refusal to accept a merely passive rôle of subordination which involves a denial of their share in the expression of the General Will. In effect, Rousseau's cardinal contribution to political theory is his assertion that will and not force is the only legitimate basis for social obligation, and that the General Will, present in every citizen, provides the only nexus between men that is consistent with reason and capable of reconciling the claims of society with those of personal freedom and self-expression. For Rousseau, the basis of society is in the will of the people, and not in the superior sagacity of a ruling caste. Sovereignty is in the people ; and this Sovereignty is for ever inalienable and in need of continuous exercise.

Now, all this may seem, to many of us, far too idealistic. Rousseau is perpetually talking about rights, whereas our problem is to deal with positive forces resting not upon abstract right but upon possession or usurpation. There is nothing in Rousseau about the struggle of classes, or the materialistic basis of social institutions, or the evolutionary character of social relationships, or the dependence of men's political ideas on the changing forces which determine their ways of living.

All this is true. Rousseau is not Marx, or his John the Baptist. He is an Idealist philosopher, thinking throughout in terms of what *ought* to be, even though he is perpetually qualifying his categorical imperatives by reference to practical probabilities. If ' ought ' is to be eliminated from the vocabulary of politics, perhaps Rousseau is to be eliminated as well. But can we so easily, even if we accept Marx, empty out the categorical imperative ? Material forces set limits to what can be achieved ; but who could feel even a moment's enthusiasm for the classless society unless he believed it to be desirable, as well as historically necessary ? Marx himself certainly never meant to empty human will out of history. On the contrary, he was insistent upon its creative rôle. And I think Rousseau can legitimately be held, with all his Idealism in a philosophical sense, to have asserted, much more challengingly and positively than anyone before him, the creative power of the common people and the practical possibility of founding the social system, not upon tradition or inertia or prescription, but upon the social will and energy latent in every citizen, and capable of responding to the cry of human suffering and of human hope.

Marx's ' Capital '

KARL MARX'S *Capital* is not an easy book to read. It is difficult in itself, because it deals with a highly difficult and abstract subject-matter, and even more because its method implies, for full understanding, a knowledge of the economic doctrines and philosophical ideas current when it was written. Marx's mind was at once highly abstract and highly critical. He was determined always to penetrate beneath the phenomenal form of things to what he conceived as a reality underlying their appearance ; and he thought most naturally by casting his ideas into the form of a criticism of preceding doctrines. Philosophers such as Hegel, economists such as Ricardo, stalk through his pages to the bewilderment of those who approach his work without some prior knowledge of the history of philosophical and economic theories.

This difficulty, considerable enough in itself, was made far greater than it need have been by the poor quality of the translations in which Marx's doctrines were presented to English readers. This did not matter so much in the case of his pamphlets, such as the *Communist Manifesto* ; for the general character of their thought was usually too plain for even the worst translation seriously to obscure it. But the understanding in England of Marx's larger works, and especially of his greatest work, *Capital*, has been greatly obstructed by an English version at all points difficult to read, and at some almost unintelligible without reference to the German original.

The recent translation, made by Eden and Cedar Paul, finally removes this obstacle, as far as the first, and most important, volume of *Capital* is concerned. For the new version is at once faithful and readable. It does say exactly what Marx said, as far as any translation can convey the meaning of an original ; and it does read, as far as any translation can read, like an original work. It is a remarkable achievement, on which I cannot forbear to congratulate both its authors and the public. And it is greatly to be hoped that it will be possible for the same translators to put the crown to their undertaking by rendering into English the later volumes of *Capital*. For these, while a large part of them is by no means equal in importance to the opening volume, are in some respects essential to a full understanding of Marx's doctrines. Indeed, the third volume contains what is, in effect, the explanation of the first.

The reader of the first volume, however, while he has not Marx's complete work before him, has all of it that was issued in Marx's lifetime, and all that has exerted a widespread influence on European thought. Most people, even most Marxists, when they speak of *Capital*, mean mainly the part of it that was published in 1867. Marxism arose, and spread over Europe to become the inspiration of a developing Socialist movement, long before the posthumous volumes of *Capital* were disinterred from Marx's papers and given to the public by his faithful friend and collaborator, Friedrich Engels. And while there are, as we shall see, some points of Marxian doctrine to which no complete answer can be found in the part of *Capital* which Marx himself lived to publish, it does contain explicitly by far the greater part of Marxism, and the rest by implication.

But even in the most excellent translation, *Capital* is not an easy book to read ; and its widespread influence therefore seems to call for some explanation. In part, the explanation is that Marx's influence does not rest on *Capital* alone. Many more people have read the *Communist Manifesto*, and such pamphlets as *Wage-Labour and Capital* and *Value, Price and Profit*, in which Marx gave a brief exposition of certain parts of his doctrine, than have even dipped into *Capital* itself. Moreover, Marx's influence, in his own lifetime, was by no means confined to his writings. He was the active organiser and practical leader of the Socialist movements of his day, as well as their theoretician. Marx expressed himself practically in the International Working Men's Association of 1864— the ' First International '—as well as theoretically in *Capital* and the *Critique of Political Economy*.

This practical side of Marxism was, indeed, vital to its influence. Men set out to master Marx's theoretical position, and felt a disposition to accept it, largely because they found themselves carried on the wave of the actual movement of working-class agitation which he had helped to organise and to inspire. This is not to suggest that Marx created this movement, which sprang essentially out of the economic conditions and class-antagonisms of the time ; but he did contribute greatly to giving it form and direction, and those who were drawn into the movement were thus readily induced to consider favourably the doctrines of its chief theoretical interpreter.

Approached from this standpoint, Marxism as a doctrine was—and is—far less formidable than Marxism enshrined in a book. For Marx's fundamental ideas, from this angle, present themselves not as difficult or elusive at all, but as perfectly straightforward and immediate in their appeal. They fit in with the working-class Socialist's experience of everyday affairs, and throw the sanction of a system over the familiar propagandist appeals of his Trade Union or his grumbling fellow worker at the bench. The notion that the poor man gets less than his due, and that the rich man lives by exploiting the poor, is not at all hard to grasp. There have been poor men who held it—and perhaps rich men too—ever since riches and poverty first existed in the world. And what is Marx's doctrine of Surplus Value but an elaborate theoretical formulation of the method by which, in capitalist society, this exploitation takes place ?

Nor is there anything hard to grasp about Marx's

second idea that ' the State is an executive committee for managing the affairs of the governing class as a whole '. The idea of ' one law for the rich and another for the poor ' is also as old as riches and poverty. It did not need Marx to invent the idea of State and law as powers external to the wills and interests of classes which were excluded from any active part in their administration. Marx formulated this popular notion into a theory of the State ; but in this, as in his theory of Surplus Value, he was building on ideas already prevalent, and not at all hard even for the simplest minds to grasp.

These two simple ideas underlie all Marx's thought. But they are conceived, not statically, but throughout in a dynamic sense. Both the economic exploitation and the political domination of class by class appear to him as manifested in a succession of great historical movements. He sees human history as a series of class struggles which are at once economic and political in their character. The opposing classes change again and again in the course of historical evolution ; but the struggle goes on, and will go on as long as production and the State are organised on a basis of class differentiation. The struggle between labourers and capitalists, which is the present phase of this evolutionary process, Marx regards as a stage—the last stage—of humanity's march towards a classless society. The historic mission of the working class—the last class left to be exploited—is, by victory in its struggle with Capitalism, to make an end of classes altogether.

Now, this idea of historical evolution, with the struggle of classes as its *motif*, is in itself a good deal harder to grasp than either the idea of exploitation or the idea of the State as an instrument of class-power. The grasping of it marks the transition from those elementary ideas which are the common stock of popular Socialist agitation to Marxism as a theory. But it is not, and above all it was not, to the more educated workers of Marx's day, really a difficult step. Even before Darwin, the idea of evolution was becoming part of the common stock of thought. It had expressed itself not only in popular science, but also in popular philosophy. Hegel's influence on ideas extended far beyond philosophical circles ; and popular geology spread the evolutionary idea long before popular biology came to reinforce it through the writings of Darwin and Huxley and Herbert Spencer. Men's minds were ready, even if they had never heard of Hegel, for an evolutionary interpretation of human history ; and Marx's ' inverted Hegelianism ', even if its form was not easy, was not in itself difficult to appreciate in its broader aspects.

It is, however, true that, until our own day, popular Marxism tended to stress the simple theory of exploitation, as expressed theoretically in Marx's doctrine of Surplus Value, more than his idea of historical evolution, as expressed in his Materialist Conception of History. Or rather, the latter tended to appear as little more than a rhetorical reference to the ' historic mission ' of the working class, whereas the former occupied a far more dominant place in Marxian propaganda and exposition.

This situation has now changed, partly as a result of the emphasis placed upon the Materialist Conception of History by the school of Marxists that has made most stir in the world of late—the Communists of Russia— but more fundamentally because the upsets and self-questionings caused all over Europe by the Great War have set men thinking more in historical terms, and made them more intent to find some unifying significance behind the welter of destruction and creation that has come upon them of late. It is now generally recognised that the Materialist Conception of History is the clue to the Marxian system and that Marx's other doctrines grouped themselves in his mind round this conception as an organising principle of thought.

One of the chief difficulties in the way of a clear understanding of Marxism is that Marx has nowhere written down any full account of this principle. It is implicit and not explicit in most of his work. In *Capital* it is present throughout in the background, guiding the course of the exposition and imposing itself upon the argument at every stage. But in *Capital* it is never formulated at all. The reader is left to infer it as a consequence of the marshalling of fact and argument round the central analysis of capitalist society. It can be inferred in this way ; but *Capital* is an easier book to read if the reader comes to it with some idea of this architectonic conception of its author's already in his mind.

This can best be got from certain of Marx's earlier writings, notably from the *Communist Manifesto* of 1848, and from the *Critique of Political Economy*, published in 1859, eight years before the appearance of the first volume of *Capital*. The *Communist Manifesto* applies the Materialist Conception of History to the social and economic struggles of nineteenth-century Europe, and thus shows that it was already the governing principle of Marx's thought almost at the outset of his career ; but the *Manifesto*, like *Capital*, does not directly expound the doctrine, but rather implies it. It is in the Preface to the *Critique of Political Economy* that Marx directly explains what is at the back of his mind—what underlies both his criticism of the orthodox economists and his attempt to construct a rival system of his own. As the *Critique* is, in essence, a preliminary sketch of *Capital*, which works out its ideas more maturely and in greater detail, the Preface to the *Critique* may well serve also as a preface to the understanding of the greater work.

The form of the Preface is autobiographical. Marx explains in it how, beginning as a student of jurisprudence and of philosophy and history, he was led to take up the study of economic questions partly by being brought into contact with the earlier schools of French Socialism, and partly by a growing dissatisfaction with the dominant schools of Hegelianism. ' I was led ', he writes, ' by my studies to the conclusion that legal relations and the forms of the State could neither be understood by themselves, nor be explained by what was called the general " progress of the human mind ", but were rooted in the material conditions of life. . . . The general conclusion which I reached, and which, once I had reached it, continued to serve as the leading thread of my work, may be summed up briefly as follows : Men, in the social production which they carry on, enter into definite relations which are indispensable and independent of their wills ; and these relations correspond to a definite stage in the development of their material powers of production. The sum-total of these relations of production constitutes the economic structure of society—the real foundation on which rise legal and political superstructures and to which definite forms of social consciousness correspond. The method of production in material life determines the general character of the social, political, and spiritual processes of life. It is not the consciousness of men that determines their being, but, on the contrary, their social being determines their consciousness.'

In other words, Marx had come to hold that the clue to the understanding of history was to be found in the development of the powers of production. Men's over-mastering need was to get the means of living ; and the ways in which they did this, and the differences in the natural resources at their disposal and in their knowledge of the use of these resources—Man's command over Nature—at different times and places determined not only how the productive system would be organised, but also how man would be related to man in the structure of society, how social classes would be formed, property relations organised, and even how men would think, because the kind and degree of their command over nature would set them the problems that they would attempt to solve. At the bottom of all great historical conditions Marx saw men's power to provide themselves with the means of living ; and behind all great historical movements he saw changes in the character and extent of this same power.

Clearly this view—the first principle of the Marxian theory of history—cannot be lightly dismissed. Every anthropologist or sociologist will agree that men's ways of getting their living have a profound effect on the structure of the societies in which they live. Contrasts between the characteristic social institutions of hunters and fishermen, pastoralists and tillers of the soil, inland plain-dwellers and maritime peoples, are the common-places of every modern sociological writer. No one will deny that such great economic discoveries as the steam-engine have revolutionised political as well as economic relationships in the modern world, or that the moment at which the progress of man's command over nature changed the ocean from a barrier into a highway was of vast consequence for the economic, political, and cultural future of the world. It will not, indeed, be so readily admitted that in the changing powers of production lies the *sole* clue to the development of human history ; but their importance as a clue will hardly be gainsaid by anyone in these days.

At this point, however, we encounter already a difficulty in the interpretation of Marx's thought. Marx conceived that his view was essentially *materialist*—an inversion of the idealistic, Hegelian view of reality. But was it ? Is it possible to conceive these ' powers of production ' in purely materialist terms ? Coal is nothing to man till he knows how to use it ; the sea is barrier or highway according to the skill and courage of those who dwell beside it. What nature provides doubtless limits man's achievement ; but nature's provision depends in effect upon man's knowledge. Would Marx answer that man discovers only what nature thrusts under his nose, and is bound to discover what nature does so put before him in nature's due time ? Unless we do hold this, it is difficult to regard the ' powers of production ' as a purely material datum. As ' powers of production ' they are essentially products of the human mind, as well as gifts of nature.

Marx, I think, is not at all concerned to deny this. Indeed, the creative rôle of humanity is stressed again and again in his work. But the mind of man appears to him as a social product and as part of the reality which he contrasts as material with the purely ideal reality of the Hegelians. Much of the prejudice against his doctrine comes from a failure to understand this. Marx's materialism is not materialistic in the sense that it excludes the action of mind, but only in that it seeks its reality in the world of men and things, and not in any universe of ideas transcending this world and its limitations.

So far, however, we have reached only the first step in the statement of Marx's doctrine. The next step brings us a good deal nearer to a comprehensive statement. The Materialist Conception of History is a doctrine, not of being, but of becoming. It sets out to explain not simply why things are what they are, but how they are in process of becoming something else. The ' powers of production ' are constantly changing as the form and extent of man's command over nature change ; and these changes in the ' powers of production ' call for corresponding changes in economic, political, and social organisation. As the ' powers of production ' are modified, men need different systems for the organisation of labour, different class relationships, different regulations of property, different forms of government, and, in general, different ways of life and thought. These adaptations, however, are not easily or smoothly made ; for each social institution, once established, gathers round it defenders who are reluctant to see it pass away, whose interests are bound up with its continuance. Accordingly, the adaptation of economic, political, and social institutions has a tendency to lag behind the evolution of the ' powers of production ', and is brought to correspond with it only by the sharp shock of revolution. In Marx's own words, ' the material powers of production in society, at a certain stage of their development, came into conflict with the existing relations of production, or—what is but a legal expression for the same thing—with the property relations within which they were previously at work. These relations of production then turn from forms of development of the powers of production into fetters upon them. Then comes the period of social revolution. With a change in the economic foundation of society the entire immense superstructure is more or less rapidly transformed. . . . No social order ever disappears until all the productive powers for which there is room within it have been developed ; and new, higher relations of production never make their appearance until the material conditions of their existence have been developed in the womb of the old society.'

It is at this point that the form of Marx's doctrine most clearly reveals his Hegelian inheritance. History, for him as for Hegel, progresses by a method of contradiction. Each social system, based on a particular stage in the evolution of the ' powers of production ', is a thesis, which calls into being its antithesis. Thus, at the present stage, the capitalist system, as thesis, is compelled, for the development of the very ' powers of production ' on which it is based, to call into being its own antithesis, the organisation of labour as a class. It must, in order to make the most of its own methods of production, aggregate the workers into factories and factory towns, and subject them to a common discipline which calls into existence the challenge of an organised Labour movement. Capitalism is, at its coming, a forward step in the organisation of the ' powers of production ', but by and by Capitalism, having done its work, will become a fetter on the development of these growing ' powers '. The processes of production will need a higher and more closely co-ordinated form of social production than Capitalism is able to supply ; and the working class, having learnt solidarity under the capitalist discipline, will be ready to assume the task of creating this higher form of organisation. The capitalists, however, will not give way without a struggle; and out of this contest between capitalist thesis and proletarian antithesis the synthesis of the new classless society will arise. Just as the capitalist class absorbed the old feudal landlords into a synthesis appropriate to the capitalist stage of development of the ' powers of production ', so in due time the proletariat will absorb the capitalists. But there will be this difference, that there will be no subject class left to exploit. With the victory of the working class, Marx proclaims, ' pre-history ends, and history begins '.

This Hegelian conception of thesis-antithesis-synthesis expresses itself in Marx's writings as a theory of the historical process working itself out through a series of class struggles. At each stage of human history, thesis and antithesis are social classes placed in a situation of mutual economic antagonism, and the synthesis is achieved by a new system of class relationships. Marx's theory of history is not only, or primarily, a theory of the dominance of economic factors in the development of society. It is above all a theory of class struggles as the form in which this ' economic determinism ' is worked out. This view is clearly stated in the sweeping generalisations of the *Communist Manifesto*; and the historical chapters of *Capital*, in which Marx describes the genesis of Capitalism (Chapter 26) and the evolution, through ' manufacture ', of the modern system of machine production (Chapters 12 and 13), are applications of the same method to the study of capitalist society. These historical chapters are easily the most readable, and in many respects the best, in the whole book. They are still the clearest accounts of the broader developments of capitalist organisation, and especially of its growth in the centuries immediately preceding the Industrial Revolution of the eighteenth and early nineteenth centuries.

Marx's Materialist Conception of History has been often misunderstood. As will be seen from the foregoing account, it has nothing whatever to do with any psychological theory of the motives which guide the actions of

individual men. Marx does not say, as some have represented him as saying, that men act only from economic motives, or solely with a view to securing their
own advantage or pleasure. His view has nothing in
common with any kind of economic Benthamism. It does
not deal at all with the question of human motives. What
Marx urges is that the broad transformations of society
from epoch to epoch arise from economic conditions, in
a wide sense, and that men, from whatever motives they
act, are in fact and in the mass guided in what they
achieve by these conditions. The development of the
' powers of production ' sets them their problems ; and
' mankind always takes up only such problems as it can
solve '. Often, men fight out their conflict in ' ideological
forms ' which serve to conceal its real character ; but
these forms have to be ' explained from the contradictions of material life, from the conflict between the social
powers of production and the existing relations of production '. In other words, an individual man may think
as he pleases, or act from what motives he pleases,
within the limitation that he cannot escape from the
ideas and problems set him by his time ; but the ideas
that become forces in world evolution are those which
can contribute to the development of the ' powers of
production ', and to the adjustment to these powers of
the economic and social relations existing among men.

This conception is the clue to the rest of Marx's
thought. His theory of Surplus Value and his criticism
of the classical economists of his own day are but
workings-out of it in the particular sphere of contemporary economic theory. The arrangement of his
book, however, serves to conceal this from his readers,
and to make the drift of his argument unnecessarily
hard to follow. For *Capital* opens, not with an account
of Marx's theory of history, but with ten chapters devoted
mainly to a detailed exposition of his theory of value.

For the modern reader who approaches Marx in any
spirit save that of blind acceptance, these chapters are

extraordinarily hard to understand. They cannot, in fact, be fully understood except in relation to the doctrines of those classical economists with whom Marx is always eager to break a lance. At the outset, Marx's main thesis in them appears to be that the ' value ' of commodities depends exclusively upon the amount of labour involved in their production. This labour, however, is not the labour of this or that particular kind of craftsman, but an abstract undifferentiated human labour which has as little regard for the qualities of different men as the conception of ' horse-power ' has for that of individual horses. All actual labour, it is argued, can be resolved into so much of this abstract labour, skilled labour counting as a multiple of it, so that an hour's labour of a skilled craftsman may count for, say, two hours of abstract labour. Secondly, the ' amount of labour ' that enters into the ' value ' of commodities is not the actual amount expended on the production of each commodity, but the amount that is ' socially necessary '—the amount required to produce the commodity under the average conditions prevailing at the time and place in question. The socially necessary amount of this abstract labour is the sole factor that can influence the value of any commodity.

All this Marx says, and much of the modern criticism of Marxism is directed to showing that this view is wrong. But it is important to observe that not one single idea in this theory of value was invented by Marx, or would have been regarded by him as an original contribution of his own to economic science. Marx merely took over this conception of value from the classical economists, omitting no doubt certain ambiguous refinements in their doctrine, but broadly repeating what they had said, and what most economists of the earlier nineteenth century implicitly believed. There is nothing specifically Marxian about Marx's theory of value ; what is novel is the use to which he puts the theory, and not the theory itself.

The contribution of Marx to the theory of value is not the idea that ' labour is the sole measure of value ', but the conception of Surplus Value which he derives from it. The classical economists had held broadly, first, that the value of commodities depends on the amount of labour incorporated in them, and secondly, that the wages of labour tend always to subsistence level. Out of these two ingredients of the classical doctrine Marx compounds his doctrine of Surplus Value. Adam Smith, Malthus, and Ricardo had all put forward, in different ways, a subsistence theory of wages ; and, in the two latter at least, this doctrine had been closely linked up with a theory of population. Wages must tend to subsistence level because, if they were above it, the population would increase, and the competition of more labourers for employment would thus tend to bring them back to it. It was, indeed, admitted that, in a society advancing in prosperity, wages might remain long enough, because of an increasing demand for labour, above an established level of subsistence to enable the labourers to incorporate a new and higher level in their standard of life. Subsistence level might thus change ; and it was recognised as possessing always and everywhere a conventional element. But, with this reservation, the wages of labour were assumed to bear a fixed relation to the price of the necessaries of life.

This doctrine, together with the ' labour theory of value ', Marx takes over from the classical economists. But he draws from both notions conclusions widely different from theirs. Of all the ' factors of production ', he holds that labour—including brain-work as well as manual work—is alone creative. The materials used up in production, the instruments of production—all things that capital can buy except labour-power—create nothing. They can only transfer to the final product unchanged the value of the labour already incorporated in them. The labourer, on the other hand, produces more than is necessary for his subsistence. But he is paid

274

only enough to enable him to subsist and to reproduce his kind. The rest of his product passes to the capitalist who has bought his labour-power for a subsistence wage. This surplus over and above the cost of the labourers' subsistence is Surplus Value, and is the source out of which rent, interest, and profits are paid. It arises because the labourer, divorced from direct access to the land or other means of production, cannot realise directly the value of his productive power, but can only sell his labour-power to a capitalist in order to get the means of life. The existence of a working class, thus divorced from the means of production, is essential to the existence of capitalism ; and the genesis of this class is also the genesis of capitalist society.

Why does this Surplus Value exist at all, or, in other words, how does it come about that the labourer is able to produce a value in excess of the cost of his subsistence ? Marx's answer is that the surplus is due to the economic benefits of co-operation and the division of labour. A number of men working together as a group can produce far more than the same number working in isolation. But they can thus work together only if they can provide themselves with a growingly expensive equipment of productive instruments. This the propertyless man cannot do ; but the capitalist can do it for him, and is thus enabled to appropriate, as Surplus Value, the entire increment of productivity due to the co-operative use of labour. The labourer is paid the value of his individual labour-power in terms of subsistence ; the capitalist gets all that is over and above this, and the surplus is, in view of the growing productivity of labour, of ever-increasing magnitude.

These are the essential elements of the Marxian doctrine of Surplus Value. Marx's critics have seldom attacked directly this part of his theory. They have preferred to concentrate their attack on the Labour Theory of Value, which he took over practically unaltered from the classical economists, rather than on the theory of

Surplus Value, thinking doubtless that, if the foundations were destroyed, the whole structure would certainly collapse. It is, however, fully possible to hold the theory of Surplus Value without holding the Labour Theory of Value on which, superficially, it appears to depend.

By all economists save the Marxists, the Labour Theory of Value has long been derided. How it came to be discarded by the orthodox schools I can best explain if, for the moment, I may leave Marx and Marxism altogether aside. In the classical economists, the Labour Theory of Value was definitely at the same time a theory of price. Ricardo and his followers were seeking for a principle underlying the relative prices of different commodities in the market. They realised that market prices might change, not only with monetary conditions, but in accordance with the daily fluctuations of supply and demand. But they held that, as monetary changes would tend to react equally on all prices, they could be ignored in considering the laws of value, and that, underlying the constant fluctuations of supply and demand, there must be some natural value to which the market price of any commodity would tend to return when supply and demand were in normal equilibrium. This natural value, they thought, must be something intrinsic in the commodity itself, or at any rate something derived directly from its conditions of production. The one quality common to most commodities seemed to be that of being products of human labour ; and accordingly, with varying reservations, they adopted the view that the relative values of commodities in exchange were determined, subject to temporary market fluctuations, by the amounts of labour incorporated in them.

This view, however, as a theory of prices, could not survive the test of practical application. It was evident that the whole cost of producing a commodity equally influenced the conditions of its supply, and that, as soon as commodities were produced with different ' compositions of capital ', so that some were made mainly by labour directly, while others involved the use of expensive machinery and a considerable lock-up of fixed capital for their production, their prices, as determined by supply conditions, could not depend solely on the amounts of labour incorporated in them. Ricardo, in two extraordinarily muddled chapters, attempted to confront this difficulty only to give it up later (in his Correspondence) as a bad job. His successors, especially John Stuart Mill, attempted to restate the theory as a ' cost of production ', or ' price of production ', theory, in which no longer the amount of labour, but all the money costs of production ranked as the determinants of normal or natural price or value. Then came Jevons, who sought a way out of the confusion by shifting the emphasis from the conditions of supply to those of demand, and representing the values, or prices, of commodities as measured in all cases, not by ' amount of labour ', or ' price of production ', but by their ' utility ' to the consumer, expressed in the prices which he was prepared to pay for them. According to this view, the price which the consumer would pay for the last ' dose ' bought—the ' marginal utility '—measured the value.

Jevons had, indeed, to recognise that there were conditions of supply as well as of demand to be taken into account. Buyers could not buy unless sellers were willing to sell ; and there were thus ' marginal supply prices ' below which producers would not go as well as ' marginal demand prices ' which buyers would not exceed. Among English economists, it was left for Alfred Marshall to restate the new theory in terms of an unstable equilibrium between the two. At different prices, suppliers would supply, and consumers purchase, different amounts. Actually, prices would settle round the points at which the quantities sellers would sell, and consumers buy, tended to coincide. In effect, Marshall hedged. Prices, he held, were determined in the short run more by demand than by supply, and in the long run more by supply than by demand.

All modern theories—if we may still leave the Marxists aside for the moment—are very far removed from the ' amount of labour ' theory which Marx took over from Ricardo and McCulloch. How, then, does it happen that the Marxists have gone on for quite half a century reaffirming Marx's view, and have remained wholly unshaken by all the criticisms that orthodox economists have been able to bring against them ? The answer, paradoxical as it may seem, is that Marx's theory in no way contradicts Marshall's, because it is not a theory of the determination of market prices. When Marx says that the *value* of commodities depends absolutely on the amount of socially necessary labour incorporated in them, he does not say that their market prices depend upon this. The reader of the first volume of *Capital* will, indeed, unless he reads with exceptional care, be apt to conclude that this is what Marx means ; for he speaks usually as if commodities had actually a tendency, subject to temporary market fluctuations, to exchange at their ' values '. But he says explicitly that he does not mean this ; and in the third volume of *Capital* he fully develops his point, and makes the inevitable divergence of prices and ' values ' abundantly clear.

It is necessary, in order to elucidate this point, to retrace some of the steps of our argument. Marx, we have seen, has contended not only that the ' value ' of commodities is measured solely by the amount of labour incorporated in them, but also—which is not the same thing—that the sole agent creative of value is human labour. Now, of the capital applied to production, a part is spent in buying labour-power, and another part in buying the materials and instruments of production. Marx holds that only the former part of the capital can be regarded as productive of value, and that the latter part can only transfer to the final commodity the value already created by the labour which produced the materials or the instruments of production which it is

278

used to buy. Capital, as we have seen, engenders surplus value because it is able to buy labour-power for less than labour, when expended, can produce. But only capital spent in buying labour-power can engender this value. Capital spent on materials or machinery has no such potency. Accordingly, Marx calls the capital expended in buying materials or machinery Constant Capital, because it only transfers its value unchanged to the finished commodity, whereas he calls capital spent in buying labour-power Variable Capital, because it has the potency of yielding a surplus to its owner.

This distinction, in the form in which it was expounded in the first volume of *Capital*, exposed Marx to formidable attacks. If he were right, it was urged, it ought to pay capitalists best to employ as much labour and as little machinery as possible ; for by doing so they would keep most of their capital in the ' variable ' form, and thus tend to realise for themselves the greatest amount of Surplus Value. In fact, however, it certainly pays capitalists to employ labour-saving machinery, even though in doing so, on Marx's showing, they reduce the proportion of their total capital out of which Surplus Value can possibly arise.

Marx's answer is twofold. In the first volume of *Capital* he replies in terms of the subsistence theory of wages and of the temporary advantage accruing to the particular capitalist who first applies improved machinery to production. Such a capitalist, it is pointed out, is able to secure a greater product in return for a given expenditure of labour. Until his competitors have adopted productive methods as good as his own, he is able to sell his wares for more than he needs in order to recoup him ; for their prices continue to be determined by the average methods of production in use in the trade. Each individual capitalist has therefore an incentive to introduce new machinery in order to reap this advantage ; and, when he has done so, his competitors are compelled to follow suit. Moreover, every labour-saving device which reduces the value, or production cost, of the means of subsistence, tends also to reduce the cost of labour's subsistence, and therefore the wages of the labourer. Thus, less of the working day is spent by the labourer in providing for his own subsistence, and more in creating Surplus Value for the capitalist. In Marxian language, the rate of Surplus Value is increased by adding to the Relative Surplus Value created.

This answer, however, is not complete. For the benefit of the cheapening of the means of subsistence, and therefore of wages, would redound to the advantage of all capitalists equally, and would thus leave unchanged the disparity of Surplus Value between those capitalists who used a high or low proportion of Constant, and a low or high proportion of Variable, Capital. The yield of Surplus Value to different capitalists would still remain widely different, according to the different compositions of their capital. What then ? Surely capitalists will rush into the occupations which, because of their high proportion of Variable Capital, have the tendency to yield the greatest Surplus Value, and will rush away from those occupations in which the opposite conditions exist.

This, says Marx, is precisely what will happen, until the competition of capitalists in the more desirable occupations, and the dearth of competition in the less desirable, so affect the prices of the various classes of goods as to bring the profits on total capital (constant and variable together) down or up to a common standard in all the competing industries. Profits have a tendency to equalisation in all employments (here again Marx is merely echoing the classical economists) ; and by this equalisation the Surplus Value realised by the exploitation of labour will be redistributed among the whole body of capitalists in proportion to the total magnitude of their invested capital.

But how does this readjustment take place ? It can occur only through the instrumentality of prices. In order that the profits of the more favourably situated capitalists may fall to the average, competition must reduce the prices they are able to charge.

If, however, prices are to serve as the means of redistributing Surplus Value, there can be no tendency for prices to coincide with ' values ' based upon the amount of labour incorporated in each commodity. It is, Marx agrees in volume three, a mere accident if, in a particular case, price and ' value ' happen to coincide.

Of what, then, is the Marxian theory of ' value ' a theory, if it is not a theory of price ? Marx's answer to this question, developed in the third volume of *Capital*, is, on the face of it, utterly paradoxical. There is, he says, in the last resort no such thing as an isolated and separate commodity, or branch of production. Capitalism is essentially associated and co-ordinated production, based on enlisting the forces of labour co-operation on the side of capitalist Surplus Value. It is all nonsense to claim for the individual labourer any ' right to the whole produce ' of his labour ; for his labour has no produce that can be separately reckoned. It is inextricably mingled with that of countless other workers. Similarly, it is impossible to isolate the product created in any factory, or any branch of capitalist production. In essence, there is but one product, but one gigantic associated capitalist, and but one many-handed labourer yoked to the task of creating Surplus Value. Prices of individual commodities are but devices by means of which the capitalist class shares this Surplus Value. The amount of labour incorporated in production measures finally the ' value ', not of this or that particular commodity, but of the social product as a whole.

Here, yet again, Marx's Hegelian affinities stand out clearly. The One is, for him, more real than the Many ; and he is always reaching out after a real Oneness underlying the phenomenal multiplicity of the capitalist world. He envisages a working class, which he had attempted to organise in the International Working Men's Association, in process of becoming one, and he sees the capitalists of the world as banded together against the working class. This oneness alone is real. The prices of individual commodities are mere appearances. What is real is the one fact of exploitation—the appropriation by the capitalist class of the economic advantages of associated production. The ' detail labourer ' is a mere abstraction ; not individuals, but only social classes, possess ultimate reality.

It is impossible thoroughly to understand Marx's thought without appreciating this mystical view of reality. Marx's view of history made him regard social classes as far more real and creative than individual persons. The theme of *Capital* is not the exploitation of individual labourers by individual capitalists, but of one whole class by another. He who would criticise Marx must begin by either accepting or attacking this fundamental concept. It conditions the entire Marxian system.

It also makes that system immune from attack by any of the ordinary methods of criticism employed by economists of the orthodox schools. For if ' values ' in the Marxian sense have no tendency to coincide with prices, what is to be said ? It cannot be demonstrated, by any argument drawn from the realm of prices, that ' values ' do not depend on the amount of labour incorporated in each commodity. It may indeed be urged, with some force, that there is no valid reason for erecting this concept of ' value ', as apart from price, at all, and that the entire Marxian theory is, on this point, a useless construction in the air, due to historical conditions, and certainly not worth preserving to-day. As far as the labour theory of value in itself is concerned, I am disposed to agree with this view ; for I feel quite sure that Marx would never have constructed a theory of ' value ' unrelated to price unless he had begun by criticising a false theory of value as related to price that was prevalent among the classical economists of his own day.

If, however, we abandon the Marxian theory of value,

does Marx's theory of Surplus Value, which was his distinctive contribution to economic doctrine, therefore fall to the ground ? I do not think it does, though much in the manner of its expression will obviously need to be modified. For the theory that the measure of the relative values of commodities is to be found in the amounts of labour incorporated in them has really nothing to do with the much more significant theory that labour, by hand or brain, is the sole positive agent in the creation of wealth, and that the owners of capital are able, by virtue of their ownership, to appropriate to themselves a large part, if not the whole, of the surplus product due to the economic advantages of associated production. This is the true foundation on which the theory of Surplus Value rests ; and it brings into relief the close relationship of the theory to Marx's doctrine of history. These two conceptions may be accepted or rejected ; but it is pertinent to point out that neither of them stands or falls with the ' Labour Theory of Value ', and that they, and not the ' Labour Theory of Value ', are the active principles of Marxian doctrine in the world to-day.

William Morris and the Modern World

THERE is no anniversary so difficult to celebrate as the centenary of a great man's birth. He is at once too near and too remote. There are many still alive who remember him as a man, and can tell how they met him and talked with him, and how he behaved in the matter of everyday living. But all too often our elders are to us in such circumstances but as ghosts speaking of ghosts. What should make the dead come alive often serves only to remind us how very dead even the living can be.

By the time a man has been dead a hundred years he has passed into history ; and we are at least beginning to know what his place in history is. When he was born but a century ago he belongs to that obscurest of all historical periods—the age of our fathers, the age that lies just outside most men's personal memory. When William Morris died, in 1896, I was just seven. I have often spoken to friends who had known him well—to some who reverenced his memory, and to others who did not reverence him at all, but regarded him as a likeable but wrong-headed old fellow with an unusually explosive temper. For on that point at any rate all the chroniclers agree. Morris was a highly explosive person, though his rage was easily consumed. He had quick passions ; and his indignation, as well as his anger, was easily aroused. He found plenty to arouse it in that Victorian England which seemed to him so alien, but to which he seems to us so thoroughly to belong.

Piecing together the legend of William Morris from the memories of living men, we who came too late to know him can get some notion of him as a man—busy, impatient, friendly, and simple-minded, with a great capacity for loving people he knew and hating public characters he did not know, with an overmastering faith that it mattered whether things were beautiful or ugly, and that ugliness was an unnatural and preventable distortion which man's wrong-headedness had brought into the world—above all, with a ceaseless itch to be doing things, making things, both for the sake of doing and making them and as object-lessons of how things should be done and made. He was a *bourgeois* knight-errant of the Victorian Age, who tilted not at windmills but at factory chimneys, and set out to rescue not fair ladies but dispossessed labourers whom the ogre of industrialism had immured. The age condemned him to make his poems, his printed books, his tapestries and cretonnes and furniture, chiefly for the immediate delectation of the few whose privileges he denounced. He wanted all men to enjoy his beautiful things, and to have and make beautiful things of their own. But the things he made were expensive ; and only the well-to-do could afford them. Nevertheless, he served a far wider public than the customers of Morris and Company and the Kelmscott Press. For what he made influenced others ; and there is not a craft that he practised but has been deeply affected by his work. Modern decoration and modern printing—the cheap as well as the dear —would both be different and worse if Morris had not set the impression of his personality upon them.

William Morris's influence is very much alive to-day ; but—let us not disguise the truth—he himself and his work are out of fashion. He has shared with Burne-Jones and Rossetti, with Ruskin and Arnold, with Browning and Tennyson, the eclipse of the Great Victorians. Some of them will come back: indeed, in the case of Tennyson the literary current is already beginning to set again that way. There is a cult of Tennyson among the new poets, in spite of *Locksley Hall*. But there is hardly a cult of Browning, whose exuberant liberal optimism is out of tune with an age that has learned to believe in little, and least of all in itself. Nor is there a cult of Morris, largely for the same reason. For Morris too was an optimist—none the less for holding that it was most doubtful whether God was in his Heaven, and certain that there was very much wrong with the world.

This fall from fashion extends to nearly all Morris's work—the best almost equally with the least successful. For there is in almost all of it a common quality ; and that quality ' dates '. All Morris's finished work—everything he made or wrote primarily as a craftsman—is essentially decorative. It sets out to adorn life, rather than to interpret it. Its concern is with beauty, in a sense in which beauty has nothing to do with stark realism, but a great deal to do with ideals, and with dreaming dreams. It is never the penny plain, but always the twopence coloured. And it is through and through romantic, rich and varied in colour and imagery, full of soft curves and voluptuous cadences, and never severe, or economical of means, or reticent in the expression of feeling. This is as true of most of Morris's poetry as of his prose romances ; and it is no less true of his richly decorated volumes printed at the Kelmscott Press, of his tapestries and stained-glass windows, his carpets and furniture, than of what he wrote.

Before I sat down to write this essay, I went to my book-shelves and cast my eye over the twenty-four volumes of William Morris's *Collected Works*. They do not include all that he wrote ; but, if he had done nothing besides, they would go far beyond the life's work of most artists. Of these twenty-four volumes, roughly eleven are poetry, including his translations from Homer and Virgil and his rendering of *Beowulf* into modern English. The greater part of two more volumes consists of prose translations—from sagas and old French and Northern stories—and these do not include the six volumes of the Saga Library, which were left out of the collected edition. Next come more than eight volumes of romances and tales, all save one those prose romances, such as *The Glittering Plain* and *The Well at the World's End*, in which Morris sought, none too profitably, to recapture the manner of Malory and *The High History of the Holy Grail*, mingling with it something from the Norse sagas, and something else, alas, that stamped it as fatally derivative and unreal. Morris's prose romances I think the world can afford to let die, keeping their stronger originals. Not so the one volume of Socialist tales and parables—*News from Nowhere* and *A Dream of John Ball*—surely among the best, as well as the most widely read, of all his writings. Finally, the *Collected Works* include one volume of his Icelandic journals—a travel diary kept for himself and not for publication, and two volumes of his lectures and essays on the arts and on Socialism. To these have been added, since the *Works* first appeared, two supplementary volumes, bringing together many more of his lectures, pamphlets, and miscellaneous writings, and some previously unpublished poems.

Here is a formidable enough array : yet it is but a fraction of its maker's work. We must add to it, for a full view of his accomplishment, the whole range of his activities as a craftsman in other arts. Anyone who visited the Exhibition that was held at South Kensington to commemorate the centenary of Morris's birth will have seen for himself how wide that range was—from furniture, carpets, tapestries, chintzes, cretonnes, and wallpapers to glass-ware and pottery, and from paintings and architectural designs to printed and illustrated books and to manuscripts illuminated with the skill of a medieval monk with nothing else to do. I am not calling upon anyone to admire or like all these works of Morris's hand and mind—much less to decorate his house to-day as a period-piece in the Pre-Raphaelite manner. It is undeniable that much of Morris's work is no longer even beautiful in any satisfying way. Much of it was too exclusively reminiscent, too much an attempt merely to imitate the past ; and much of it has now only the value and interest of fruitful experiment. There is better furniture than Morris's : there are better founts of type than those which he designed, too ornamentally, for the Kelmscott Press. But would these better things have existed without his influence ? Moreover, at any rate some things that he made have stood purely and simply, and apart from any historical interest, the test of time. His cretonne, The Strawberry-Thief, for example, or some of his tapestries, with Philip Webb's birds. I have had both these in my house for a good many years ; and my pleasure in them is as fresh and intense to-day as it has ever been.

When a man does many things, there is always a risk that he will do none of them superlatively well. There are indeed two risks—that he may fall short in craftsman-ship, and that he may put too little of the substance of his mind and spirit into any one thing. Morris ran both these risks. As a craftsman he had, in almost any art that he chose to practise, a quite astonishing skill. The crafts came easily to him, including the craft of poetry ; and now and then they came too easily. But it was not as a craftsman that Morris often fell short, but rather by resting content with craftsmanship. The second risk found him out, above all else as a writer. He found writing so easy that often he was content merely to write with less than half his mind, making his poetry a by-product of more exacting labours. Of the best of his poetry this is not true at all—above all it is not true of *Sigurd the Volsung* or of the best of his shorter poems. But a good deal of his poetry falls short of greatness, because he did not try to make it great, but only pretty and pleasant and workmanlike.

Yet, though a man's work may fall short of greatness if he attempt too many things, it does not at all follow that he would have done better to attempt less. For the truth may be that he wants to do and say so much that he is more concerned to get it done and said than to do one thing, or a few things, supremely well. He may have the power of expressing himself, and of serving his fellow men, rather in many things than in a few ; and though no one thing mark him out as master, his mastery may appear none the less plainly in them all. This, I think, is true of William Morris. He is greater as a man and as an influence and in his work as a whole than in any one part of what he wrote or made.

The clue to the understanding both of Morris as a man and of his accomplishment is to realise that he was above all else a workman who enjoyed his work. He enjoyed it so much that he wanted to be always working ; and he could imagine nothing that would have made him more miserable than having nothing to do. And yet there was another condition that seemed to him hardly less wretched—to be forced to work at a task that was both irksome in itself and useless in its outcome, as much of the work that men are made to do in the world to-day appeared to him to be. He was happy, because he had found ready to his hand work that both needed doing and was pleasant and satisfying to do—work that both fulfilled the creative impulse that was in him and passed on a product that was worth while to his fellow men.

Morris did not want to keep this happiness to himself. He was not prepared to regard it as the prerogative of a special and limited class of artists. He saw a vision of a world in which all men would share, at least in some degree, in the privileges which he enjoyed, and all work would have in it a quality of worth-whileness that would redeem it from being mere drudgery. With passion and conviction, he wanted to make that vision a reality. That was what he had in mind when he claimed again and again that no act of production could pass the ultimate test of value unless it were a source of pleasure to the maker and also a source of pleasure to the user of the thing made.

This notion William Morris got largely from Ruskin, whose *Stones of Venice* first made him formulate it clearly in his own mind. But it came to him also largely from the experience of his own work. He began by applying it, without any political moral, to the condition of the arts, denouncing the decadence of the useful arts and the fatal division between designer and craftsman that had come in with the Renaissance. He wanted everyone who made anything to be making something of his own, with freedom to shape the detail and the method for himself, however much he might be working in with a larger design. Morris set to work to revive and develop the crafts, in the hope by this means of giving back to the craftsman his lost freedom as a creator, and therewith his lost sense of pleasure in his work.

But the more Morris worked at reviving the crafts—and even the greater his success in reviving them—the more he came to realise that no regeneration of the work of Society could come about in that way alone. He could achieve no more as an artist-craftsman than the making of exceptional things for exceptional people, whereas he wanted to be making for ordinary people ordinary things of everyday use. He came to see that, however successfully he printed and wove and dyed and decorated, the life of the great mass of the people would go on as before, totally unaffected by his activities. He cried out in his revolt against this impotence, ' I do not want art for the few, any more than I want education for a few, or freedom for a few '. But how was he to work to win for all that happiness which he found, above all else, in the making of beautiful things ?

It was because of this contradiction, which sank more and more deeply into his mind, that Morris's view of art brought him at last to Socialism, as it half-brought Ruskin to Socialism. But Morris became a much more thorough-going convert than it was ever possible for Ruskin to be. Ruskin went on hoping that the rich and the artistic would at length set to work to educate and to elevate the poor, whereas Morris, democratic by temperament as well as by belief, came round to the view that the poor would have to educate and to elevate themselves, and that the rich and cultivated, so far from helping them, would for the most part stand solidly and obstinately in their way. Morris read Marx, confessing to a sore struggle over the sections dealing with the theory of value, but finding in the historical chapters of *Das Kapital*, and in Marx's account of the development of class-struggles from the Middle Ages, a view of Society which seemed to him as valid as Ruskin's, and its essential complement. He became a Socialist, not merely in the sense of wishing and hoping for a different sort of Society, but in the sense of working for it, preaching for it at street-corners, and shocking a great many of his admirers by throwing himself heart and soul into a working-class movement which was in those days very much less respectable than it has since become.

Morris, in turning Socialist, did not in the least abandon or modify his artistic ideals. He continued to regard the arts as the most important part of life, because he held that the quality of the arts was the expression of the quality of life as a whole. He believed that art ought to be, and would be in any healthy society, not a thing set apart from the ordinary everyday work of men, but a quality present in the products of all men's labour, though necessarily present in different degrees in different types of work and in different people. The distinction between rough work and fine work he understood and recognised as valid : that between art work and work that was merely utilitarian he refused to recognise at all—except as a sign of deep-seated social disease. He held that it was fully possible, in a decently ordered Society, for all work to partake of the essential quality of art—that of giving pleasure to the doer as well as combining beauty with utility in the thing made.

Many critics of William Morris have dismissed this belief of his as the merest piece of romanticism—a delusion for which he can be the more readily forgiven because it is too absurd to be taken seriously. He has been charged with imagining a craftsman's paradise which it is impossible to imagine as extended to the majority of men—an artists' Utopia which would be quite beyond the comprehension or enjoyment of most people, even if its extension to them could be regarded as practicable. Most men, it is said, do not want or expect pleasure in labour : their pleasure is, and must be, solely in the rewards which labour yields, and not in the labour itself. At most, it is urged, ordinary labouring men and women can be expected to distinguish only between labour that is merely neutral and labour which is positively irksome ; and it is quite beyond the bounds of probability that any change in the forms of social organisation could affect this attitude or make most men capable of seeing or feeling as the artist-craftsman sees and feels. Moreover, it is argued, the attempt to give all work a creative and artistic quality, even apart from its lack of appeal to the majority of men, would involve so tremendous a diminution of output as to cause much more misery by the fall in the standard of life which would ensue upon it than it could possibly remove by lessening the unpleasantness of labour.

There is of course some substance in this criticism ; for it is true enough that Morris, especially in his earlier writings and speeches, did regard all work from the special standpoint of the artist-craftsman, and did hanker after the hand-made thing and incline to wage war upon the machine. He denounced mass-production, because it seemed to him to involve the destruction of all pleasure, or even tolerableness, in the work that men were called upon to do. In his later writings he seems to have become conscious of previous exaggeration, and to have recognised more clearly that there would be a place for machinery in Utopia ; but he never ceased to believe that Socialism would bring with it, together with the liberation of the producers, a great increase in hand-work as the corollary to the freeing of the artistic impulse. He felt this impulse as a force so strong and valuable in himself that, being a good democrat, he felt impelled to affirm and demand it as a possession which all men should be entitled to enjoy.

Yet, if Morris exaggerated the strength of the artistic impulse in most men, and the possibility of remaking most of the world's work in the image of his own, I feel very positive that in a deeply important sense he had taken hold of a living truth. His most fundamental faith was that the quality of work and the quality of living could not be dissociated, and that men whose daily labours were to them no better than an irksome round of toil, satisfying no part of their natural impulses, could by no means live happily or fruitfully merely by making the best of their leisure. The quality of their working hours would penetrate and poison their lives, making them worse and less happy as friends or lovers, as citizens, and as men. Can anyone deny that this is true, or that the irksomeness and nervous strain of much modern factory labour are powerful causes of unhappiness, ill-temper, and thwarted or twisted personality in the world of to-day ? The happiest among us, I verily believe, and the most at peace with the world—however much we find ourselves at war with its abuses—are those of us who are able to enjoy our work.

Where Morris went wrong was not in affirming the need for pleasure in labour, but in resting the hope of this pleasure on too narrow a basis. For pleasure in work is not, in fact, the monopoly of artists and writers and handicraftsmen, who enjoy in a peculiar sense the pleasure of purely individual creation. A skilled mechanic can enjoy operating a machine, provided that the process gives him a chance of putting the machine through its paces well—or ill—provided, that is, there is skill or at least a high degree of dexterity in the task. Still more of course can a technician, whose work it is to plan the action of vast machines, or an inventor, who devises new and more cunning instruments of production, or an administrator who plays at human chess upon the huge board of modern industry or government, enjoy his work and find in it an absorbing and unending source of pleasure. Morris always respected the work of the architect ; and the modern architects of industry are the administrators and the engineers.

In the world of to-day, these men are on the whole happy ; but the main body of the manual workers in most countries are not, for most labour lacks the creative quality which the work of the engineer and the administrator undoubtedly possesses. But I doubt if the irksomeness of most modern labour comes, nearly as much as Morris thought it did, from the mere fact that most men have to work at routine tasks upon machines. It comes rather from two other sources, to both of which Morris himself gave a considerable measure of recognition. The first of these is that the technician and the administrator, in planning the use of machinery, commonly pay much closer attention to its effects on the money-costs of production than to its reactions upon the lives of those who tend it. This may be their misfortune rather than their fault ; for they can get their chance to show their prowess and to play about with the machines they love only on condition of regarding them as instruments for the extraction of profit. Consideration of the effect of the machine upon human happiness, unless this is seen to be likely to react on its profit-making capacity, is compelled to take second place, even where the technician is imaginative enough for it to enter into his mind as a factor worth taking into account. Thus it comes to pass that the machine, which should lighten and ease the labour of men, all too often increases the nervous strain, even where it lessens the purely muscular effort of work. This happens apart from the tendency for modern machinery to make many kinds of craft-skill superfluous, and thus to throw skilled men idle, and leave them to rot away in an enforced and ironically named ' playing ' which is worse and more destructive of happiness and manhood even than irksome employment.

Secondly, Morris's criterion of happy work was always that it should create a worth-while product. Waste labour seemed to him to be necessarily painful labour, because it was bound to be accompanied by a sense of futility. By this test he held that a great deal of the labour of the modern factory workers, often irksome in itself besides, stood decisively condemned. Modern civilisation he regarded as a great engenderer of unwanted wants, which multiplied toil at the same time as they stamped it with futility. This was partly because wealth was wrongly distributed, so that a great deal of effort was expended in producing ugly things valued only for the ostentation of wealth, and not for any real service. Indeed, the abuse went much further than this ; for even the poor wanted many things only by imitation of their economic ' betters '. Morris firmly believed that a society of economic equals would want fewer things, and want them of better quality and design, so that the making of them would call for better kinds of labour. He believed too that the pleasure of making things would be much the greater if the worker had the assurance that they would serve, when they had been made, to fulfil a real need.

Morris's belief in the joy of labour was, then, based on the postulating of two conditions—that the work in itself should be pleasant, or at least not irksome in the doing, and that its product should serve a social or human purpose which the doer could accept as his own. These two conditions were so much on his own mind that he never clearly distinguished between them— regarding Socialism as the means of satisfying them both together. It is, however, important to draw the distinction, however close the connection between the two may be. For the hope of making most work yield, by its own inherent quality, the same sort of pleasure as an artist derives from the act of creation is indeed forlorn. But the hope of giving to most work a character not irksome to the doer, and at the same time redeemed from mere negativity by its real contribution to a useful social end, is by no means mere romanticism, but present possibility.

It is indeed much less difficult than Morris's way of stating the case would lead us to suppose. For he saw but imperfectly, when he saw at all, that the pleasure he found in handicraft could come out of the handling of machinery as well as out of the older types of craft. It is easier for us to see this, as we watch the endless round of tinkering with motor-cars and radio sets and every sort of mechanical gadget begotten of our time, and realise that the sense of craftsmanship is being reborn in our children as the sense of the machine. What is wrong with our age, as Morris himself half saw at times—in his essay on *A Factory as it might be*, for example—is not that it uses machinery, but that it abuses the men and women who mind it—in fact, not that it uses machinery, but that it has not learned how to use it in the service of human living.

For the pleasure of the machine, very strong in the technician and often hardly less strong in the youth who has just got his first motor-bicycle or small car, is at present wholly denied an outlet among the great body of workers in industry. The rank-and-file worker operates the machine; but he can play no tricks with it, and display no prowess in its use. He is not the cunning or dexterous craftsman, showing his mastery, but the unhonoured and unskilled attendant, with whose growingly monotonous and unenterprising labour the eager technician is always happily thinking out new ways to dispense.

It would be some alleviation of this lot if the ordinary worker could feel, as a tremendous effort is being made to get the workers to feel in Russia, that behind this monotony of labour lies a clear and acceptable social purpose, so that, even if the toil be irksome in itself, it can be made a labour of faith expressed in works. But, as Morris plainly saw, for the majority of men this sense of acceptable social purpose is at present almost wholly lacking. Most things are to be made, not because they are needed—even if they are needed—but because a profit is expected from their sale ; and though the orthodox economists have spent a century in trying to persuade us that this profit affords clear evidence of a social purpose being truly served, the conviction does not strike home. Give men the sense that their labour is worth while, and, whether that sense be well or wrongly based, most of them will both work the harder and better for it and be far less weary when the work is done. That happens in war, when men believe, rightly or wrongly, that they are fighting in a righteous cause. It happens constantly, in all sorts of work that men undertake because they believe in its value, rather than for the sake of its material rewards. It is happening to-day in Russia, on an unprecedented scale, in the ordinary labour of mine and factory. I dare say something of it is to be found in Nazi Germany and in Fascist Italy, where men are being induced by all the arts of propaganda to work hard and well for the honour and greatness of the State. A bad cause as well as a good one can excite belief and enthusiasm, and can make men happy in working for it. But I am sure this experience is not happening to most men in England or in the United States, or in any humdrum capitalist country where there is no sense of revolutionary struggle to sublimate the ordinary business of life.

It is Morris's message—the most living part of it—that men will not be happy unless their work is so organised as to be plainly worth doing, because it serves a purpose they can accept as their own. This involves, I think, another condition—that they must have freedom to arrange the doing of it in their own way. The task, if it is to be accepted by a man as his own, must be in a real sense self-imposed. It may involve working under a discipline, as most work is bound to do—including the work of supervision and control ; but there is all the difference in the world between a leadership of which men recognise the validity and accept the purpose, and a merely imposed authority. I do not suggest that even a self-imposed social purpose can for most men turn a distasteful task into a pleasure, day in and day out, for years on end ; but it can make all the difference to the quality of a task that is not in itself distasteful, but merely unexciting.

This promise of tasks energised more by the sense of a useful and acceptable purpose than by their inherent craft quality falls, undoubtedly, far short of Morris's Utopia, in which every man would find his work pleasant in itself as well as in its purpose. But this is not the whole story. For if work can be prevented from being a positive burden of dreariness and ill-ease, the quality of leisure can be improved as it cannot be under the conditions which now exist. Machinery, if it is used to supersede dirty and irksome rather than skilled and interesting work, can be so applied as to save labour for the preservation instead of the undoing of man. The hours of necessary labour can be cut down, and the strain of it reduced ; and men can come out of the factory ready for the recreation of interesting work of their own individual choosing. The arts can burgeon from men's leisure, as well as from their hours of organised service. This cannot happen as long as the quality of paid labour is deadening or nerve-racking and destructive of the sense that work can be a source of pleasure. It can and will happen as soon as men find release from the double drudgery of dull labour whose purpose they cannot accept as their own.

When you read *News from Nowhere*, if you have read it, what did you make of it ? I have heard a good many people say that they could not bear to live in so easeful a paradise, any more than they could bear to keep perpetual holiday. I have heard it said that in so placid a society as Morris describes, the wits and wills of men would wither away, and civilisation decay into a second childhood of fecklessness and inanition. So they would, though there is not much chance of their having to run the risk. For Morris's Utopia is not at all likely ever to become real : nor, I am sure, did he ever suppose that it would. The man who admired so greatly the old Norse sagas, with their endless record of heroism and struggle against desperate odds—the man who, visiting Iceland, was struck above all else by the *smallness* of the lives men led there in modern times against the background of those tales of giants—was not of a sort really to rest content with a world in which all good things were to be had merely for the asking. Morris knew, as well as another, that the good life involves striving and reaching out after things unattained. He did not think that the getting of Socialism would solve all human problems, and leave mankind to spend the rest of time with nothing difficult to desire. *News from Nowhere* is not a prophecy, but, as its author told us, a pleasant dream. It is an aspect of life, and not the whole : one man's answer to other men's very different dreams, expressing a hope Morris cherished, not without cherishing many others besides. *News from Nowhere* should be read so, as dream, not Utopia—above all, as a dream of that human fellowship which, in the mouth of John Ball, Morris proclaimed as the true heaven on earth.

But in that fellowship there will be much to do and to make—much that will not come easy. Even in Morris's dream, men had found it hard work to achieve their freedom ; and they had come to their Utopia only through the heat and torment of civil war. His account of this struggle has in it fully as much of the essential Morris as what comes after—the same quality that appears again and again in his epic, *Sigurd the Volsung*, or in his Socialist poem of the Paris Commune, *The Pilgrims of Hope*. He would have found not merely work to do, but hard things to strive for, even in Utopia ; and a paradise without hard tasks worth attempting would have been for him no paradise at all. But he did not believe that the striving and struggling need be directed against other men : he wanted to strive in fellowship with others to improve the quality of life.

Nevertheless, it is true that his conception of sheer beauty had in it too much of languorousness for our taste. He loved dearly the warm quietude of summer days up the river, the thick scent of mingled perfumes in enchanted gardens, the glamour of that too passive and reposeful beauty which Rossetti knew well how to paint. In these days we want our pleasures sharper-edged, and more strident, more angular and less of a sort to lull the senses asleep. In fact, Morris too wanted these things in his life, and in his art ; and he got them along with the others, out of Norse sagas and Socialist street-corner meetings. He was no natural tub-thumper, and he found Socialist speechifying difficult and, in itself, irksome work. He had no instinct for meetings and committees ; and he often wished the ' comrades ' at the devil when they kept badgering him about points of order, and above all when they would set to quarrelling one with another. But he kept hard at these things, and I think it is safe to say that he extracted from them some of the salt of life. So did he from his business ; for running Morris and Company was no sinecure. It involved constant experiments with new and difficult processes, constant efforts to learn and teach new crafts, constant problems that had to be struggled with, and taxed the mind and will. From these problems Morris would come home to write poetry or prose tales ; and the character of much of his writing is that of recreation after the hard part of the day's work was done.

It is good to do battle against ugliness, even if one can but half see beauty. And it is good to do battle against injustice and oppression, even if the vision of Utopia be but dim in the haze of distance. But it is best to fight against ugliness and oppression together, knowing them for the two-headed giant that they are. Woe unto them that cry out upon the ugliness and ignorance of the poor, and yet would deprive them of goodly nurture for mind and body. But blessed be those who, loving beauty, cannot bear that all men should not love and possess it too. The roots of ugliness are two—riches and poverty. Men use ugly things either because they are poor and must make shift with shoddy till they grow used to it, and even come to think it good ; or because they are rich, and want not something good in itself, but something their neighbours cannot aspire to. Men make ugly things, either because they despise the poor, and think anything good enough for them if only it be cheap, till they come to think things good mainly because they are cheap ; or because they adulate riches, and adorn things into ugliness in order to make them dear. But it is not natural to man to make ugly things, unless he makes them so deliberately, as a savage may make, with astonishing vitality, the hideous visage of a malevolent god. Simple things are not ugly things ; and cheap things need not be ugly, even if they are machine-made. Some ugliness there must always be, in both things and men. But how much of the world's ugliness is sheer uglification—the making of a thing ugly when it would be just as cheap and easy, and far more natural, to make it at the least passably pleasant !

Morris fought against ugliness ; and though he fought with too narrow a vision of beauty in his mind, that matters relatively little. The point is that he fought to give all men the chance of making their own sense of beauty and value a power in their lives. In fighting for this, he had to fight for fellowship ; and in fighting for fellowship he had to fight for Socialism. For he did not believe that either beauty or fellowship could be realised in a society that held men divided into classes, and made of some men means to other men's ends.

In all this I may seem to have said too little of Morris as a creative artist, and too much of his ideas about art and life. This is not because his creative work is unimportant ; for I am sure there is much of it to which

men will come back again and again for its intrinsic
beauty, and not only because Morris's work occupies a
key position in the development of the arts. There are
short poems not far below the very greatest in our
language : *Sigurd the Volsung* belongs to the very small
company of long poems that deserve the name ' epic ' :
A Dream of John Ball is not merely a parable, but a piece
of singularly beautiful English prose ; and *News from
Nowhere* is the only English Utopia since More's that
deserves to be remembered as literature. No collection
of English printed books will ever be representative without examples from the Kelmscott Press ; and the best
of Morris's tapestries are, among modern work, in a
class wholly by themselves. Yet I admit that there is
much of Morris's work for which no such claim to
personal immortality can be made. Achieving decorative
beauty, it falls short of greatness, because it fails either
to express or classically to eschew passion. It is neither
simple enough nor impassioned enough to force its way
through time to the appreciation of later ages. It is of
an age which it does not transcend.

But how few artists, even the greatest, are there of
whose lesser works the same cannot be said ? If it has
to be said in a special sense of Morris, that is because in
his lesser work he was not only prolific, but also deeply
influential. We cannot forget these lesser things, and
concentrate on what is best, because they too are an
essential part of his legacy to our time. In diffusing his
energy over many things, he came to count for more as a
man than as artist or writer, however well he wrote or
made when he was at his best. For this reason, it is true
that his ideas, as well as his purely artistic or literary
productions, constitute a necessary element in our
appreciation of him.

It has often been said that in these ideas there was
nothing novel—no more than Ruskin interpreted in the
light of Marx. But to interpret *The Stones of Venice* in
the light of *Das Kapital* is in itself a highly original and

creative idea. Ruskin expounding the ' nature of Gothic ' to an unbelieving generation became the arch-critic of the orthodox Political Economy, demanding of it that it should correct its study of prices by taking into account the real values of human welfare. But Ruskin, for all his excursions into Economics, remained to the end a voice crying in the drawing-room without a Messiah to proclaim. He could never perform the final act of faith that would have brought him to a belief that, even if in the struggle for freedom all art should die, it would be born again out of the creative energy of the common people— provided only that they could become free to remake society in their own way. Ruskin, in *Fors Clavigera*, saw glimpses of this faith ; but he never embraced it or held it fast. He never gave up hope of the regeneration coming from above—through the helpful humanitarianism of a section of the cultivated class.

Morris, though he, like Ruskin, supported Art and Craft movements and made many appeals to the rich and cultivated to help the arts, did see beyond this limited horizon. Beginning in the faith that the arts were the key to life, he came to see that life was the key to art, and that the arts could flourish as he wished them to flourish only as the expression of a quality of living. In the end, he came to care more about the living than about the art, not because he cared less for art, but because he cared more for men.

That, I think, is why his often hastily written lectures on Socialism and the arts, and his Socialist poem, *The Pilgrims of Hope*, are actually better writing than much of his more finished literary work. There is more real feeling in them, as well as more thought ; and in them Morris breaks through the forms and frills of medievalism which so often made an artificiality in his earlier writing. In *A Dream of John Ball*, the hedge-priest stepped down out of the tapestry and became a man ; and in the essays and lectures, when the decorative impulse was set aside, Morris's personality came through, simple and friendly, with a great love of simple things and simple people and a great hatred of all things that were ' cheap and nasty ' and stultified life and happiness. I have quoted before, but I must quote again, the words he wrote in one of these papers in praise of England, both for what it says and for how it is said :

The land is a little land ; too much shut up within the narrow seas, as it seems, to have much space for swelling out into hugeness : there are no great wastes overwhelming in their dreariness, no great solitudes of forests, no terrible untrodden mountain-walls : all is measured, mingled, varied, gliding easily one thing into another : little rivers, little plains, swelling, speedily changing uplands, all beset with handsome orderly trees ; little hills, little mountains, netted over with the walls of sheepwalks : all is little, yet not foolish and blank, but serious rather, and abundant of meaning for such as choose to seek it : it is neither prison nor palace, but a decent home.

That is praise of this land of ours by a man who loved it, and loved its people too ; for he loved the land not as a spectacle only, but as a home. Beside that vision of the unspoilt England set this other—of the England that is yet to be made out of what Englishmen have marred—the vision, shall we say, of Hull or Manchester as it might be, but by no means as it, or any other city, is. Morris is speaking of the new art—the popular art—that will come when men have achieved not only liberty, but ' equality, which, and which only, means fraternity, and so have leisure from poverty and from all its griping, sordid cares'.

That art will make our streets as beautiful as the woods, as elevating as the mountain-sides : it will be a pleasure and a rest, and not a weight upon the spirits, to come from the open country into a town ; every man's house will be fair and decent, soothing to his mind and helpful to his work : all the works of man that we live amongst and handle will be in harmony with nature, will be reasonable and beautiful : yet all will be simple and inspiriting, not childish nor enervating ; for as nothing of beauty and splendour that man's mind and hand may compass shall be wanting from our public buildings, so in no private dwelling will there be any signs of waste, pomp, or insolence, and every man will have his share of the *best*.

It is a dream, you may say, of what has never been, and never will be ; true, it has never been, and therefore, since the world is alive and moving yet, my hope is the greater that it one day will be : true, it is a dream : but dreams have before now come about of things so good and necessary to us, that we scarcely think of them more than of the daylight, though once people had to live without them, without even the hope of them.

If that is the country we would wish to preserve, and that the city we would wish to build, but if some of us feel the task hopeless and are reconciled to a world that must seek for beauty in the nooks and crannies of the ugliness it miscalls wealth, let us remember that what Morris said in his day is far truer in ours—the physical means of creating abundance as well as beauty are in our hands, if we can find but the wit to use them. Morris's picture of *A Factory as it might be* is much less Utopian to-day than it seemed to those who read it when it first appeared. We have even done something to make our newer factories cleaner and healthier, and even less deliberately ugly in their design. Perhaps we have even done a very little to make the work that has to be done in them less laborious—though I fear that in many modern factories speeding-up has made the nervous strain increase further than the muscular strain has been reduced. We have done something in certain ways to improve our standards and ideals, even if we have done all too little towards cleaning up the sordid mess that industrialism has made of our country. Moreover, the power to create all necessary things in all required abundance is ours to-day in fuller measure than when Morris proclaimed it half a century ago ; for to-day human productivity has run much further ahead of human wisdom than it had then. We need not be so simple in our tastes now as then in order all to have enough ; and we can afford the more readily, and with the less regard for cheapness, to seek beauty as well as

305

abundance. But we shall not seek either to good purpose unless we make our quest in the mood of fellowship. For in the words Morris put into the mouth of John Ball, ' Fellowship is heaven, and lack of fellowship is hell : fellowship is life, and lack of fellowship is death ; and the deeds that ye do upon earth, it is for fellowship's sake that ye do them, and the life that is in it, that shall live on and on for ever, and each one of you part of it, while many a man's life upon the earth from the earth shall wane. Therefore, I bid you not dwell in hell but in heaven, or while ye must, upon earth, which is a part of heaven, and forsooth no foul part.'

That faith in fellowship, that faith in the power of common men to make an earthly paradise, that faith that art and life will flourish together among men who are free, and that the quality of life and human happiness depends on the quality and character of the labour that men are called upon to do—in these things lies the substance of what Morris has to say : and the world has by no means learned these lessons yet. But I value not least in Morris that in preaching his gospel he was never a prig, but a very human person who could lose his temper and roar at times, but, however angry he grew at his fellow men's follies and cruelties, never stopped liking them, individually as well as in the mass, and being liked by them as a friendly sort of fellow from whom it was no hardship to take a scolding. For Morris was never bitter, even when he was violent. Yeats called him ' The Happiest of the Poets '. I like to think of him as the Happiest of the Socialists.

Henry Ford

I SHOULD hate to be a workman in the Ford motor works at Detroit. So would Henry Ford. He has said as much himself, in one of his books. He admits that to him the idea of repetitive labour—' the doing of one thing over and over again and always in the same way '— is nothing less than ' terrifying '. ' I could not possibly do the same thing day in and day out ', he writes ; but he goes on to say that ' to other minds, perhaps I might say to the majority of minds, repetitive operations hold no terrors. . . . To them the ideal job is one where the creative instinct need not be expressed.' On this belief, that his own mind is somehow utterly different from the minds of the majority of men, Henry Ford has built up his resounding success as the man who has made a million motor-cars grow where one grew before. Mankind has to judge how far he is right, both in his view of what human beings are like, and in acting upon it.

In the chapter of *My Life and Work* in which this revealing passage occurs, Henry Ford goes on to argue that most men do not want, and will positively go out of their way to avoid, responsibility. Although his system makes the majority of jobs merely repetitive— the sort a man can learn to do in a day or a week, and can do thereafter without fresh creative effort—he says that his difficulty is still to find enough men able and willing to take on the responsible or difficult jobs that remain. He holds firmly that the ordinary workman does not want to ' control ' his industry, or to be at the trouble of creative thinking about his work, but wants to be told what to do, and to get good money for doing it. Ford believes strongly in high wages, and he wants above most things to raise the standard of life for as many people as possible. But he has no use at all for ' democracy in industry ' ; and provided that jobs are done under healthy conditions, in well-lighted, well-ventilated, clean, and sanitary factories, he does not think it matters one iota that the great majority of the tasks men perform in these factories are entirely devoid of interest or creative quality. He denies altogether that it demoralises a man to spend his working life in utterly monotonous labour, or that a business man needs to think of anything else than getting goods produced in the most efficient and cheapest ways it is possible to devise—for in his view efficiency involves healthy working conditions. His ceaseless cry is for ' more and cheaper goods ' ; for in his view man the producer is simply an instrument for serving the ends of man the consumer. In consuming the products of labour most men find their satisfactions, and in earning the good money that will enable them to consume. To find satisfaction in work as well as in consumption is a privilege reserved for a fortunate minority —of whom Henry Ford is one.

This is undoubtedly a comforting doctrine. For there is no doubt at all about man's ability, by applying Ford's methods with even half his ruthless efficiency, to make goods on a scale big enough to flood the world. If all industrialists were Henry Fords, and these industrialists successfully kept the financiers in their place, as, being Henry Fords, they most certainly would—the problem of material poverty—dearth of goods—would be very speedily solved. There would soon be common consent to a drastic reduction in the hours of labour ; and men would find themselves with more leisure as well as more goods to enjoy. Capitalism would be safe for a long time to come from any working-class onslaught : Plato's ' city of swine ' would soon be with us at a level of material plenty far outrunning Plato's most daring imaginations.

Is that what we want ? If so, there is at any rate one reason why we are not likely to get it—a dearth of Henry

Fords. For the majority of leaders of ' Big Business ',
however full of hustle and ' efficiency ' they may be, and
heartily as they will echo Ford's sayings about what the
workers want, are as unlike him as a Ford car is unlike
Boadicea's chariot. They agree with him that workmen
ought to work hard and under discipline, that there must
be no coddling and that Trade Unionism is a nuisance,
that most workmen have minds and needs differing
radically from their own ; but they by no means follow
his faith that if you look after the efficiency of your
service, profits will come of themselves, or that the
prosperity of industry can be built only on a foundation
of high and ever-increasing wages. Henry Ford worships
plenty ; but most of his fellow employers cannot rid
their minds of the gospel of scarcity, or realise that the
only way to extend sales is to widen the market by raising
the standard of life.

For that reason, even if we are content to accept
Henry Ford's doctrine, we are not likely to get his results
spread wide over the whole field of industry—unless we
can master the art of mass-producing not only Ford
cars but also the mind that lies behind their making.
This is far harder than even to mass-produce ' Golden
Arrows ' ; for in all the world there never was a more
individual mind than Ford's. His individuality appears
in his very simpleness. When he is not talking about
motor-cars, or at any rate about making things, he is
capable of talking the most abysmal nonsense—for
example, about Jews. But he was apparently born with
a simple, direct, over-mastering will to make a cheap
motor-car. That is his heart's desire : that provides him
with his simple religion. On that subject, whether he be
right or wrong, what he has to say is not nonsense, but
plain realism for good or ill. You have to accept it, or to
fight against it : you cannot merely brush it aside.

I come back, then, to the question whether Henry
Ford is right or wrong in believing that most people are
radically unlike himself, and in acting on that belief.

He tells me that I am quite wrong in supposing that most people are like him in finding terrifying or intolerable the prospect of a life spent, as far as its working hours are concerned, in purely repetitive labour of a necessarily monotonous kind. ' Those who have what might be called the creative type of mind and who thoroughly abhor monotony are apt to imagine that all other minds are similarly restless and therefore to extend quite unwanted sympathy to the labouring man who day in and day out performs almost exactly the same operation.'

On the facts, I partly agree with Mr. Ford. It is true that only a minority of the workers consciously hates purely repetitive and uninteresting labour, so as to prefer to it harder but more interesting work, or to value the creative quality of labour above a difference in monetary reward. He is right in saying that most men are not irked by mere monotony as it would irk him, or you, or me. I can write ' you ' because those whom it does not irk will not read this essay. He is right when he says that most people would choose a higher standard of material living, or more leisure, in preference to more interesting or responsible work. He says he is sorry to believe this, and perhaps he is ; but being sorry does not alter facts—and on the facts he is, so far, right.

But whereas, to Henry Ford, that seems to be the end of the argument, it cannot end it for me or, I hope, for mankind. Slavery would never have been ended if men had waited for the slaves to end it, or even to revolt against it in their minds. A contented slave—even a whole population of contented slaves—is not a sufficient defence of slavery, and would not have been so even if slave-labour had been efficient labour, which it never was.

For the case against slavery was that society ought, by making the slaves free in their bodies, to give them a chance of becoming free in their minds as well. That they did not want to be free in their minds was no answer at all ; for how can a man want to be free in his mind until he is free ? A man can want freedom of body without wanting freedom of mind. Being free in his mind he can want, or even cease to want, freedom of body. But he cannot want freedom of mind until he has it ; for to want it is to have it. If men are as Henry Ford believes they are, is that a reason for acting on their being so, or is it not rather a powerful reason for so acting as to make them different ?

' When you come right down to it ', Mr. Ford goes on, ' most jobs are repetitive.' That again is true ; but it is also true that Mr. Ford's methods make jobs much more repetitive than they were before. His chief object in planning production has been to eliminate every sort of waste. Applied to labour, that means eliminating waste motions. He has done that, with extraordinary success. But to eliminate waste motions is to eliminate variety—the wasteful variety which men, however unconsciously, introduce into doing a repetitive job, if they are left to do it in their own way. Made to do it in the Ford way, they produce more ; but their labour does become definitely more monotonous than it was. Mr. Ford pins them down to a narrower task ; and he also sets a pace which means that the task can be done only if a fixed set of motions is scrupulously followed. More output, more wages, probably in due course more leisure, but also undoubtedly more monotony of labour, are the result.

The fundamental question is whether monotony is bad for men or not. Even if most men do not rebel against it, but even choose it in preference to less monotonous work at lower pay, does it allow them to be happy ? Does it allow them to be men of as good ' quality ' as they are capable of being ? With John Ruskin and with William Morris, I say without hesitation that it does not. I say this sort of monotonous labour makes men unhappy, even if they are not conscious of the source of their unhappiness. I say that it is bad for the quality of human living.

But, says Henry Ford, if you reject my gospel, you reject plenty for poverty ; for if you set out to give men more interesting work, you must also keep them poor. I do not believe it. I agree that Henry Ford could never have made his motor-cars so cheap if he had been unable to get men to serve as mere attendants upon his machines; but I am not prepared to agree that this subjection of men to machines makes, over industry as a whole, for the achievement of plenty. It makes docile machine-tenders ; and, for every one who serves a machine at the orders of a Henry Ford, there are thousands who serve other masters whose aim is not plenty but profit. Their docility, inbred in them by their servitude to the machine, creates not plenty, but scarcity. They are offered up on the altar of high production in order to create not wealth, but unemployment.

Mr. Ford agrees with these strictures on his fellow-employers ; but he thinks the remedy is to remake other capitalists in his own image. It will never be done. As long as masters can get docile labour, most of them will exploit that labour. To sacrifice freedom and pleasure in labour for plenty is to lose all three. No society of slave-owners ever made even the material well-being of its slaves its end, whatever a slave-owner here and there may have done.

And yet there is substance in Henry Ford's assertion that ' when you get right down to it, most jobs are repetitive '. Not only that : they are bound to be repetitive, at least for a long time to come, however we reconstruct the social system. For assuredly the world is not yet ready to renounce the higher productivity which comes of mechanisation. Some people talk as if the problem of production had been so completely solved that all mankind could now without difficulty enjoy simultaneously three boons—a higher standard of living, shorter working hours, and a pleasant and satisfying quality of labour. But, in fact, of these things the first two clash with the third. We cannot have a higher standard of living and an increase of leisure for all the people except at the price of accepting, for most, a considerable degree of the monotony in labour which mechanisation involves. If labour is to be made less monotonous, the output of industry is bound to be smaller than it would be if all industry were run on Henry Ford's principles.

It is useless to run away from this fact; and, if we reject Mr. Ford's answer to the problem it presents, we must be prepared to find another. My answer is that men must be made free to choose for themselves, and that, without throwing mechanisation aside, we must be prepared to face some loss of possible output in order to safeguard their freedom of choice. Mr. Ford, with his deeply rooted individualism, has always refused to have any dealings with Trade Unions. That was one of the principal causes of his quarrel with President Roosevelt's Government over the acceptance of the National Recovery ' Code ' for the automobile industry. He does not, he explains, refuse to let his employees belong to a union if they wish to ; but he will not negotiate with any union, or recognise even among his own men any claim to bargain collectively. He fixes wages and conditions ; and the men he employs are free to take or leave what he offers. That, in his view, is the end of the matter ; and, because he does pay higher wages than most other employers, he has so far been able to make his ban on Trade Unions effective. Nor must we forget that the corruption of American Trade Unionism has provided some excuse for his attitude. The American Trade Unions—up to the quite recent emergence of the ' New Unionism ' of the Committee for Industrial Organisation, which is now at last attempting to organise the Ford workers—have mostly followed a selfishly sectional and restrictive policy wherever they have been strong. There has been far too much of the ' boss ' about the typical American Trade Union leader.

But this cannot be the end of the matter. It is not

X

enough to pay men good wages, if these wages are paid on conditions which rob men of their freedom. If we are to use automatic machines which condemn men to dull and monotonous labour, we must also place in men's hands some more effective means of protest than the right to look for another job—in which they may find themselves subject to the same conditions. We must recognise, and even encourage, their claim to protest against irksome conditions of labour, and be prepared to modify the conditions, even at some sacrifice of productivity. More and cheaper production is a very important object of human effort, but it is not, as Mr. Ford seems to imagine, the only end. If he is right in holding that most men are only fit for dull and monotonous work, and will not mind it, even if they are free, well and good : they will not protest against it, as long as it brings in good money. But we ought to give them every facility to protest ; and, when they do protest, we ought to be ready to devote as much pains to meeting their claim for a better quality of work as Henry Ford devotes to cutting down the manufacturing cost of his cars. Mankind has to strike a balance between cheap goods and decent human conditions of labour ; and the balance ought to be struck, not by the fiat of the employer, but by the democratic decision of those who feel the pinch.

Henry Ford will never see this because such a recognition of the humanity of labour would get in the way of his plans for cheapening production. He takes his stand on his view of men as they are, and refuses to consider whether they would not be different if they were more free. Man the consumer he has a limitless passion to supply ; for he sees in this service an endless opportunity for the exercise of personal power, and man as consumer, remaining strictly impersonal, never gets in his way. Man the producer is another affair ; for his personality is liable to hit up against Mr. Ford's projects. Therefore his personality must not be allowed to interfere with production. If he has personal qualities that will fit into the Ford scheme, well and good. He can be made into a foreman, or a technician, or perhaps a manager. But if his personal qualities do not fit, either they must be ground to powder or he must take his notice and be off somewhere else. The Ford Motor Company has no room for men who do not fit. That men must be made to fit, or must go, is the first article in the creed of Henry Ford. Where they are to go is not his affair, which is to produce cheap cars. Everything must give way to that.

That is why Henry Ford and his son, Edsel, own the entire capital of the Ford Motor Company. Mr. Ford has bought out all other stockholders, in order to make sure of having not only a free hand, which he had before, but a complete absence of responsibility to anyone else. He is a man who is by temperament quite unable to work with equals or colleagues : he can work only with subordinates who will carry out his will. When the Company started in 1903, he held a quarter of the shares. In 1906 he had 51 per cent, which gave him control. But that was not enough. In 1919 his son, acting for him, bought out all the other stockholders. It cost seventy million dollars to buy them out ; but it established an absolute hereditary monarchy in the Ford line, and it got rid of the need for even formally consulting anybody else. Mr. Ford insists on having a free hand, both with things and with people.

From childhood he has been single-minded. His father, an emigrant from County Cork and a farmer, wanted him to be a farmer too, whereas Henry Ford wanted to be an engineer. As a boy of twelve, he gratified his passion by repairing every watch he could lay hands on. He left school at fifteen and went on to the farm. But at sixteen he virtually ran away from home, and apprenticed himself to a machine shop in Detroit, working for a jeweller in the evenings to eke out his earnings. Then he shifted to an engine shop, to get varied experience, and then to a firm which dealt in farm machinery. He went back to the farm to live, and made himself an engineering shop in a shed, where he built a steam tractor, which was not a success. His father, to get him away from engineering, gave him land of his own to clear. He cleared it, sold the lumber, and used the money to experiment with engines. Incidentally he married, and built himself a log house on his farm. But before long he was back in Detroit, as engineer to the Edison Company ; and in Detroit, in 1892, he built his first motor-car, in his spare time. He had become convinced that the future for road and farm work was not with steam, but with the internal combustion engine.

Motor-cars were not quite a novelty then. Daimler had introduced his internal combustion engine in 1885, and in the same year Benz in Germany and Butler in England had devised motor-tricycles. Levassor had built the first workable motor-car in 1887 ; and the Germans and French had been hard at work devising improvements during the next few years. There were motor-car makers in the United States before Henry Ford started producing on a commercial scale. He did not invent the motor-car : what he did was to make it light and cheap. He made his experiments for himself, little influenced by other makers. He was the first man to conceive of the motor-car not as an expensive luxury, but as a universal need, that must be made and sold at a low price.

Mr. Ford made more cars after 1892. But it was not till 1899 that he threw up his job with the Edison Company, and set out to manufacture cars for the market. A company was formed—the Detroit Automobile Company—with Henry Ford as chief engineer. But most of the capital was not his ; and there were soon differences of opinion. The other directors wanted to make expensive cars like other makers : they did not believe in the possibility of a wide market. They would not take up his plans for cheap mass-production. In 1902 he resigned and prepared to start again on his own. But, for a send-off, he wanted a good advertisement.

316

In his heart, Henry Ford has no use for racing cars. He likes making cars for sober, useful service—not for showing off. But he realised that, if he wanted a market for cheap cars, he would have to advertise his wares. Motor-racing, introduced from France, was then very much in fashion. In 1902 Edge had won the Gordon-Bennett Cup from the French, previously regarded as supreme. Henry Ford built two cars purely for speed, and won every race in which he competed. Thereupon, in 1903, he launched the Ford Motor Company. In 1927, when he abandoned his familiar ' Model T ' for the new ' Model A ', he had sold fifteen million cars. In the first years he had built a number of different models, each on quite a small scale. From 1909, sure of his market, he concentrated on ' Model T ', in order to get the last cent of economy out of mass-production.

No one will deny that he did get the last cent of economy, at the expense of every cost except wages. Or rather he got the last cent of economy in labour-cost as well ; but he got it by raising wages, not by cutting them down. For he found that he could make men work harder if he paid them well ; and he also maintained stoutly that if you wanted to sell more goods, you had to give people the money to buy them. Mr. Ford does believe in the ' economy of high wages ' ; and he believes too in getting his money's worth in return. He gets it, as he gets most things he wants. Really single-minded people do : there are not enough single-minded people to get in their way. Only twice has he plainly failed to get what he wanted—once when he stood as senatorial candidate for Michigan in 1918, and once when he chartered his ' Peace Ship ' in 1915 and set out to make Europe see reason and end the war. But when he stood for the Senate he was not single-minded. He did not care whether he won or not ; and he took no part in the campaign. He was lucky not to be elected ; for, lacking utterly the faculty of collaboration, he would make a hopeless politician. As for the ' Peace Ship ', on that occasion he did fail, as he was bound to do. The war seemed to him idiotic, and he wanted to stop it. Till the United States entered the war he absolutely refused to make munitions. Thereafter he put all his resources at the Government's disposal. The Ford tractor was the outcome of his war experience—a light tractor for everyday use, cheap and easy to handle, like his cars. He made them by thousands to help the Allies to solve the problem of food supply in face of labour shortage ; and after the war he went on making them for farmers all over the world.

There was a time when merely to mention a Ford car was regarded as an excellent joke. That was when the motor-car was still a luxury, and a cheap car was scorned like a ready-made suit in Savile Row. In England there came to be rather more than that in the joke ; for ' Model T ', built to suit American road conditions of a generation ago, did look rather funny on modern roads some time before its creator himself saw the joke, and totally changed his design. About the modern Fords there is nothing funny ; and they are doing service all over the world. There is not just one Ford factory where they are made, but a host, scattered all over the United States, with assembling works in all important countries, and the great European factory at Dagenham as well as the parent plants at Detroit. More and more, Ford decentralises his production, setting up plants in many different places, where his materials are found, and specialising each plant more and more for the making of a single part or product. He saves transport by sending his parts straight to each big market, and assembling his cars near where they are to be sold. He has begun to experiment with factories in which men work only part of their time, spending the rest in agricultural work. Incidentally, that makes it easier to stand men off in order to meet seasonal changes in demand. Mr. Ford upholds it as good for the men ; but he sees to it that it pays him as well. When he was asked to give money to the hospital at Detroit, his reply was to take it over, lock, stock, and barrel, and run it as a self-supporting concern. His firm belief is that the best philanthropy is that which is on a paying basis. He hates charity. He has always stood on his own feet, and he thinks everybody else ought to do the same.

Of course, Henry Ford was born into a society that just suited him. Acutely individualistic, knowing exactly what he wanted to do, and determined to go his own way, he found American society intensely congenial to his ideas. That did not prevent him from quarrelling fiercely, not only with the bankers who wanted to get him into their grip by financing him, but also with his fellow employers, whom he fought over patent rights and whose association he resolutely refused to enter, just as he refused in 1933 to become subject to President Roosevelt's ' Code '. He is quite incapable of working with others, or of any sort of give and take. He insists on having everything his own way. As a manufacturer of motor-cars, he is a very great man, and a real maker of the modern world. But in making motor-cars he does not make men ; nor is he capable of understanding that man does not live by cars alone—that cheapness can be bought at too high a human price. He treats men as what they are in his factories—auxiliary power-plant to serve his machines. He would have them keep all their human qualities outside the works, where they are not wanted, and become as nearly automatic as possible in their motions during working hours. He is sure they do not mind, provided that they are well paid. But whether most men mind or not, with their conscious intelligences, is not the point. The question is whether their not minding is not a sign of something radically wrong with their working lives. Russia may seem to justify Mr. Ford ; for Russia too, faced with a vast problem of poverty, is busy subordinating the man to the machine. The world, as William Morris said long ago, is destined to use more machinery before it can use less ; for till we have solved

319

the problem of sheer poverty we shall not begin to think seriously about the quality of human work. But our ambition, I think, must be not Henry Ford's, but Morris's —not to make more and more things, in an endless multiplication of ' supplies ' and ' demands ', each supply creating a new demand for ever and ever, but in the last resort to give men work they can enjoy, and make our ' demands ' for goods square with the condition that each man's work shall be, as far as we are able to make it, ' a joy to the maker and the user '. Under any system, there will be some men who will not want to create, and will not mind repetitive labour if only the hours of work are short. As long as they have freedom to choose, and are educated and encouraged to use that freedom, well and good. They can be used for repetitive labour without shame. But they must have freedom to choose, and it must be a real freedom, not a merely passive acceptance of the yoke. Henry Ford cannot see that ; and therefore he is only a great capitalist maker of motor-cars, and not a leader of men. For to make men, and not cars, is the supreme task of leadership.

The Webbs : Prophets of the New Order [1]

I F any man deserves to be regarded as the prophet of
a planned Socialist economy, that man is Sidney Webb
—for he prefers to be called by that name rather than
by the title of Lord Passfield, which he consented to
take only because the British Labour Government needed
his services in the House of Lords. And if anyone
deserves to be regarded as the first person to recognise
the vital parts which Trade Unionism and Co-operation
—the two great voluntary movements of the wage
earners—will be called upon to play in the working of
a Socialist community, that credit belongs to Beatrice
Webb, who must on no account be called ' Lady
Passfield ', for she has steadfastly refused to accept the
title, on the ground that she is under no obligation to
share in her husband's enforced ennoblement.

These two remarkable people's vision of how
Socialism is likeliest to come into being may have proved
to be in many respects very wide of the mark. Their
Socialism, as a political policy, may have suffered from
the lack of assured and clear-cut philosophical foundations. They may have made many mistakes, about
measures as well as about men. But they have never lost
hold of two things—their belief in a planned and orderly
basis for the economic life of society and their assurance
that such a society can be securely built up only on the
foundation of a strongly knit and active working-class
movement, and on public ownership and control of the

[1] The following essay was written during Mr. and Mrs. Webb's
visit to Russia in 1932, and of course before they had written their
book on *Soviet Communism*. It appeared in *Current History* in
November 1932, after their return, in a somewhat altered version.
I have here reinstated the form in which it was originally written.

essential instruments of production, distribution, and exchange.

Now, after giving their lives to preaching the virtues of ' gradualism ' as a way of approach to the new social order which they want to see in being ; after being above all other leaders at the back of the gradualist policy of the British Labour Party, and after being content to work for Socialism through any and every human instrument, Socialist or non-Socialist, that has come to their hand, they find their most cherished ideas actually being carried into practice by a body of Socialists armed with a method and ideology radically different from their own. As I write these words they have just set off upon a visit to Russia in order to see for themselves what a planned Socialist community is like.

Before we consider the ideas for which they stand, let us set down the main facts of their careers. On July 13, 1932 Sidney Webb was seventy-three years old. At the age of nineteen he entered the Civil Service, where he worked for thirteen years, chiefly in the Colonial Office. During this time he was called to the Bar. The year after he resigned his Civil Service post, in 1891, he was elected to the London County Council as a candidate endorsed by the Fabian Society, which he had helped to organise in 1884. For eighteen years he remained on the Council, and at each of his four re-elections he was returned at the head of the poll. His chief interest during this period was in the Technical Education Board, of which he was chairman. From 1903 to 1906 he served on the Royal Commission on Trade Union Law, set up as a result of the Taff Vale Judgment, and on other important public bodies. He had married Beatrice Potter, six months his senior, in 1892. Mrs. Webb was already a writer on economics and sociology in her own right and had been in close personal contact with Herbert Spencer, who for some time had a considerable influence on her thought. At the time of her marriage she was already the author of *The Co-operative Movement in Great Britain*

(1891), and a contributor to Charles Booth's *Life and Labour of the People of London*, having served her apprenticeship, as she calls it, to the science of social investigation as a worker upon this famous survey.

The Webbs' first important essay in joint authorship was their *History of Trade Unionism*, published in 1894 ; and this was followed by numerous other joint works, including their series of volumes on the history of English local government and the famous Minority Report of the Royal Commission on Poor Laws and Unemployment, of which Mrs. Webb was a member. After that their intellectual influence in the British Labour movement grew steadily. They played an important part in building up the London School of Economics and Political Science, where Sidney Webb became Professor of Public Administration. They were chiefly responsible for the founding of the weekly *New Statesman* in 1913. Mr. Webb was a member of the Labour Party executive from 1915 to 1925. Elected to Parliament for the first time in 1922, he became President of the Board of Trade in the first Labour Government of 1924. In the second Labour Cabinet of 1929–31 he served successively as Secretary of State for Dominion Affairs and for the Colonies.

For a lifetime the Webbs have laboured in the most selfless and devoted fashion to make Socialism a practical working plan of social reorganisation as well as a vision of a new kind of society. They have never forgotten their idealism ; but they have severely disciplined it and kept it in check. They have felt an insatiable curiosity about the foundations of the movement with whose aid they have been attempting to build up the new social system. At a time when many other Socialists were denouncing Trade Unionism as a reactionary movement, a mere aristocracy of skilled workers shut up within the ideology of the wage system, they set out to write its history and to prescribe for it a Socialist faith and doctrine. Almost alone, they have been the candid friends of the consumers' Co-operative Movement, criticising its working and its methods of organisation and trying to help towards reshaping it as a necessary element in a Socialist community. Deeply impressed with the importance of local government institutions within the national State, they have devoted years of laborious work to writing the history of English local government and to trying to work out the right relationship between national and local institutions under a Socialist system. No labour has been too great for them to undertake ; and no failure to recognise the importance of their work has for a moment deterred them from going on with it in their own way.

They have their limitations, no doubt. They have seldom, at any rate till quite lately, been internationalist enough or conscious enough that the British political conditions, on which they have based their schemes, have been in the nature of a curious historical accident. But the fact remains that they have done more original Socialist thinking than any one since Karl Marx, and that they have been always extraordinarily ready to modify their ideas and plans in the light of changing conditions, as well as singularly devoid of intellectual pride. I believe they have never in their lives resented a criticism, however unmannerly ; and I am sure, from personal experience, of their humane and generous readiness to turn the other cheek to the arrogance of their juniors.

Wide as are the differences between the Marxist Communism of Lenin and Stalin and the Fabian Socialism with which the Webbs are inseparably associated, the points of identity between what they have been aiming at all their lives and what is now actually being accomplished in Soviet Russia go far deeper and are far more important than the differences. The Webbs' fundamental Socialist faith and intellectual candour are such that they were bound to realise this and base their judgment upon the Russian experiment on an essential community of aim. The differences, indeed, concern mainly the means of bringing about Socialism, and not the character of its institutions and economic system when the Socialists have attained to power ; they are the product partly of the different political and economic conditions of Great Britain and Russia and partly of a real divergence of mind and outlook. While the Communists were still struggling to obtain power they seemed to have little in common with the Fabian Socialists ; but, when power was once securely in their hands, they turned unhesitatingly to the building up, in their own way, of a society in many ways very like that which Mr. and Mrs. Webb have been advocating for the past forty years.

At the time when the Webbs began their work in England there was no Labour Party, only a small and not very influential Socialist movement, and not the smallest adumbration of an English Socialist revolution. There were a few English Marxists ; but most of these had not read Marx, or at any rate had not understood him. The Webbs, if they studied Marx at all, got very little out of him. What he had to say seemed to their minds too remote from the actual situation which they were called upon to face. They came to Socialism out of a very different economic and political tradition— from John Stuart Mill and Stanley Jevons, the heirs of Jeremy Bentham and the apostles of the developed utilitarian doctrine in economics and politics.

This doctrine was in essence critical, selective, reasonable in the sense of trying to see the pros and cons of every particular project, and, above all else, cool and suspicious of large generalisations and enthusiasms. It passed, by way of Mill, from an insistence on individualism and *laisser-faire* towards a kind of Socialism that was mainly made up of particular social reforms, each of which was justified as contributing to the ' greatest happiness of the greatest number '. It aimed at getting these reforms adopted piecemeal, one by one, and it was ready to accept help from any quarter in securing their adoption. It did this the more readily because it had combined its utilitarianism with a profound belief in evolution, as applied to the processes of social growth. It looked forward to the new Socialist society as a thing that would emerge gradually out of capitalism, by a series of piecemeal changes, and hardly less fast even if there were no Socialist movement to hasten its coming. It was held—and no one held the view more firmly than the Webbs—that the force of evolution was working swiftly and surely on the Socialist side.

Karl Marx, in his own way, held this doctrine of social evolution no less firmly than the Webbs, and was no less under the influence of evolutionary ideas. But whereas Marx, working with a materialist dialectic, after the manner of his ' inverted Hegelianism ' thought of social evolution as proceeding by means of a succession of class struggles and to the accompaniment of recurring social revolutions, the Webbs conceived of the evolutionary process as essentially gradual and unviolent. This difference arose partly because Marx was thinking mainly in terms of Continental countries to which the forms of parliamentary democracy were denied, whereas the Webbs grew up in an England where, except for woman suffrage, parliamentary democracy seemed already well on its way to acceptance, and there seemed to be no inherent impossibility in supposing that the parliamentary machine could be used for the gradual building-up of the Socialist State. The thing had not then been tried. There had been no Labour Governments to come up against the real difficulties in the way. It seemed quite possible to imagine that the successful and flourishing capitalist system—successful and flourishing, that is, from the standpoint of profit-making—would go on working with reasonable efficiency until, bit by bit, the Socialists were ready to take it over. Nor did it appear impossible to envisage a period of transition during

326

which semi-Socialist and capitalist institutions would be functioning more or less smoothly side by side.

But the Webbs, however convinced they were in those days of the ' inevitability of gradualness ', were never content with a merely partial and piecemeal vision of the Socialism they were trying to build up. Interested deeply in the machinery, as well as in the ideals, of Socialism, they wanted to see—and to make other people see—what a Socialist community in full and complete working order would be like. They never ceased to attack the planlessness and meaningless disorder of the capitalist world, or to set up against these evils their vision of an ordered and planned economic system, based on the co-ordinated control of the resources at men's command. They wanted industries to be publicly owned and administered. But they wanted much more than that ; they wanted public ownership as the means to rational planning of the community's economic life, to an orderly proportion in the production of different types of goods and services, and to a distribution of incomes that would fit in with the new order of production and provide an effective demand for all the useful things that the community decided to produce in the service of human welfare.

In short, the entire idea of a planned national economy, as it is being practised in Russia to-day, is contained in the Webbs' Socialist writings and has from the first lain at the back of their unremitting propaganda. This comes out with perfect clarity in many of their earlier pamphlets—in Sidney Webb's *Towards Social Democracy*, for example—and in many of the anonymous tracts published by the Fabian Society under their influence. They taught British Socialists the idea of economic planning—and not British Socialists only, for their influence on foreign Socialist movements was also very wide and deep. Most clearly of all, this notion of a planned economy comes out in the Socialist books which they wrote after the war—*A Constitution for the Socialist*

Commonwealth, and *The Decay of Capitalist Civilisation*.
There is much in these books, especially on the
political side, that is as the poles apart from the ideology
of Soviet Communism. The Webbs have always—or at
least until very recently—tended to do their thinking in
British terms, and in relation to the political situation in
Great Britain. They have hardly argued about the basis
of parliamentary democracy, for they have tended to take
its existence for granted and to consider only how its
forms and its working can be improved. They have
worked out their theories on a basis of persuasion rather
than of force, and have envisaged a Socialist community
operated by the methods of parliamentary democracy,
with an unmuzzled press and a free force of private
criticism always bearing upon it. Indeed, when they took
for their slogan, in their *Constitution for the Socialist
Commonwealth*, the principles of ' measurement ' and
' publicity ', they were clearly thinking of a society in
which criticism of any and every sort should be given
the fullest play, and as much as possible to feed on, by
the most complete disclosure of the actual working of
every governmental institution.

This is, of course, in certain respects, very different
from the Communist attitude. Stalin and his colleagues
would doubtless endorse every word the Webbs have
written about the need for the most careful and scrupu-
lous measurement of the efficiency of a socialised system
in ' delivering the goods '. That is of the essence of the
' control figures ' by means of which the operation of
the Five-Year Plans in Russia is continuously being
checked. It is at the back of the constant self-searchings
of the Communist Party and of the unceasing vigilance
to prevent slackness or sabotage in any part of the
economic system. But publicity, in the sense in which
the Webbs have envisaged it, has been quite another
matter. For, in their view, publicity has implied an
unrestrained freedom of criticism, not only of the
sectional efficiency of this or that particular organ of

the Socialist economy, but also of the Socialist system as a whole. It has implied the toleration of non-Socialist or anti-Socialist criticism, or at any rate, of brands and forms of Socialism out of harmony with the views of the dominant group.

Since political as well as religious toleration within certain fairly wide limits is a very long established British tradition, won as the reward of prolonged and embittered conflicts, it comes hard to an Englishman to think in terms of dictatorship, because it seems to mean turning his back on so many past victories for reason and sanity in public affairs. Toleration has been of great value to the cause of social progress in Great Britain, and it is the soil in which British Socialism has grown up. That is not to say that the forms of freedom and toleration to which we in Great Britain have been accustomed will be able to stand the strain of a direct and immediate challenge by Socialism to the capitalist system ; but it explains why most people in Great Britain—even Socialists—are so reluctant to cast this ' liberalism ' aside. It is a thing of great value in itself, and hitherto it has permitted the advocates of change to thrive and to win converts. Must it now be given up ? Was Marx right, after all, in envisaging the coming of Socialism as involving a desperate and unrestricted struggle between class and class ?

It is hard, even to-day and in face of what has happened not only in Russia but still more in Germany and Italy, for British Socialists to believe this, because the simple categories of the class struggle still seem to fit so ill the actual alignment of classes in Great Britain. Instead of a simple confrontation of wealthy capitalists and propertyless proletarians, there exists between the two extremes a far greater diversity, with a big and multiform middle section of highly skilled artisans, salaried workers and technicians, professional men, small traders and small capitalists. These intermediate groups exist, of course, in other countries besides Great Britain. But nowhere do they both exist to the same extent and provide so many active converts to, at any rate, some Socialist doctrines. Among them chiefly did the Fabian Society find its converts, and they form an important and influential element in almost every local Labour Party to-day.

The gradualist Socialism of the Webbs, with its conception of a planned economy emerging gradually and painlessly out of the capitalist system, has appealed especially to people of this sort, not only because they have a good deal to lose, fear chaos and disorder, hate conflict and prefer toleration and easy living with their fellows, but also because the planned order and system of the Socialist economy makes a strong appeal to their minds. They are in a position to see how wasteful and disorderly the present system is, and they would like to play their part in setting it straight—provided that they are not required to risk too much in the process. They have their little independence and their established position, and they hate the thought of violent revolution and of civil war.

The importance of these elements in the working as well as in the middle classes has so far prevented Communism from taking any deep root in Great Britain. But of late, in the minds of many people, and not least, I think, of the Webbs themselves, doubts have been growing whether the transition to Socialism which they once envisaged is likely to come about as painlessly as once seemed fully possible. The failure of the two Labour Governments—both ' Minority Governments ' though they were—to make any impression at all on the structure of capitalism has fed these doubts, and as some instalments of collectivism are infused into the economic system, it is increasingly realised how little difference it makes to transfer an industry to public ownership, if it has still to be managed in an environment determined by the necessities of capitalist profit-making. Nor can it be denied that, as long as capitalism determines the conditions of employment, *any* Government must so govern as not to destroy ' capitalist confidence ' in the prospect of profit, or that the increased taxation of the rich has so far made singularly little progress in bringing about an effective redistribution of wealth or incomes.

These doubts, I think, bit sooner and deeper into the mind of Beatrice than of Sidney Webb, for she has the quicker and the more imaginative, and he the more orderly and systematic, way of thought. Moreover, he was in office in both Labour Governments and was pre-occupied with their day-to-day affairs, while she, from outside, could see more plainly what was happening to them. I think it was she, rather than he, who felt irre-sistibly the desire to go to Russia, while he, rather than she, was the real progenitor of the idea of national plan-ning which the Russians are now putting into effect.

At all events, Sidney and Beatrice Webb, well on in years and with an unequalled record of disinterested service to the cause of British Socialism behind them, set off this year (1932) on a pilgrimage in order to see for themselves the astonishing new world that the Russian Communists are straining every nerve to build. And in Russia they are being received as no other country in the world could receive them—as the honoured prophets of the new order which they had the vision and sanity to imagine a generation before the chance actually to create it anywhere arose.

Associated though they have been with the idea of a gradualist and evolutionary Socialism in Great Britain, they will not, I think, find anything shocking in the disciplined dictatorship which the Russian Communists, fully conscious of the instinctive unpunctuality and haphazardness of the Russian temperament, are en-deavouring to use as the instrument of Socialist con-struction. When the Webbs went round the world a generation ago, I remember well that they came back full of admiration for Japan, where people knew what they wanted and had a way of getting it done, but with

331

a marked failure to appreciate the good qualities of the people of China. China offended them by its shapelessness and incapacity for collective organisation, whereas they found in Japan all the qualities needed for a well-conducted Socialist State—except the will to Socialism. The Webbs have no love for anarchists of any kind, at all events in political affairs. They are fond of describing world affairs as an everlasting conflict between the ' A 's and the ' B 's—between the anarchists on the one hand and those who love order, system, and disciplined control on the other. They will tell you, and not weary of telling you, that they belong to the ' B 's, and I doubt not they have found that Stalin also is a ' B '. Trotsky, of course, is an ' A ', but is not that precisely why Trotsky, his work in helping to achieve the revolution done, is now in exile and ' Trotskyism ' the Russian word for deadly political sin ? The control in Russia has passed from the ' A 's to the ' B 's, as the revolution has passed out of the combative into the constructive stage. The Webbs might have been fishes out of water in the Russia of 1920 ; they will, I think, find themselves thoroughly at home in the Russia of 1932.

So the apostles of ' gradualism ' have set off for Russia to survey the working of a Socialist revolution brought about by catastrophic means. I think they will find amid all the differences of method and idea a society whose fundamental structure fits in very closely with their own vision of the Socialist future. They went in order to see after what fashion their dreams of a lifetime were coming true, and they are far too open-minded to be put off because Lenin and his successors have worked toward the common goal by methods which are not their own. Bernard Shaw, disciple in economic matters of the Webbs, came back from Russia an enthusiast for the Soviet system. It will not surprise me if his masters, after their more critical and less extravagant fashion, celebrate their return by presenting Leninism with a no less decisive tribute.

NOTE

A NUMBER of the studies included in this volume have been previously published, though in most cases they have been revised, and in some completely rewritten, before republication. DANIEL DEFOE appeared in a volume entitled *From Anne to Victoria*, edited by Bonamy Dobrée, and published by Messrs. Cassell. DEFOE'S ENGLAND is based on my Introduction to the edition of Defoe's *Tour Through the Whole Island of Great Britain*, published by Mr. Peter Davies. TOWN LIFE IN THE EIGHTEENTH CENTURY is reprinted from *Johnson's England* (Oxford University Press). LONDON—ONE-FIFTH OF ENGLAND has not been published previously in its present form ; but I used a part of it for an article in the *Fortnightly Review*. ROADS, RIVERS, AND CANALS is new. A STUDY IN LEGAL REPRESSION is also largely new ; but a section of it appeared as a chapter in *The Martyrs of Tolpuddle*, the centenary volume issued by the Trade Union Congress in 1934. WILLIAM COBBETT was published in *Great Democrats* (Ivor Nicholson & Watson). RURAL RIDES is taken from the Peter Davies edition of Cobbett's *Rural Rides*, for which I was responsible jointly with my wife. This study is the joint work of the two editors. ROBERT OWEN AND OWENISM incorporates my Introduction to Owen's *New View of Society*, in Everyman's Library (Dent), but has been a good deal enlarged. MARX'S 'CAPITAL' is based on my introduction to the first volume of *Capital*, in Everyman's Library. WILLIAM MORRIS AND THE MODERN WORLD was originally delivered as a centenary lecture at University College, Hull, but is here published for the first time. HENRY FORD first appeared in *Great Contemporaries* (Cassell). Finally, THE WEBBS : PROPHETS OF THE NEW ORDER embodies an article written for *Current History* at a time when the Webbs were about to make their first visit to the Soviet Union.

I have to thank all those collaborators and publishers who have given me permission to make use of the various studies.